HAMLYN NEW
ALL COLOUR
COOKBOOK

HAMLYN NEW
ALL COLOUR
COOKBOOK

TED SMART

Front cover shows, clockwise from top right, *Citrus Queen of Puddings (193), Beef in Beer (61), Carrot Cake (261), Fish Kebabs (41)*

Title spread shows, clockwise from top right, *Vegetable Pancakes (129), Wholemeal Bread (241), Rich Tuna Mousse (25), Roast Chicken (81)*

Back cover shows, clockwise from top right, *Chicken Liver Risotto (145), Sausage Layer Pie (169), Chilled Strawberry Creams (217), Coffee and Hazelnut Gâteau (285), Baked Potatoes (105), Iced Cucumber Soup (1)*

Photography by David Jordan and Timothy Rose
Styling by Pip Kelly

Line drawings by Roberta Colegate-Stone and Gay John Galsworthy

First published in Great Britain in1986
This edition published in 1992
by Reed Consumer Books
part of Reed International Books Limited
for The Book People
Guardian House, Borough Road
Godalming, Surrey GU7 2AE

Reprinted 1992, 1993

A catalogue record for this book is available
from the British Library.

ISBN 1 85613 125 4

Produced by Mandarin Offset
Printed and bound in China

Contents

Soups 1–24

Starters and Snacks 25–40

Fish Dishes 41–60

Casseroles and Stews 61–80

Roasts and Grills 81–104

Vegetables and Salads 105–128

Vegetarian Recipes 129–144

Rice and Pasta 145–168

Pies, Pasties and Flans 169–192

Hot Puddings 193–216

Cool Desserts 217–240

Breads and Scones 241–260

Family Cakes and Biscuits 261–284

Fancy Cakes 285–304

Useful Facts and Figures

Notes on metrication

In this book quantities are given in metric and Imperial measures. Exact conversion from Imperial to metric measures does not usually give very convenient working quantities and so the metric measures have been rounded off into units of 25 grams. The table below shows the recommended equivalents.

Ounces	Approx g to nearest whole figure	Recommended conversion to nearest unit of 25	Ounces	Approx g to nearest whole figure	Recommended conversion to nearest unit of 25
1	28	25	9	255	250
2	57	50	10	283	275
3	85	75	11	312	300
4	113	100	12	340	350
5	142	150	13	368	375
6	170	175	14	396	400
7	198	200	15	425	425
8	227	225	16 (1 lb)	454	450

Note: When converting quantities over 16 oz first add the appropriate figures in the centre column, then adjust to the nearest unit of 25. As a general guide, 1 kg (1000 g) equals 2.2 lb or about 2 lb 3 oz. This method of conversion gives good results in nearly all cases, although in certain pastry and cake recipes a more accurate conversion is necessary to produce a balanced recipe.

Liquid measures The millilitre has been used in this book and the following table gives a few examples.

Imperial	Approx ml to nearest whole figure	Recommended ml	Imperial	Approx ml to nearest whole figure	Recommended ml
$\frac{1}{4}$	142	150 ml	1 pint	567	600 ml
$\frac{1}{2}$	283	300 ml	1½ pints	851	900 ml
$\frac{3}{4}$	425	450 ml	1¾ pints	992	1000 ml (1 litre)

Spoon measures All spoon measures given in this book are level unless otherwise stated.

Can sizes At present, cans are marked with the exact (usually to the nearest whole number) metric equivalent of the Imperial weight of the contents, so we have followed this practice when giving can sizes.

Oven temperatures
The table below gives recommended equivalents.

	°C	°F	Gas Mark		°C	°F	Gas Mark
Very cool	110	225	$\frac{1}{4}$	Moderately hot	190	375	5
	120	250	$\frac{1}{2}$		200	400	6
Cool	140	275	1	Hot	220	425	7
	150	300	2		230	450	8
Moderate	160	325	3	Very Hot	240	475	9
	180	350	4				

Notes for American and Australian users

In America the 8-fl oz measuring cup is used. In Australia metric measures are now used in conjunction with the standard 250-ml measuring cup. The Imperial pint, used in Britain and Australia, is 20 fl oz, while the American pint is 16 fl oz. It is important to remember that the Australian tablespoon differs from both the British and American tablespoons; the table below gives a comparison. The British standard tablespoon, which has been used throughout this book, holds 17.7 ml, the American 14.2 ml, and the Australian 20 ml. A teaspoon holds approximately 5 ml in all three countries.

British	American	Australian
1 teaspoon	1 teaspoon	1 teaspoon
1 tablespoon	1 tablespoon	1 tablespoon
2 tablespoons	3 tablespoons	2 tablespoons
3½ tablespoons	4 tablespoons	3 tablespoons
4 tablespoons	5 tablespoons	3½ tablespoons

An Imperial/American guide to solid and liquid measures

Imperial	American	Imperial	American
Solid measures		**Liquid measures**	
1 lb butter or margarine	2 cups	$\frac{1}{4}$ pint liquid	$\frac{2}{3}$ cup liquid
1 lb flour	4 cups	$\frac{1}{2}$ pint	1¼ cups
1 lb granulated or caster sugar	2 cups	$\frac{3}{4}$ pint	2 cups
1 lb icing sugar	3 cups	1 pint	2½ cups
8 oz rice	1 cup	1½ pints	3¾ cups
		2 pints	5 cups (2½ pints)

Note: When making any of the recipes in this book, only follow one set of measures as they are not interchangeable.

Introduction

Hamlyn's New All Colour Cookbook is a must for those starting to cook basic dishes as well as for experienced cooks who wish to enlarge their repertoire of dishes for family meals, dinner parties and other special occasions.

Every recipe is illustrated by a colour photograph so that you can see just what the finished dish should look like as you are following the recipe. Attractive presentation of food greatly increases the pleasure of a meal, so the opportunity to check on the garnish and appearance of the dish provided by the photograph is invaluable. Not only does every one of this huge collection of recipes give excellent results, each is easy to follow and accompanied by a microwave, freezer, or cook's tip, describing a technique for use in all kinds of basic food preparation and cookery. Detailed drawings beside the tips give further clarification. And for weight and health-conscious cooks, the calorie count of each recipe is provided.

When you want to plan an ideal meal or dinner party, this book will give you numerous appetising ideas. Just leaf through from soups and starters at the beginning of the book, to fish, main dishes, vegetables and cool and hot desserts, and be tempted to try something new. There is a section of vegetarian meals for those who want to limit the amount of meat in their diet and another on rice and pasta dishes. Nor is home baking forgotten, there are chapters on pies, pasties and flans, breads and scones, family cakes and biscuits and fancy cakes for those seasonal and special occasion teas.

There is no need to worry about how long preparation of a meal will take, because a further indispensable feature of the Hamlyn New All Colour Cookbook is that preparation and cooking times are given above each recipe, so that you can see at a glance whether you have time to make a particular dish.

All the recipes have been tried out in the Hamlyn Test Kitchen and we are sure you will agree that they not only look and taste delicious, but that they are easy and quick to prepare.

Note When this book was first published cling film was used in the microwave oven.
Since then, it has been recommended that *ordinary cling film should not be used for microwave cooking.*
Substitute **special microwave cling film**, a plate, or a suitable lid to cover food.

Soups

Home-made soups are delicious and very versatile. A chilled or light cream soup makes a simple, cook-ahead starter for a dinner party. More substantial soups such as minestrone or French onion make a tasty light lunch, when served with hot herb bread. Chunky chowders or soups with pasta or dumplings are welcome weekend supper dishes on cold evenings. In this chapter there is a wide variety of soups to suit every occasion.

1 | Iced Cucumber Soup

Preparation time
5 minutes, plus 1 hour to chill

Cooking time
25 minutes

Serves 6

Calories
85 per portion

You will need
1 large cucumber
1 onion
900 ml/ 1½ pints chicken stock
25 g/ 1 oz butter or margarine
25 g/ 1 oz plain flour
salt and pepper
150 ml/ ¼ pint natural yogurt

Garnish
18 ice cubes
mint sprigs
cucumber slices

Dice the cucumber, and finely chop the onion. Place the cucumber in a saucepan with the stock and onion. Bring to the boil, cover and simmer for about 20 minutes, or until the cucumber is tender. Cool, then blend in a liquidiser until smooth.

Melt the butter or margarine in a saucepan, stir in the flour and cook for 1 minute. Gradually add the cucumber purée. Bring to the boil, stirring frequently, then reduce the heat and simmer for 2 minutes. Season to taste. Add the natural yogurt and leave to cool thoroughly.

Garnish each serving with ice cubes, mint sprigs and cucumber slices.

2 | Spanish Soup

Preparation time
10 minutes, plus 2 hours to chill

Serves 6

Calories
90 per portion

You will need
½ cucumber
450 g/ 1 lb tomatoes
1 red pepper
1 green pepper
2 large Spanish onions
1 clove garlic
100 g/ 4 oz fresh white
  breadcrumbs
about 450 ml/ ¾ pint water
2 tablespoons red wine vinegar
1 teaspoon salt
2 teaspoons olive oil
½ teaspoon paprika
chopped parsley to garnish

Chop the cucumber, peel and chop the tomatoes, deseed and chop the peppers. Chop the onions and garlic.

In a bowl mix the vegetables with the garlic, breadcrumbs, water, vinegar and salt. Blend the mixture in a liquidiser until smooth, then return it to the bowl and whisk in the oil and paprika.

Cover the soup and put it in the refrigerator for 2 hours.

Before serving the soup, stir well, then ladle into chilled soup bowls. Garnish each serving with parsley.

Cook's Tip

Before adding the yogurt, whisk a tablespoon of mint jelly into the hot soup until dissolved.

Cook's Tip

To peel tomatoes, put them in a basin, cover with boiling water, leave for 30 seconds, then strip off skins.

3 | *Vichysoisse*

Preparation time
*25 minutes, plus 1
hour to chill*

Cooking time
20 minutes

Serves 6

Calories
260 per portion

You will need
*2 large leeks
1 onion
1 large potato
50 g/ 2 oz butter or margarine
600 ml/ 1 pint hot vegetable stock
300 ml/ $\frac{1}{2}$ pint milk
150 ml/ $\frac{1}{4}$ pint double or whipping
   cream
150 ml/ $\frac{1}{4}$ pint natural yogurt
salt and pepper
dash of Tabasco sauce
2 tablespoons chopped chives*

Wash and trim the leeks, then cut into thin rings. Finely chop the onion. Peel and dice the potato.

In a saucepan cook the onion and leeks in the butter or margarine until softened. Add the potato and stock. Bring to the boil, reduce the heat and simmer gently for 20 minutes. Add the milk. Blend the soup in a liquidiser until smooth. Transfer to a bowl and whisk in the cream, yogurt, salt and pepper and Tabasco.

Leave the vichysoisse to cool. When cold, chill for at least 1 hour.

Serve the soup in individual bowls and garnish each serving with freshly chopped chives.

4 | *Chilled Lemon Soup*

Preparation time
*5–10 minutes, plus 1
hour to chill*

Cooking time
25 minutes

Serves 6

Calories
195 per portion

You will need
*1 onion
1 clove garlic
50 g/ 2 oz butter or margarine
25 g/ 1 oz plain flour
900 ml/ 1 $\frac{1}{2}$ pints chicken stock
grated rind and juice of 2 lemons
salt and pepper
300 ml/ $\frac{1}{2}$ pint single cream*

Garnish
*thin lemon slices
freshly chopped mint*

Finely chop the onion and garlic. In a saucepan, cook the onion and garlic in the butter or margarine until softened. Reduce the heat, stir in the flour, then gradually add the stock, stirring continuously, and bring to the boil. Add the lemon rind, juice and seasoning to taste. Reduce the heat and simmer gently for 20 minutes.

Blend the soup in a liquidiser, then pour it into a large tureen and stir in the cream. Cool and chill for at least one hour.

Just before serving garnish with slices of lemon and freshly chopped mint.

Cook's Tip

To clean leeks thoroughly, trim roots and tough green leaves off leeks. Slit leeks lengthwise to centre, then hold root end uppermost under cold running water to wash out dirt.

Freezer Tip

Boil home-made stocks rapidly until greatly reduced and concentrated. Cool, freeze in ice cube trays then pack cubes in freezer bags. Use as required, diluting with water.

5 | Hot Avocado Soup

Preparation time
20 minutes

Cooking time
20 minutes

Serves 6

Calories
300 per portion

You will need
3 ripe avocados
2 tablespoons lemon juice
1 onion, finely chopped
2 cloves garlic, finely chopped
1 green chilli, deseeded and
    thinly sliced
50 g/ 2 oz butter or margarine
25 g/ 1 oz plain flour
900 ml/ 1½ pints chicken stock
150 ml/¼ pint milk
salt and pepper
150 ml/¼ pint soured cream

Quarter the avocados. Remove the stones and peel and discard. Cut off a few thin slices of avocado and reserve them for garnish. Brush with a little of the lemon juice to prevent discoloration. Roughly chop the remaining avocado and mix it with the remaining lemon juice.

Cook the onion, garlic and chilli in the butter or margarine until softened. Reduce the heat, add the flour, cook for 2 minutes stirring. Add the chicken stock and milk, stirring all the time. Bring to the boil, add the avocado and seasoning, then reduce the heat and simmer gently for 2–3 minutes. Blend in a liquidiser until smooth. Return the soup to the saucepan and over a very low heat stir in the soured cream.

Pour the soup into individual soup bowls and garnish each serving with the reserved slices of avocado. Serve immediately.

6 | Carrot Soup

Preparation time
10 minutes

Cooking time
25 minutes

Serves 6

Calories
200 per portion

You will need
675 g/ 1½ lb carrots, sliced
salt and pepper
1 onion
2 celery sticks
25 g/ 1 oz butter or margarine
25 g/ 1 oz plain flour
900 ml/ 1½ pints chicken stock
1 (400- g/ 14- oz) can evaporated
    milk
2 teaspoons lemon juice

Garnish
grated carrots
2 tablespoons chopped parsley

Cook the carrots in boiling salted water for 15 minutes, then drain them.

Chop the onion and celery and fry in the butter or margarine until softened, but not browned. Reduce the heat and stir in the flour. Add the carrots. Slowly add the stock and evaporated milk, stirring continuously. Add the lemon juice. Bring to the boil, reduce the heat and simmer gently for 5 minutes. Season to taste. Blend the soup in a liquidiser, then return it to a saucepan and reheat.

Pour the soup into individual soup bowls and garnish with grated carrot and freshly chopped parsley.

Cook's Tip

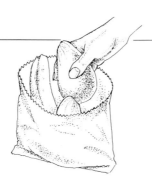

To ripen avocados quickly, place in a brown paper bag with a ripe banana or tomato.

Microwave Tip

Put all prepared vegetables in a bowl and add 300 ml/½ pint boiling stock. Cover with cling film, leaving a gap for the steam to escape, and cook on full power for 18–20 minutes. Blend in a liquidiser. Mix the flour to a smooth paste with a little cold water, stir in the remaining boiling stock and add to the soup. Stir in evaporated milk, seasoning and lemon juice. Heat for 5–7 minutes to thicken before serving.

7 | Tomato and Orange Soup

Preparation time
10 minutes

Cooking time
20 minutes

Serves 6

Calories
130 per portion

You will need
1 onion, chopped
2 cloves garlic, crushed
50 g/ 2 oz butter or margarine
25 g/ 1 oz plain flour
1 (800-g/ 28-oz) can chopped
*   tomatoes*
900 ml/ 1½ pints chicken stock
grated rind and juice of 2 oranges
2 teaspoons sugar
salt and pepper

Garnish
150 ml/¼ pint single cream
grated rind of 1 orange

Fry the onion and garlic in the butter or margarine until softened. Stir in the flour, then the tomatoes. Stirring continuously, add the stock and the orange rind and juice. Reduce the heat and simmer gently for 15 minutes, stirring occasionally. Add the sugar and season to taste. For a smooth soup, blend in a liquidiser.

Pour the soup into individual bowls and garnish each serving with a swirl of cream and a sprinkle of orange rind.

8 | Cream of Watercress Soup

Preparation time
10 minutes

Cooking time
10 minutes

Serves 6

Calories
225 per portion

You will need
1 onion, chopped
2 cloves, garlic, crushed
50 g/ 2 oz butter or margarine
50 g/ 2 oz plain flour
600 ml/ 1 pint chicken stock
600 ml/ 1 pint milk
2 bunches of watercress, trimmed
*   and chopped*
salt and pepper
¼ teaspoon grated nutmeg
juice of ½ lemon
150 ml/¼ pint single cream
watercress sprigs to garnish

In a saucepan, fry the onion and garlic in the butter or margarine until softened. Reduce the heat and stir in the flour. Gradually add the stock and milk, stirring all the time. Stir in the watercress, salt and pepper, nutmeg and lemon juice. Simmer gently for 5 minutes. Reduce the heat, then stir in the single cream. Reheat without boiling.

Pour the soup into individual soup bowls and garnish each serving with a sprig of watercress.

Freezer Tip

Pour cooled soup into a rigid plastic container, leaving head space for expansion, label and freeze. To serve, dip container in hand-hot water, reheat soup in a saucepan slowly to boiling, stirring frequently.

Cook's Tip

To quickly chop watercress, trim off the stalks and place the leaves in a food processor. Pulse the blades on and off for 1 minute. Remember to utilize your food processor for chopping the onion too.

9 | *Borscht*

Preparation time
10 minutes

Cooking time
1 hour

Serves 6

Calories
60 per portion

You will need
450 g / 1 lb raw beetroot
2 carrots
1 onion
bay leaf
1.15 litres / 2 pints beef stock
salt and pepper
150 ml / ¼ pint natural yogurt to
  garnish

Grate or finely chop the beetroot. Finely chop one carrot and the onion. Grate the second carrot. Put the vegetables, bay leaf, stock and seasoning into a saucepan. Bring to the boil, reduce the heat and simmer for 1 hour. Taste the soup and adjust the seasoning.

   Pour the borscht into individual soup bowls and top each serving with a spoonful of natural yogurt.

10 | *Minestrone*

Preparation time
25 minutes, plus
overnight soaking

Cooking time
1 hour 15 minutes

Serves 6

Calories
220 per portion

You will need
50 g / 2 oz dried haricot beans
1 onion, chopped
1 clove garlic, crushed
2 tablespoons oil
4 rashers rindless bacon, diced
1 (425-g / 15-oz) can tomatoes
1.15 litres / 2 pints chicken stock
1 leek, cut into rings
2 carrots, diced
¼ small white cabbage, finely
  shredded
salt and pepper
50 g / 2 oz pasta shapes
1 tablespoon grated Parmesan
  cheese to serve

Cover the haricot beans with plenty of cold water and soak overnight. Drain. Fry the onion and garlic in the oil in a large saucepan, then add the bacon and continue cooking for a further few minutes.

   Stir in the tomatoes, stock and haricot beans, then bring to the boil, cover and simmer gently for 45 minutes. Add the leek, carrot and white cabbage and continue simmering for a further 15 minutes. Season to taste, add the pasta and cook for 10 minutes, or until the pasta is tender but firm.

   Pour the minestrone into individual soup bowls and sprinkle each serving with Parmesan cheese.

Cook's Tip

Traditional borscht contains shredded cabbage and cubes of beef. Dice braising steak and add to the soup with the beetroot. Add the cabbage for the last 15 minutes cooking time.

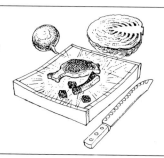

Cook's Tip

To save on soaking time, substitute 1 (425-g / 15-oz) can white cannellini beans for the dried haricot beans. Add the drained canned beans to the soup with the pasta.

11 | Curried Parsnip Soup

Preparation time
10 minutes

Cooking time
25 minutes

Serves 6

Calories
160 per portion

You will need
1 onion
2 cloves garlic
675 g/ 1½ lb parsnips, peeled
1 tart dessert apple, peeled and cored
2 tablespoons oil
1 tablespoon curry powder
40 g/ 1½ oz flour
1.15 litres/ 2 pints chicken stock
salt and pepper
150 ml/¼ pint natural yogurt to garnish

Chop the onion, garlic, parsnips and apple. Heat the oil in a saucepan, add the curry powder, vegetables and apple, cook for 5 minutes. Reduce the heat and stir in the flour. Gradually add the stock, stirring all the time, bring to the boil, season to taste and simmer gently for 20 minutes.

Blend the soup in a liquidiser until smooth. Return the soup to the saucepan, reheat, then pour into individual dishes and garnish each serving with a swirl of yogurt.

12 | Quick Apple and Cashew Soup

Preparation time
5 minutes

Cooking time
10 minutes

Serves 4

Calories
145 per portion

You will need
1 onion
100 g/ 4 oz button mushrooms
100 g/ 4 oz cashew nuts
600 ml/ 1 pint apple juice
salt and pepper
¼ teaspoon dried mixed herbs
1 teaspoon yeast extract

Chop the onion and halve the mushrooms. Put all the ingredients into a large saucepan, bring to the boil and reduce the heat to simmer gently for 10 minutes.

Pour the soup into individual soup bowls and serve with warmed French bread.

Cook's Tip

Cook some lightly oiled poppadums under a hot grill until puffed and golden. Do not put the grill pan too near the heat or the poppadums may burn.

Cook's Tip

If you have a garden, then try drying some herbs for the winter. Sage, thyme and tarragon, for example, can be tied in bunches and hung in a cool, dry place.

13 | Mulligatawny Soup

Preparation time
5 minutes

Cooking time
1 hour

Serves 6

Calories
145 per portion

You will need
1 apple
1 large carrot
2 onions
2 tablespoons oil
50 g/ 2 oz plain flour
1 tablespoon curry powder
1.15 litres/ 2 pints beef stock
1 tablespoon chutney
50 g/ 2 oz sultanas
pinch of sugar
salt and pepper
1 teaspoon lemon juice
a few coriander sprigs to garnish

Dice the apple, carrot and onions. Heat the oil in a saucepan, add the apple and vegetables and cook for 5 minutes. Stir in the flour and curry powder. Gradually pour in the stock, bring to the boil and simmer for 5 minutes. Add the remaining ingredients and simmer together for about 45 minutes to 1 hour.

Blend the soup in a liquidiser until smooth, then return it to the pan to reheat. Taste the soup, adjusting seasoning if necessary, and add a little extra sugar or lemon juice if required.

Garnish with coriander sprigs.

14 | Celery and Stilton Soup

Preparation time
10 minutes

Cooking time
25–30 minutes

Serves 6

Calories
290 per portion

You will need
1 head of celery
1 onion
100 g/ 4 oz walnuts
50 g/ 2 oz butter or margarine
50 g/ 2 oz plain flour
1.15 litres/ 2 pints chicken stock
salt and pepper
100 g/ 4 oz blue Stilton cheese
2 tablespoons port (optional)

Garnish
celery curls and leaves, or
  croûtons

Chop the celery, onion and walnuts. Cook the vegetables in the butter or margarine until softened. Reduce the heat, stir in the walnuts and flour. Gradually add the stock, stirring all the time. Bring to the boil, reduce the heat and simmer gently for 20 minutes.

Season the soup, then transfer it to a liquidiser and blend until smooth. Return the soup to a saucepan and reheat over a low heat. Crumble the Stilton and add it to the soup, then stir in the port, if using.

Pour the soup into individual soup bowls and garnish with celery curls and leaves or croûtons.

Cook's Tip

Use a heavy pestle and mortar to grind whole spices; use as curry powder. Cinnamon sticks, coriander, cumin and mustard seeds can be combined with ground ginger and chilli powder.

Microwave Tip

To make croûtons, cut thick slices of bread into cubes, discarding crusts. Place on absorbent paper and microwave until hard, 3 or 4 minutes, turning often. Melt 40 g/ 1½ oz butter and mix until butter is absorbed.

15 | Cheese and Onion Soup

Preparation time
10 minutes

Cooking time
10 minutes

Serves 6

Calories
490 per portion

You will need
2 onions
50 g / 2 oz butter or margarine
50 g / 2 oz plain flour
600 ml / 1 pint chicken stock
600 ml / 1 pint milk
225 g / 8 oz matured Cheddar
   cheese, grated
150 ml / ¼ pint dry or medium dry
   cider
¼ teaspoon grated nutmeg
salt and pepper

Garnish
grated cheese
croûtons

Chop the onions and cook in the butter or margarine for 3 – 5 minutes until soft. Reduce the heat and stir in the flour. Slowly add first the stock, then the milk, stirring all the time. Bring to the boil and cook for 3–4 minutes. Remove the saucepan from the heat, add the Cheddar and stir until all the cheese has melted. Over a low heat, stir in the cider and seasoning. Do not allow the soup to boil.

Pour the soup into individual bowls and garnish with grated cheese and croûtons.

16 | French Onion Soup

Preparation time
5 minutes

Cooking time
25–30 minutes

Serves 6

Calories
235 per portion

You will need
450 g / 1 lb onions
50 g / 2 oz butter or margarine
1 litre / 1¾ pints beef stock
150 ml / ¼ pint dry red wine
salt and pepper
6 slices French bread, buttered
100 g / 4 oz Cheddar cheese,
   grated

Chop the onions and fry in the butter or margarine until soft and golden brown. Pour in the stock, bring to the boil, then reduce the heat and simmer gently for 25 minutes. Add the wine and seasoning, stir well and heat the soup for a further few minutes.

Put a slice of French bread into each heatproof soup bowl and pour over the soup. When the bread rises to the surface sprinkle the top with the Cheddar, put under a hot grill until golden. Serve immediately

Cook's Tip

To chop an onion, cut a peeled onion in half lengthwise; place the flat side on a chopping board. Holding opposite sides, slice finely first lengthwise, then across.

Cook's Tip

Coarsely grate and freeze small leftover pieces of cheese – they are often useful for recipes such as this one. Pack the cheese in polythene bags, allowing plenty of room in the bag so that the cheese does not become compressed in a lump. Use straight from the freezer.

17 | *Mushroom and Sherry Soup*

Preparation time
10 minutes

Cooking time
20 minutes

Serves 6

Calories
170 per portion

You will need
450 g/ 1 lb button mushrooms
1 onion, chopped
2 cloves garlic, crushed
50 g/ 2 oz butter or margarine
50 g/ 2 oz plain flour
300 ml/ ½ pint milk
600 ml/ 1 pint chicken stock
2 tablespoons sherry
salt and pepper

Garnish
150 ml/ ¼ pint single cream
1 tablespoon chopped parsley

Thinly slice the mushrooms. In a saucepan, cook the onion and garlic in the butter or margarine until softened. Add the mushrooms and cook gently for a few minutes. Stir in the flour. Gradually blend in the milk and stock. Bring to the boil, reduce the heat and simmer gently for 15 minutes. Stir the soup frequently to ensure a smooth consistency.

Add the sherry and season to taste. Pour into soup bowls. Garnish the soup with a swirl of cream and sprinkle with parsley.

Cook's Tip

For a soup low in calories and fat, omit sautéed onion, butter and flour. Simmer sliced mushrooms in 900 ml/ 1½ pints stock. Add some chopped spring onions and the sherry. Omit the milk; serve without cream.

18 | *Cock-a-Leekie Soup*

Preparation time
10 minutes

Cooking time
1 hour

Serves 6

Calories
100 per portion

You will need
1 chicken carcass
1 onion
bouquet garni
1.15 litres/ 2 pints chicken stock
about 100 g/ 4 oz cooked chicken
3 carrots
450 g/ 1 lb leeks
100 g/ 4 oz no-need-to-soak prunes
salt and pepper
1 tablespoon chopped parsley to garnish

Simmer the chicken carcass, onion and bouquet garni in the stock for an hour, then strain the liquid into a large saucepan.

Slice the chicken meat into strips. Thinly slice the carrots and leeks. Add the chicken, vegetables and prunes to the stock. Bring to the boil and simmer gently for 20 minutes. Season with salt and pepper.

Serve the soup garnished with freshly chopped parsley.

Cook's Tip

To chop a small amount of parsley, place a few parsley sprigs in a large cup or mug and snip with scissors, turning the cup with one hand, rather than using a knife and chopping board.

19 | Cream of Chicken Soup

Preparation time
5 minutes

Cooking time
1 hour 10 minutes

Serves 6

Calories
165 per portion

You will need
1 chicken carcass
1 onion
bouquet garni
1.15 litres/2 pints chicken stock
about 100 g/4 oz cooked chicken
300 ml/½ pint milk
50 g/2 oz plain flour
2 tablespoons water
1 tablespoon lemon juice
¼ teaspoon grated nutmeg
salt and pepper
150 ml/¼ pint single cream
croûtons to garnish

Simmer the carcass, onion and bouquet garni in the stock for an hour. Strain the liquid, return to the saucepan.

Neatly dice the cooked chicken meat. Add the chicken meat and milk to the stock. Blend the flour with the water, then slowly add the mixture to the stock, stirring all the time. Bring to the boil, reduce the heat and simmer gently for 10 minutes. Season the soup with lemon juice, nutmeg, salt and pepper.

Stir in the cream, pour the soup into individual soup bowls and garnish with croûtons.

20 | Scotch Broth

Preparation time
10 minutes

Cooking time
2½ hours

Serves 6

Calories
110 per portion

You will need
50 g/2 oz pearl barley
225 g/8 oz neck of mutton or
lamb, or stewing beef
2 leeks
2 carrots
1 onion
2 celery sticks
1 small turnip
1.15 litres/2 pints water
bouquet garni
salt and pepper
1 tablespoon chopped parsley to
garnish

Blanch the pearl barley in boiling water for 3 minutes, then strain. Cut the meat into small cubes. Slice the leeks, carrots, onion and celery. Dice the turnip.

Bring the water, pearl barley, meat, bouquet garni and seasoning to taste slowly to the boil in a saucepan. Skim. Reduce the heat, add the vegetables and simmer gently for 1½ hours, skimming off any foam that may appear on the surface of the broth. Remove the bouquet garni.

Pour the broth into individual soup bowls and garnish each serving with chopped parsley.

Cook's Tip

Instead of small square croûtons, use cocktail cutters or small biscuit cutters to make attractive shapes.

Cook's Tip

To make a fresh bouquet garni, tie a sprig each of parsley and thyme and a bay leaf together with thin string. Tie to the saucepan handle so that the bouquet garni can be removed easily before serving.

21 | *Beef Soup with Dumplings*

Preparation time
15 minutes

Cooking time
1 hour 20 minutes

Serves 6

Calories
340 per portion

You will need
450 g/1 lb braising steak, cubed
25 g/1 oz plain flour
50 g/2 oz butter or margarine
2 onions, finely chopped
2 cloves garlic, crushed
1 teaspoon marjoram
1 teaspoon paprika
salt and pepper
1.15 litres/2 pints beef stock

For the dumplings
2 day-old bread rolls
6 tablespoons lukewarm milk
1 onion, finely chopped
1 tablespoon oil
2 tablespoons chopped parsley
salt and pepper
1 egg

Coat the beef in flour. Melt the fat in a large saucepan, add the onion and garlic and fry for 3 minutes. Add the meat and fry until browned on all sides. Add the marjoram and seasoning. Gradually blend in the stock, bring to the boil, reduce the heat and simmer for 1 hour. Cut the rolls into thin slices and soften with the warmed milk. Cook the onion in the oil. Mix together the bread, onion, parsley, seasoning and egg. With wet hands, form the mixture into six small balls.

Add the dumplings to the soup and simmer for a further 15 minutes. Serve each portion of soup with a dumpling.

Freezer Tip

Before adding the dumplings, cool soup quickly and freeze. Make and freeze the dumplings separately. To reheat, bring the soup to the boil, add the defrosted dumplings, and cook as above.

22 | *Bacon and Split Pea Soup*

Preparation time
10 minutes, plus
overnight soaking

Cooking time
1 hour 10 minutes

Serves 6

Calories
295 per portion

You will need
100 g/4 oz split peas
1 small turnip
1 carrot
2 leeks
2 tablespoons oil
8 rashers rindless smoked streaky
  bacon, diced
1.4 litres/2½ pints ham or chicken
  stock
salt and pepper
½ teaspoon dried mixed herbs
150 ml/¼ pint single cream
1 tablespoon chopped parsley to
  garnish

Cover the split peas with cold water and soak them overnight. Drain well. Dice the turnip and carrot. Slice the leeks into rings.

Cook the vegetables in the oil for 5 minutes, add the bacon and continue cooking for a few minutes. Add the stock and split peas. Season well with salt, pepper and the mixed herbs. Simmer gently for an hour. Blend the soup in a liquidiser until smooth.

Return the soup to the saucepan and reheat over a low heat. Stir in the cream. Pour into individual soup bowls and garnish each serving with chopped parsley.

Cook's Tip

Reserve the cooking liquid from a joint of bacon or gammon for this soup. Omit the streaky bacon. Cool and chill the liquid, then skim off any fat before use.

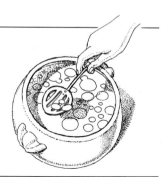

23 | Seafood Soup

Preparation time
15 minutes

Cooking time
30 minutes

Serves 6

Calories
245 per portion

You will need
600 ml/1 pint water
350 g/12 oz haddock
1 bay leaf
1 lemon, cut into wedges
salt and pepper
1 onion, chopped
2 cloves garlic, crushed
1 tablespoon oil
25 g/1 oz plain flour
600 ml/1 pint milk
350 g/12 oz cooked peeled
   prawns and bottled mussels
   (mixed)
$\frac{1}{4}$ teaspoon ground mace
2 tablespoons lemon juice
2 tablespoons dry white wine
   (optional)
4 tablespoons single cream
croûtons to garnish

Bring the water, haddock, bay leaf, lemon wedges and seasoning to the boil and simmer gently for 15 minutes. Drain the fish, reserving the cooking liquid. Discard the bay leaf and lemon wedges. Skin, bone and flake the fish.

In a large saucepan, cook the onion and garlic in the oil until softened. Reduce the heat, add the flour, then gradually pour in the milk, stirring all the time. Add the seafood, mace, lemon juice, wine (if using) and seasoning to taste, simmer for 5 minutes, then add the fish and simmer for a further 5 minutes. Remove from heat. Stir in the cream. Garnish each serving with croûtons.

24 | White Fish Chowder

Preparation time
10 minutes

Cooking time
25–30 minutes

Serves 6

Calories
295 per portion

You will need
2 rashers bacon
450 g/1 lb coley, haddock or cod
50 g/2 oz butter or margarine
4 medium potatoes, peeled and
   diced
2 leeks, sliced into rings
50 g/2 oz button mushrooms
600 ml/1 pint milk
salt and pepper
pinch of grated nutmeg
1 (227-g/8-oz) can tomatoes
1 tablespoon chopped parsley to
   garnish

Dice the bacon and fry in its own fat until crisp; remove from the pan. Cut the fish into small pieces, removing skin and bones.

Heat the butter or margarine in a saucepan, then add the fish, potato, leek and mushrooms. Cook for 2 minutes. Add the milk, then simmer gently for 15–20 minutes. Season with salt and pepper and the nutmeg. Stir in the bacon and tomatoes and heat through gently.

Pour the chowder into individual soup bowls and garnish with freshly chopped parsley.

Cook's Tip

Mace is the outer covering of the nutmeg. It is used to season savoury dishes like pâtés, baked meats and soups.

Freezer Tip

Frozen cod steaks are ideal for this chowder. Defrost for about 15 minutes, then cut into cubes and cook while still partially frozen.

Starters and Snacks

A starter should be light, well-flavoured and provide a contrast in texture and flavour to the courses which follow. A well chosen starter should whet the appetite for the meal, not blunt it. Many of the recipes in this chapter are suitable to serve as starters and also for a snack lunch or supper, whilst later recipes are for more substantial snacks.

25 | Rich Tuna Mousse

Preparation time
25 minutes

Cooking time
25 minutes, plus 1 hour to set

Serves 4

Calories
880 per portion

You will need
1 onion
2 (198-g/7-oz) cans tuna
50 g/2 oz butter
3 tablespoons dry white wine
1 tablespoon gelatine
3 tablespoons boiling water
1 teaspoon horseradish sauce
300 ml/½ pint mayonnaise
6 tablespoons double cream
salt and pepper
lime slices to garnish

Finely chop the onion. Drain and flake the tuna. Beat the butter until creamy. Blend the onion, fish and butter together with a fork.

Pour the wine into a bowl. Sprinkle in the gelatine, then pour in the boiling water, stand over a pan of simmering water and stir until the gelatine has dissolved. Cool the mixture slightly. Blend in the horseradish and mayonnaise. Put the tuna mixture in a liquidiser, add the gelatine mixture and blend until smooth.

In a bowl, beat the cream until stiff. Fold the fish mixture into the cream and season to taste. Turn the mousse into individual ramekins.

Refrigerate for about 1 hour, until set.

Garnish each serving with a twist of lime and serve with brown bread or vegetable crudités.

26 | Smoked Haddock Pâté

Preparation time
10 minutes

Cooking time
20 minutes

Oven temperature
200 C, 400 F, gas 6

Serves 4

Calories
165 per portion

You will need
2 large fillets smoked haddock, cooked
2 hard-boiled eggs
75 g/3 oz wholemeal breadcrumbs
1 thick slice onion, finely chopped
150 ml/¼ pint natural yogurt
salt and pepper
1 tablespoon chopped parsley
1 tablespoon grated lemon rind
lemon slices to garnish

Finely flake the fish. Finely chop the hard-boiled eggs. Mix together the fish, eggs, breadcrumbs, onion and yogurt. Beat until smooth. Season with salt and pepper, then fold in the parsley and lemon rind.

Spoon the mixture into four individual ramekins. Smooth the top of the pâté with the back of a teaspoon, then bake in a moderately hot oven for 20 minutes.

Garnish the pâté with lemon twists and serve immediately with hot triangles of toast.

Variation
This dish can also be served cold. Follow the recipe above, but chill the pâté for an hour before serving. Serve with brown bread and butter.

Cook's Tip

For crudités, prepare matchstick carrots, tiny cauliflower florets, celery sticks, button mushrooms, strips of pepper and scrubbed radishes.

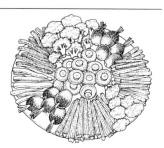

Cook's Tip

If you want to use just one slice of onion, cut it off the whole unpeeled onion. Wrap the remainder in cling film and put it in the refrigerator. It will keep for up to a week.

27 | Potted Prawns

Preparation time
20 minutes, plus 30
minutes to chill

Cooking time
5 minutes

Serves 4

Calories
555 per portion

You will need
4 spring onions
450 g/ 1 lb peeled cooked prawns
150 ml/ ¼ pint mayonnaise
2 teaspoons horseradish sauce
2 tablespoons lemon juice
pinch of cayenne
salt and pepper
100 g/ 4 oz butter

Garnish
whole prawns
watercress sprigs
curly endive (optional)

Thinly slice the spring onions. Place 225 g/8 oz prawns in a liquidiser, add the mayonnaise, horseradish, spring onions and lemon juice. Blend the mixture to a paste. Mix the remaining prawns into the paste. Add the cayenne, salt and pepper. Press the prawn mixture into individual ramekins.

Melt the butter in a small saucepan, then pour it over the potted prawns, dividing the quantity evenly between the ramekins. Refrigerate until the butter is firm, about 30 minutes.

Garnish the potted prawns with whole prawns, water-cress, and curly endive, if liked, and serve with hot buttered toast.

28 | Quick Taramasalata

Preparation time
10 minutes, plus 1
hour to chill

Serves 4

Calories
305 per portion

You will need
100 g/ 4 oz smoked cod's roe
75 g/ 3 oz fresh white bread
2 tablespoons milk
large clove of garlic, crushed
100 ml/ 4 fl oz olive oil
juice of ½ lemon

Garnish
lemon slices
parsley sprigs

To retain pink flecks, skin the roe rather than scoop out the middle. Trim the crusts from the bread and soak the slices in the milk for 15 minutes, remove and squeeze dry. Mash with the cod's roe and crushed garlic.

Place the mixture in a liquidiser. Pour in the oil gradually, while blending, then add the lemon juice and blend until smooth. Chill for an hour before serving.

Garnish with lemon slices and parsley sprigs and serve the taramasalata with a selection of packeted savoury snacks and a green salad.

Microwave Tip

To defrost prawns, spread over a double thickness of absorbent kitchen paper. Cover with absorbent kitchen paper and cook on full power for about 3 minutes (for 450 g/ 1 lb).

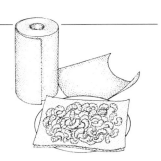

Cook's Tip

Serve stoned black olives and warm pitta bread with the taramasalata. To quickly stone olives use a cherry stoner.

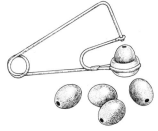

29 | *Chicken Liver Pâté*

Preparation time
20 minutes

Cooking time
15 minutes, plus 2
hours to chill

Serves 6

Calories
280 per portion

You will need
1 onion
1 clove garlic
1 tablespoon oil
450 g / 1 lb chicken or turkey
   livers, trimmed
100 g / 4 oz butter
salt and pepper
pinch of grated nutmeg
1 teaspoon mixed herbs
2 tablespoons dry sherry
2 tablespoons double cream

Line and grease a 450 g / 1 lb loaf tin. Finely chop the
onion and garlic. In a saucepan cook the onion and garlic
in the oil until softened. Add the chicken or turkey livers,
cover the pan and cook over low heat for 10 minutes.
Cool slightly, then blend the mixture in a liquidiser until
smooth.

Melt the butter in the saucepan already used. Add the
seasonings, mixed herbs, sherry and cream. When heated through, add the mixture to the liver purée and blend
until the consistency is of whipped cream. Pour the purée
into the prepared tin and chill, covered, for 2 hours or
more.

To serve, turn out the pâté on to a serving plate and
remove paper. Accompany each serving with a fresh
tomato and Chinese leaves, or a small side salad, and
melba toast.

30 | *Salad Niçoise*

Preparation time
15 minutes

Serves 4

Calories
270 per portion

You will need
a few lettuce leaves
1 (198-g / 7-oz) can tuna
1 green pepper, deseeded
1 onion
2 tomatoes
2 hard-boiled eggs
100 g / 4 oz French beans, cooked
4 tablespoons French dressing
   (recipe 125)
salt and pepper

Garnish
1 (50-g / 2-oz) can anchovy fillets
a few black olives, halved and
   stoned

Arrange the lettuce leaves on four small plates. Drain the
tuna and break it into chunks with a fork. Cut the pepper
into strips. Thinly slice the onion into rings. Quarter the
tomatoes and eggs.

Lightly toss all the ingredients together in the French
dressing, then season to taste.

Spoon the salad over the lettuce leaves and garnish
with the anchovy fillets and black olives. Serve with hot
French bread.

Cook's Tip

To make melba toast,
remove crusts from
medium-thick sliced bread.
Lightly toast on both sides.
Slice horizontally, then
toast the second side of
each thin piece until curled.

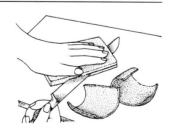

Cook's Tip

To prevent black rings
forming around the yolks of
hard-boiled eggs, drain and
leave in the saucepan under
a running cold tap for about
2 minutes.

31 | Eggs Mayonnaise

Preparation time
15 minutes

Cooking time
10 minutes

Serves 4

Calories
230 per portion

You will need
4 eggs
4 tablespoons mayonnaise
3 tablespoons double cream or
  whipping cream
2 teaspoons lemon juice
¼ teaspoon paprika
salt
8 lettuce leaves
1 tablespoon freshly chopped
  chives to garnish

Hard-boil the eggs for 10 minutes, then plunge them into cold water at once to prevent a dark line forming around the yolk. Leave the eggs to cool. Remove the shells and halve the eggs lengthways.

Mix together the mayonnaise, cream, lemon juice and seasoning. Arrange two lettuce leaves on each of four individual serving plates. Top the lettuce with two egg halves. Pour the mayonnaise mixture over the egg halves.

Garnish each serving with a sprinkle of chopped chives and serve with brown bread and butter.

32 | Stuffed Mushrooms

Preparation time
15 minutes

Cooking time
30 minutes

Oven temperature
180C, 350F, gas 4

Serves 4

Calories
295 per portion

You will need
12 large mushrooms
1 clove garlic, crushed
1 onion, finely chopped
50 g/2 oz butter
3 tablespoons oil
50 g/2 oz fresh breadcrumbs
50 g/2 oz Parmesan cheese,
  grated
salt and pepper

Garnish
tomato wedges
watercress sprigs

Remove the stems from the mushrooms and chop the stems finely. In a small saucepan, cook the garlic and onions in 25 g/1 oz of the butter and 1 tablespoon of the oil until soft. Add the chopped mushroom stems and stir over a moderate heat for about 5 minutes. Remove from the heat. Mix in the remaining oil, the breadcrumbs and Parmesan. Season to taste.

Stuff the mushroom tops with the mixture. Top each cap with a dot of the remaining butter.

Arrange the mushrooms in a shallow well-oiled ovenproof dish and bake in a moderate oven for about 25 minutes. Serve hot, garnished with tomato wedges and watercress sprigs.

Cook's Tip

To make spicy egg mayonnaise, add 2 teaspoons of curry powder to the mayonnaise mixture and garnish with parsley sprigs and lemon slices.

Microwave Tip

Microwave the onion and garlic on full power for 4 minutes. Add chopped mushroom stems and cook 2 minutes. Cook filled mushroom tops in two batches (as shown) on full power for 3–4 minutes.

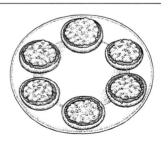

33 | Individual Onion Quiches

Preparation time
20 minutes

Cooking time
35 minutes

Oven temperature
200 C, 400 F, gas 6

Serves 4

Calories
625 per portion

You will need
225 g / 8 oz plain flour
pinch of salt
100 g / 4 oz margarine
2 tablespoons cold water

For the filling
2 large onions, sliced into rings
2 tablespoons oil
2 eggs
150 ml/¼ pint milk
salt and pepper
100 g / 4 oz Cheddar cheese,
   grated

Garnish
onion rings (optional)
coriander sprigs (optional)

Sift the flour and salt into a mixing bowl. Rub in the fat until the mixture resembles fine breadcrumbs. Gradually add the water and form the mixture into a ball. Put the pastry on a lightly floured board. Roll it out and use to line four 11-cm/4½-in quiche rings or flan dishes.

Cook the onion rings in the oil until soft. Beat the eggs lightly, then beat in the milk, season and add the cheese. Divide the onions equally amongst the quiches. Pour over the egg mixture.

Bake the quiches in a moderately hot oven for 30 minutes.

34 | Avocado Dip

Preparation time
10 minutes, plus 15
minutes to chill

Serves 4

Calories
130 per portion

You will need
1 onion
1 green chilli
1 tomato
2 avocados
juice of 1 lemon
1 or 2 cloves garlic, crushed
salt and pepper

Finely chop the onion. Slit, deseed, rinse, dry and finely chop the green chilli. Peel, deseed and chop the tomato.

Peel and stone the avocados. Mash to a chunky consistency in a bowl. Add the lemon juice, onion, garlic and chilli. Mix thoroughly, then season to taste with salt and pepper. Stir in the chopped tomato, then transfer the dip to a serving bowl or four individual bowls.

Chill for at least 15 minutes. Serve with taco chips, salted crisps, or vegetable crudités.

Freezer Tip

Place the cooled quiches on a baking tray, covered with cling film. Put in freezer until hard, then pack into two polythene bags, seal, label and return to the freezer. Use within 1 month.

Cook's Tip

Wash your hands well after handling chillies and do not rub your eyes when cutting them. The juice can irritate skin. Remove the hot seeds inside, and rinse the chillies under cold running water.

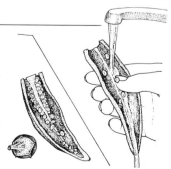

35 | Grilled Grapefruit

Preparation time
5 minutes, plus 10
minutes standing time

Cooking time
5 minutes

Serves 4

Calories
85 per portion

You will need
2 grapefruit
50 g/2 oz brown sugar
2 tablespoons rum, brandy or
   vermouth
few sprigs of mint to decorate

Halve the grapefruit, loosen the segments from the skin and from the centre with a grapefruit knife or other sharp knife, so they are easy to remove. Sprinkle each half with sugar. Pour over the rum, brandy or vermouth. Leave to stand for 10 minutes to allow the sugar and alcohol to soak right through the grapefruit.

Cook the grapefruit halves under a hot grill for about 5 minutes. Serve immediately decorated with a sprig of fresh mint.

36 | Melon and Black Grape Cocktail

Preparation time
10 minutes, plus 1
hour to chill

Serves 4

Calories
50 per portion

You will need
1 small honeydew melon
225 g/8 oz black grapes
2 teaspoons mint sauce
1 teaspoon caster sugar
few sprigs of mint to decorate

Halve the honeydew melon and scoop out the seeds. Use a melon baller to remove the fruit in neat balls into a bowl. Halve and remove the seeds from the black grapes. Add the grape halves to the melon, then add the mint sauce and sugar.

Cover the cocktail and chill for about an hour, tossing occasionally. Check the flavour, adding a little more sugar if required.

Serve the cocktail in glasses and decorate with fresh mint.

Cook's Tip

Using a sharp pointed knife, cut around the middle of the grapefruit in towards the centre in a zig-zag pattern. Pull the halves apart gently. This sort of edge is called vandyke.

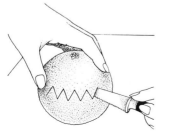

Cook's Tip

For special occasions, frost the tops of the glasses by dipping the rims lightly in beaten egg white then sugar.

37 | Toasted Sandwiches

Preparation time
10–15 minutes

**Each filling
makes 3**

Calories
276 per sandwich with
Filling 1
236 per sandwich with
Filling 2

You will need
12 slices bread
50 g/ 2 oz butter or margarine
watercress sprigs to garnish

Filling 1
3 slices cooked ham
50 g/ 2 oz Cheddar cheese grated
salt and pepper

Filling 2
1 (120-g/ 4¼- oz) can sardines in
tomato sauce
2 slices onion, finely chopped
salt and pepper

Remove and discard the crusts from the bread. Butter each slice. For filling 1, place a slice of ham on the unbuttered side of each of three slices of bread. Sprinkle with cheese and seasoning, then cover with second slices of bread, buttered side out, place in a sandwich toaster and cook for 5 minutes, or until crisp and golden.

For filling 2, remove the bones and mash the sardines. Spread the sardines on the unbuttered side of each of three slices of bread, sprinkle the onion on top, season and cover with second slices of bread, buttered side out, and toast as above.

Garnish with watercress sprigs and serve with celery sticks and tomatoes.

38 | Speedy Pizzas

Preparation time
10 minutes

Cooking time
20–25 minutes

Serves 4

Calories
530 per portion

You will need
1 small French loaf
50 g/ 2 oz butter
1 onion, finely chopped
1 clove garlic, crushed
1 tablespoon oil
100 g/ 4 oz button mushrooms
1 (425-g/ 15- oz) can tomatoes
100 g/ 4 oz mozzarella cheese
100 g/ 4 oz Cheddar cheese
salt and pepper
¼ teaspoon oregano

Cut the French loaf in half horizontally and butter each half. Cut each half across the middle so that you have four pieces of bread.

Cook the onion and garlic in the oil until soft. Add the mushrooms and cook for a few minutes, then add the tomatoes. Simmer vigorously for 10 minutes or until the tomato is reduced and thickened. Meanwhile dice the cheeses into small pieces.

Spread the French sticks with the tomato mixture, sprinkle over salt, pepper and the oregano. Dot the cheese evenly on the top (be careful not to put it too near the edges).

Brown under the grill for 5–10 minutes, or until the cheese has melted and the pizzas are heated through.

Cook's Tip

If you do not have a sandwich toaster, then make the sandwiches and brown both sides under a hot grill. Or try quickly shallow frying the sandwiches. Drain on absorbent kitchen paper.

Microwave Tip

Instead of browning them under the grill, halve the pizzas and cook on full power in the microwave for about 5 minutes, until heated through.

39 | Welsh Rarebit

Preparation time
5 minutes

Cooking time
8–10 minutes

Serves 4

Calories
390 per portion

You will need
225 g / 8 oz Cheddar cheese
25 g / 1 oz butter
25 g / 1 oz plain flour
salt and pepper
pinch of cayenne
pinch of mustard powder
150 ml / ¼ pint milk or beer
few drops of Worcestershire
    sauce
4 slices bread
butter for spreading

Grate the cheese. Melt the butter in a saucepan, reduce the heat, add the cheese, flour, seasonings, milk or beer and Worcestershire sauce. Heat the mixture gently, stirring occasionally, until a smooth, thick sauce is formed.

Toast and butter the bread. Top with the cheese mixture and brown under the grill for 2–3 minutes.

Serve immediately with grilled tomatoes, or garnished with tomato wedges and a coriander sprig.

40 | Cocktail Kebabs

Preparation time
15–20 minutes

Cooking time
20–25 minutes

Makes 16

Calories
230 per portion

You will need
1 onion, finely chopped
1 tablespoon oil
1 (227-g / 8-oz) can tomatoes
2 teaspoons tomato ketchup
½ teaspoon chilli powder
few drops of Worcestershire
    sauce
salt and pepper
8 rashers rindless bacon, halved
8 cocktail sausages
4 large cubes of pineapple
4 stuffed green olives

First make the spicy dip: cook the onion in the oil until softened, add the tomatoes and bring to the boil. Add the tomato ketchup, chilli powder, Worcestershire sauce and seasoning. Simmer gently for 5–10 minutes, or until reduced. Blend the mixture in a liquidiser until smooth, then pour it into a small serving bowl.

Pleat four halved bacon rashers on to a metal skewer. Wrap the remaining rashers around the sausages and the pineapple cubes and thread on to metal skewers.

Cook the kebabs under a hot grill for 10–15 minutes. Use a metal fork to slide the cooked ingredients off the metal skewers on to a double-thick piece of absorbent kitchen paper. Mop any excess fat off the top with another piece of absorbent kitchen paper. Thread the bacon on to wooden cocktail sticks with the olives. Thread the sausages on sticks with the pineapple.

Arrange the cocktail kebabs in a serving dish and serve with the dip.

Cook's Tip

Make satisfying and tasty buck rarebit by topping the Welsh rarebit with a poached egg. Add roughly chopped parsley for colour.

Cook's Tip

To remove items from skewers, use the prongs of a fork. Remember to protect your hand with a double-thick tea-towel if the skewers are hot from the grill.

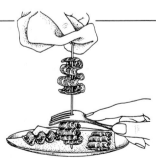

Fish Dishes

Delicious, nutritious, low in calories, and quick to cook, fish is a near-perfect food and yet has been underrated for many years. Fortunately, it has become much more widely appreciated recently, both for its nutritional worth and for its versatility. These recipes include all the popular fresh fish as well as making use of ready-prepared canned and frozen fish.

41 | Fish Kebabs

Preparation time
15 minutes, plus 1 hour to marinate

Cooking time
12 minutes

Serves 4

Calories
300 per portion

You will need
4 frozen cod or coley steaks, defrosted
1 large green pepper, deseeded
100 g/4 oz button mushrooms
8 bay leaves
4 tablespoons olive oil
2 cloves garlic, crushed
1 tablespoon lemon juice
salt and pepper
1 teaspoon dill weed
1 (340-g/12-oz) can pineapple chunks, drained
2 kiwi fruit, peeled and quartered
1 (410-g/14½-oz) can apricot halves, drained

Cut the fish steaks into 2.5-cm/1-in cubes. Cut the pepper into 2.5-cm/1-in squares. Wipe the mushrooms. Place the fish, pepper, mushrooms and bay leaves in a glass dish. Mix together the oil, garlic, lemon juice, salt and pepper and dill weed and pour over the fish mixture. Cover and chill for an hour, then remove the kebab ingredients, reserving the marinade.

Thread the peppers, pineapple, fish, bay leaves, kiwi fruit, mushrooms and apricots on to the skewers, continuing until all the ingredients have been used up.

Heat the grill to medium heat. Place the kebabs on a rack in the grill pan, and cook for 12 minutes, turning the kebabs as necessary and basting frequently with the marinade. Serve immediately with Saffron Rice (see recipe 149).

42 | Grilled Cod Steaks with Parsley Butter

Preparation time
10 minutes

Cooking time
12–16 minutes

Serves 4

Calories
270 per portion

You will need
4 fresh cod steaks
salt and pepper
100 g/4 oz butter
1 tablespoon chopped parsley
1 tablespoon lemon juice

Garnish
lemon wedges
coriander sprig (optional)

Season the fish generously with salt and pepper on each side. Cover and chill while preparing the parsley butter.

Beat the butter until soft and creamy. Work in the parsley, lemon juice and seasoning to taste. Using half the butter spread a little over each side of each fish steak.

Turn the grill on to medium heat. Place the cod steaks on a sheet of foil and grill for 6–8 minutes on each side or until the fish is cooked through.

Top the cod steaks with the remaining parsley butter and garnish with lemon wedges and a coriander sprig, if liked. Serve at once.

Cook's Tip

Saffron strands should be pounded in a pestle and mortar until reduced to a powder. Add a little hot water and stir to extract the maximum colour and flavour.

Microwave Tip

Microwave chilled butter on full power for about 15–30 seconds to soften. Defrost frozen butter for about 45–60 seconds – but remember to remove foiled wrapping first.

43| Fish au Gratin

Preparation time
15 minutes

Cooking time
12–16 minutes

Serves 4

Calories
205 per portion

You will need
*50 g/ 2 oz fresh white
   breadcrumbs
4 fresh cod steaks
salt and pepper
25 g/ 1 oz butter or margarine
50 g/ 2 oz Cheddar cheese, grated
¼ teaspoon mustard powder
lemon twists to garnish*

Spread the breadcrumbs on a sheet of foil and grill until golden and crunchy, then leave to cool.

Season the cod steaks generously with salt and pepper on each side. Dot the butter or margarine over one side of the fish. Turn the grill on to medium heat. Place the cod steaks buttered side up on a sheet of foil and grill for 6–8 minutes. Turn them over, mix together the breadcrumbs, cheese, mustard and seasoning to taste, sprinkle over the fish and grill for a further 6–8 minutes.

Place the cod steaks in a hot serving dish, garnish with lemon twists and serve at once with jacket potatoes and a green vegetable.

44| Haddock in Cider

Preparation time
20 minutes

Cooking time
30 minutes

Oven temperature
180 C, 350 F, gas 4

Serves 4

Calories
320 per portion

You will need
*10 shallots, peeled
100 g/ 4 oz button mushrooms
1–2 tablespoons oil
2 celery sticks, thinly sliced
1 green pepper, deseeded and
   diced
4 fresh haddock steaks
salt and pepper
300 ml/½ pint dry cider
25 g/ 1 oz butter or margarine
25 g/ 1 oz plain flour
150 ml/¼ pint single cream
chopped parsley to garnish*

Fry the shallots and mushrooms in the oil until golden. Transfer to a casserole dish. Add the celery and pepper to the pan and cook for a few minutes. Add to the casserole. Place the haddock steaks in the casserole, season with salt and pepper. Pour over the cider and bake in a moderate oven for 25 minutes or until the fish flakes easily when tested with the point of a knife. Transfer the fish and vegetables to a serving plate, cover and keep warm. Carefully drain off the cooking liquor. Melt the butter or margarine in a small saucepan, add the flour, then gradually add the cooking liquor, stirring continuously. Bring the sauce to the boil, season to taste, reduce the heat and simmer gently for 1–2 minutes. Stir in the cream and reheat without boiling. Pour the sauce over the fish, garnish with chopped parsley and serve immediately.

Cook's Tip

**A quick way to make
breadcrumbs: take a large
piece of bread and rub it on
the coarse side of a grater.**

Cook's Tip

**To avoid runny eyes when
peeling shallots or pickling
onions, peel them in a bowl
of water. Drain and discard
the skin when all are
peeled.**

45 | Haddock Crumble

Preparation time
20 minutes

Cooking time
30 minutes

Oven temperature
200 C, 400 F, gas 6

Serves 4

Calories
740 per portion

You will need
675 g/ 1½ lb haddock fillets
6 tablespoons water
salt and pepper
For the sauce
1 small onion, chopped
50 g/ 2 oz butter
40 g/ 1½ oz plain flour
600 ml/ 1 pint milk
juice of ½ lemon
50 g/ 2 oz mature Cheddar cheese, grated
For the topping
50 g/ 2 oz butter or margarine
100 g/ 4 oz plain flour
50 g/ 2 oz jumbo oats
1 tablespoon chopped fresh dill
knob of butter
dill sprig to garnish

Put the haddock, water and seasoning in a pan. Cover and poach for 5 minutes. Reserve any liquor and flake the fish, discarding skin. Fry onion in butter for 3 minutes, then add the flour. Gradually stir in the milk. Bring the sauce to the boil, add the lemon juice, seasoning and strained fish liquor. Simmer for 2 minutes. Add the cheese and fish to the sauce, then pour into an ovenproof dish.

Rub the fat into the flour until the mixture resembles fine breadcrumbs. Stir in oats, dill and seasoning. Spread on top of the fish. Dot with butter and bake in a moderately hot oven for 30 minutes or until the crumble is golden. Garnish with dill.

46 | Plaice Véronique

Preparation time
10 minutes

Cooking time
15 minutes

Oven temperature
190 C, 375 F, gas 5

Serves 4

Calories
315 per portion

You will need
8 medium plaice fillets, skinned
salt and pepper
150 ml/ ¼ pint dry white wine
1 tablespoon lemon juice
100 g/ 4 oz seedless grapes, plus
a few extra to garnish
(optional)
25 g/ 1 oz butter or margarine
25 g/ 1 oz plain flour
150 ml/ ¼ pint milk

Roll up each fillet skinned side inwards. Place the fish rolls in a greased ovenproof dish. Season the fish with salt and pepper, pour over the wine and lemon juice. Cover and bake in a moderately hot oven for about 15 minutes, or until the fish flakes easily when tested with the point of a knife. Transfer the fish to a serving dish and keep warm. Reserve the cooking liquor for the sauce.

Place the grapes in boiling water, boil for one minute, then drain. Heat the butter or margarine over a gentle heat, add the flour, then gradually add the milk, seasoning and reserved cooking liquor, stirring continuously. Bring the sauce to the boil, reduce the heat and simmer gently for 2 minutes, stirring occasionally. Pour the sauce over the fish and garnish with the grapes adding a few unblanched grapes if you like. Serve at once.

Cook's Tip

To skin fish fillets, place skin side down on a board. Rub salt on your fingers to hold the tail end. With a sharp knife cut at an acute angle, using a sawing motion between the flesh and skin.

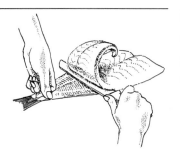

Microwave Tip

Arrange the rolls round a shallow dish. Cover with cling film and microwave for 5 minutes on full power. Mix in remaining ingredients, cover and cook for 5 minutes. Add grapes, cook 1 minute and serve.

47 | Stuffed Plaice Rolls

Preparation time
20 minutes

Cooking time
20–25 minutes

Oven temperature
180 C, 350 F, gas 4

Serves 4

Calories
390 per portion

You will need
8 small plaice fillets, skinned
100 g / 4 oz white breadcrumbs
grated rind and juice of 1 lemon
1 tablespoon chopped fresh dill
50 g / 2 oz cream cheese
salt and pepper
1 egg, lightly beaten
25 g / 1 oz butter or margarine
25 g / 1 oz plain flour
300 ml / ½ pint milk
150 ml / ¼ pint dry white wine

Garnish
dill sprigs
lemon twists

Put the fillets on a board, skinned side uppermost. Mix together the breadcrumbs, lemon rind and juice, dill, cream cheese, salt and pepper. Mix in enough egg to make a soft consistency. Place a spoonful of the stuffing on to each fillet and roll up. Place in an ovenproof dish and cover with greased foil. Bake in a moderate oven for 20–25 minutes.

To make the sauce, melt the butter or margarine over a gentle heat, add the flour, then gradually add the milk and wine and bring the sauce to the boil, stirring continuously. Reduce the heat and simmer gently for 2 minutes. Season to taste and pour over the stuffed plaice fillets. Garnish with fresh dill and lemon twists and serve immediately.

48 | Baked Stuffed Trout

Preparation time
10 minutes

Cooking time
20–25 minutes

Oven temperature
200 C, 400 F, gas 6

Serves 4

Calories
445 per portion

You will need
1 onion, finely chopped
25 g / 1 oz butter or margarine
100 g / 4 oz frozen chopped
   spinach
100 g / 4 oz fresh brown
   breadcrumbs
50 g / 2 oz flaked almonds,
   roughly chopped
grated rind of 1 lemon
¼ teaspoon grated nutmeg
salt and pepper
1 egg, lightly beaten
4 medium trout, cleaned, washed
   and dried
2 tablespoons olive oil

Garnish
lime twists
dill sprigs

Cook the onion in the butter or margarine until soft. Cover the spinach with boiling water, boil for 2 minutes, drain and squeeze dry. Mix together the onion, spinach, breadcrumbs, almonds, grated lemon rind, nutmeg and seasoning. Combine this stuffing with the egg. Divide into four and use to fill the cavity in each fish.

Place the fish in a shallow ovenproof dish, brush with the oil and bake in a moderately hot oven for 20–25 minutes or until the flesh flakes easily. Serve immediately, garnished with lime twists and fresh dill.

Cook's Tip

To make lemon twists, thinly slice a lemon and cut a slit in to the centre of each slice. Twist the slices from the cuts.

Freezer Tip

To freeze whole fish, like mackerel or trout, stuff the body cavity with a small roll of foil so that the fish stays a good shape. Remove the foil, stuff the fish (if required) and cook straight from frozen.

49 | *Trout with Almonds*

Preparation time
10 minutes

Cooking time
10 minutes

Serves 4

Calories
445 per portion

You will need
salt and pepper
25 g / 1 oz plain flour
4 medium trout, cleaned, washed
 and dried
100 g / 4 oz butter or margarine
50 g / 2 oz flaked almonds
2 tablespoons lemon juice
2 tablespoons chopped parsley

Garnish
lemon wedges
parsley sprigs

Add the seasoning to the flour and coat the trout with the flour.

Melt half the butter or margarine in a large frying pan and fry two trout gently over a medium heat for 4–5 minutes on each side, or until golden. Drain the fish and transfer to a serving dish to keep warm. Fry the remaining trout in the same way.

When the fish are cooked, add the remaining butter to the frying pan and return it to the heat. When the fat is hot, fry the almonds until golden, quickly add the lemon juice, chopped parsley, and seasoning to taste. Stir well.

Pour the sauce over the trout, garnish with lemon wedges and parsley sprigs. Serve immediately with Duchesse Potatoes (see recipe 106) and a green vegetable.

50 | *Piquant Mackerel*

Preparation time
20 minutes

Cooking time
25 minutes

Serves 4

Calories
390 per portion

You will need
4 mackerel, halved and filleted
1 tablespoon oil
salt and pepper
juice of 1 lemon
25 g / 1 oz butter or margarine
25 g / 1 oz plain flour
300 ml / ½ pint milk
2 teaspoons mustard powder
1 teaspoon white wine vinegar
1 teaspoon honey
1 tablespoon chopped parsley

Garnish
sprigs of flat-leaved parsley
lemon slices
lime slices

Place the mackerel fillets on a sheet of greased foil and brush with the oil. Season generously with salt and pepper, sprinkle over the lemon juice. Fold the fillets into little parcels, wrap them securely in the foil. Cook in a steamer for 20–25 minutes. Meanwhile, melt the butter or margarine over a gentle heat, add the flour, then gradually add the milk, stirring continuously. Bring the sauce to the boil, reduce the heat, add the remaining ingredients, season to taste and simmer for 2 minutes.

Unwrap the fish and transfer to a serving dish, reserving the cooking liquor. Keep the fish warm. Add the cooking liquor to the sauce and simmer for a further few minutes, then pour over the mackerel. Garnish with parsley sprigs and halved slices of lemon and lime.

Microwave Tip

Cook two whole trout with about 25 g / 1 oz butter in a covered dish for 12 minutes on full power. Brown 50 g / 2 oz flaked almonds with 25 g / 1 oz butter in a mug for 4 minutes.

Cook's Tip

A good lemon squeezer is a useful kitchen utensil. Decide which type you prefer and invest in a sturdy one.

51 | *Herrings with Soured Cream Sauce*

Preparation time
15 minutes

Cooking time
12 minutes

Serves 4

Calories
435 per portion

You will need
4 fresh herrings
1 tablespoon oil
1 tablespoon white wine vinegar
salt and pepper
4 spring onions, chopped
300 ml/½ pint soured cream
1 teaspoon mustard powder
cayenne
1 tablespoon chopped fresh dill

Garnish
cayenne
halved lemon slices
1 teaspoon chopped fresh dill,
*   plus a few sprigs*

Scale and gut the herrings. Wash the insides and outsides of the fish and pat dry. Cut slits down both sides of each fish. Brush the fish with oil, then spoon the vinegar into the slits and season the fish generously.

Heat the grill to medium heat and grill the herrings on one side for 6 minutes. Turn the fish over, brush with a little more oil and cook for a further 6 minutes. Transfer the herrings to a serving plate and keep warm.

Mix the remaining ingredients together. Pour the sauce into a small serving bowl, and sprinkle with cayenne and dill. Garnish the fish with halved lemon slices and sprigs of dill and serve with the sauce.

52 | *Salmon Mousse*

Preparation time
15 minutes, plus 1 hour to chill

Serves 4

Calories
365 per portion

You will need
1 tablespoon gelatine
2 tablespoons hot water
1 (213-g/ 7½-oz) can salmon
150 ml/¼ pint natural yogurt
150 ml/¼ pint mayonnaise
1 tablespoon tomato ketchup
salt and pepper
2 egg whites

Garnish
orange slices
lime slices
parsley sprigs
dill sprigs

Sprinkle the gelatine on to the hot water in a bowl. Stand the bowl over a saucepan of simmering water and stir until dissolved.

Flake the salmon into a bowl, remove any remaining bones, and add the natural yogurt. Stir in the mayonnaise, then the tomato ketchup, gelatine and seasoning. Whisk the egg whites until stiff but not dry and fold into the salmon mixture. Pour the mixture into a serving bowl and chill for an hour or until set.

Garnish the mousse with orange and lime slices, dill and parsley sprigs and serve with triangles of toast and a salad.

Cook's Tip

To make your own soured cream, add 1–2 tablespoons lemon juice to 150 ml/¼ pint single cream.

Cook's Tip

The mousse can be set in a fish-shaped mould for elegant presentation. Serve turned out on a flat serving platter.

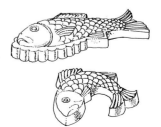

53 | Fish Ragoût

Preparation time
15 minutes

Cooking time
20–25 minutes

Oven temperature
200 C, 400 F, gas 6

Serves 4

Calories
180 per portion

You will need
450 g/1 lb cod, coley or haddock
  fillets, skinned
1 onion, sliced into rings
1 clove garlic, crushed
1 green pepper, deseeded and
  sliced into rings
100 g/4 oz button mushrooms
1–2 tablespoons oil
1 (400-g/14-oz) can of chopped
  tomatoes
150 ml/¼ pint dry white wine
½ teaspoon chopped fresh basil
salt and pepper

Garnish
fresh basil leaves
1 tablespoon chopped parsley

Rinse the fish, cut it into cubes, then put into an ovenproof dish. Fry the onion, garlic, pepper and mushrooms in the oil for 2–3 minutes, then add to the fish. Mix together the tomatoes, wine, basil, salt and pepper. Pour over the fish mixture. Cover the dish with foil and bake in a moderately hot oven for 20–25 minutes.

Serve immediately with parslied boiled rice, garnishing with fresh basil leaves and chopped parsley.

54 | Fish Cakes

Preparation time
20 minutes

Cooking time
20 minutes

Serves 4

Calories
390 per portion

You will need
225 g/8 oz coley, cubed
knob of butter
salt and pepper
225 g/8 oz mashed potatoes
100 g/4 oz Cheddar cheese,
  grated
25 g/1 oz plain flour
1 egg, lightly beaten
100 g/4 oz fresh white
  breadcrumbs
oil for frying

Garnish
lemon slices
lime slices
parsley sprigs

Place the fish on a buttered flameproof plate, season and cover with foil. Steam over a pan of boiling water for 10–15 minutes or until the fish flakes easily.

Flake the fish and mix with the potato and cheese. Season, divide the mixture into eight portions and pat each into a round cake. Coat the fish cakes in the flour, dip into the egg and then into the breadcrumbs. Heat the oil in a frying pan and fry the fish cakes until golden brown on the underside, then turn and cook until golden on the other side. Drain on absorbent kitchen paper.

Garnish the fish cakes with lemon and lime slices and parsley sprigs.

Cook's Tip

Fresh basil tastes significantly superior to its dried counterpart. Grow your own in a pot indoors, positioned on a light windowsill – purchase in plant form or nurture from seed.

Freezer Tip

For real speed, use instant mashed potato. Freeze the cakes before frying – put them on a baking tray covered with cling film and open freeze. Pack in freezer bags when hard.

55 | Fisherman's Pie

Preparation time
20 minutes

Cooking time
35 minutes

Oven temperature
200 C, 400 F, gas 6

Serves 4

Calories
760 per portion

You will need
450 g/ 1 lb cod or coley, cubed
knob of butter
salt and pepper
1 teaspoon lemon juice
1 quantity white sauce (recipe
  156)
1 (198-g/ 7-oz) can sweetcorn,
  drained
175 g/ 6 oz Cheddar cheese, grated
1 tablespoon chopped parsley
salt and pepper
pinch of mustard powder
4 hard-boiled eggs, roughly
  chopped
450 g/ 1 lb mashed potato with a
  little milk, butter and seasoning
  added

Place the fish on a buttered flameproof plate and season with salt, pepper and lemon juice. Cover the plate with foil or another plate and steam over a pan of boiling water for 10–15 minutes or until the fish flakes easily. Strain any juices and reserve for the sauce.

Bring the sauce to the boil, add the reserved fish stock and the sweetcorn, reduce the heat and simmer for 2 minutes, stirring occasionally. Remove the pan from the heat, blend in the cheese, parsley, salt, pepper and mustard. Finally add the eggs and the flaked fish. Pour into an ovenproof dish. Spread or pipe the prepared potato over the fish and bake in a moderately hot oven for 20 minutes or until the top is golden.

Microwave Tip

Instead of steaming the fish over a saucepan of water, put it in a shallow microwave-proof dish with 2–3 tablespoons hot water. Cover with cling film and cook on full power for about 15 minutes, or until the fish is only just cooked.

56 | Crispy Fish Sticks

Preparation time
20 minutes

Cooking time
5–10 minutes

Serves 4

Calories
355 per portion

You will need
8 whiting fillets
25 g/ 1 oz plain flour
salt and pepper
1 egg, beaten
100 g/ 4 oz sage and onion
  stuffing mix
2–4 tablespoons oil

For the sauce
150 ml/¼ pint thick-set natural
  yogurt
50 g/ 2 oz cucumber, diced
1 tablespoon wholegrain mustard
salt
cayenne

Garnish
lime twists
dill sprigs

Skin the whiting fillets and cut the flesh into fine strips. Mix the flour with the seasoning and use to coat the fish strips. Dip each fish strip into the beaten egg and then into the stuffing mix, pressing it on well. Heat the oil in a frying pan, add the fish strips and fry them, turning once or twice, until golden and crisp. Drain on absorbent kitchen paper, transfer to a serving dish and keep warm.

To make the sauce, mix all the ingredients together, seasoning to taste, and pour into a small serving bowl. Serve as an accompaniment to the fish sticks. Garnish the fish sticks with lime twists and dill sprigs.

Cook's Tip

To dice cucumber, cut into three or four slices lengthways, then place these, one or two at a time, cut side down on the board. Cut into fairly thin strips lengthways, then across.

57 | Fish Balls

Preparation time
10 minutes

Cooking time
10 minutes

Serves 4

Calories
245 per portion

You will need
450 g / 1 lb white fish, for
  example, hake, whiting, or cod
50 g / 2 oz fresh white
  breadcrumbs
25 g / 1 oz sesame seeds
1 egg, lightly beaten
1 teaspoon Worcestershire sauce
1 tablespoon soy sauce
2 tablespoons tomato ketchup
1 tablespoon chopped parsley
salt and pepper
oil for frying

Garnish
tomato rose
parsley sprig

Skin the fish and chop the flesh, removing any bones.
Mix the chopped fish with the remaining ingredients.
Take small spoonsful of the fish mixture and roll into balls
the size of marbles.

Heat the oil in a saucepan and fry the fish balls a few at
a time for 3–4 minutes or until golden. Drain on
absorbent kitchen paper and keep warm until all the fish
balls are cooked.

Serve hot with boiled rice and stir-fried vegetables,
garnishing with a tomato rose and parsley sprig.

58 | Seafood Curry

Preparation time
20 minutes

Cooking time
25–30 minutes

Serves 4

Calories
260 per portion

You will need
450 g / 1 lb white fish fillets, for
  example, haddock, coley or
  whiting, skinned
1–2 tablespoons oil
2 onions, finely chopped
2 cloves garlic, crushed
1 green pepper, deseeded and
  diced
2 tablespoons curry powder
2 teaspoons chilli powder
25 g / 1 oz plain flour
600 ml / 1 pint hot water
100 g / 4 oz cooked mussels
100 g / 4 oz peeled cooked prawns
4 tomatoes, peeled, deseeded
  and quartered
salt and pepper

Garnish
whole prawns
coriander sprigs

Cut the fish into cubes. Heat the oil in a frying pan, add
the onions, garlic and pepper and fry until softened, but
not browned. Add the spices and flour and cook gently.
Gradually add the water, stirring all the time. Bring the
mixture to the boil, reduce the heat and simmer gently,
then add the white fish and cook for 15 minutes.

Add the mussels, prawns and tomatoes, season to
taste and continue cooking for a further 5–10 minutes.

Garnish with whole prawns and coriander sprigs and
serve at once with boiled rice and poppadums.

Cook's Tip

**To prevent this fish mixture
sticking to your hands as
you shape it, dampen your
hands with cold water. If
the mixture begins to stick,
dampen your hands again.**

Cook's Tip

**If you cook poppadums in a
frying pan, use two fish
slices to prevent them from
curling up as they cook.**

59 | Kippers with Lemon Butter

Preparation time
10 minutes

Cooking time
5–8 minutes

Serves 4

Calories
375 per portion

You will need
8 kipper fillets
1 small onion, thinly sliced
75 g / 3 oz butter
grated rind and juice of ½ lemon
1 tablespoon chopped parsley
salt and pepper

Garnish
lemon twists
parsley sprigs

Skin the kippers and remove any obvious bones. Brush a grill grid with oil, place the kippers on top and arrange the onion rings on top.

Beat the butter until pale and creamy, then gradually work the rind and juice of the lemon into the butter. Beat in the parsley and seasoning. Dot the lemon butter over the fish.

Grill the kippers for 5–8 minutes. Garnish with lemon twists and parsley sprigs, and serve with a fresh green salad and wholemeal bread.

60 | Quick Tuna Bake

Preparation time
10 minutes

Cooking time
20–25 minutes

Oven temperature
200 C, 400 F, gas 6

Serves 4

Calories
480 per portion

You will need
2 (198-g / 7-oz) cans tuna, drained
4 spring onions, chopped
1 (425-g / 15-oz) can mushroom soup
100 g / 4 oz Cheddar cheese, grated
1 teaspoon chopped fresh dill
¼ teaspoon Worcestershire sauce
salt and pepper
225 g / 8 oz fresh brown breadcrumbs
knob of butter
dill sprig to garnish

Flake the tuna and mix together with the onion, soup, cheese, dill, Worcestershire sauce, salt and pepper.

Pour some of the fish sauce into an ovenproof dish. Add a layer of breadcrumbs, followed by a layer of sauce. Continue layering in this fashion until all the ingredients have been used up. Finish with a layer of breadcrumbs on the top, dot the surface with the butter and bake in a moderately hot oven for 20–25 minutes. Serve immediately, garnished with a sprig of dill and accompanied by a green salad.

Cook's Tip

To make an interesting, crunchy green salad, include some bean sprouts, fine strips of celery and sliced avocado with the lettuce and other traditional ingredients.

Cook's Tip

A quick way of 'chopping' spring onions: wash and trim them, then hold them over a bowl and snip them up from green end toward the root.

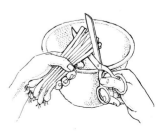

Casseroles and Stews

When casseroling or stewing, the cheaper cuts of meat are used as this moist cooking method tenderises and extracts the flavour. The addition of vegetables makes many of these recipes all-in-one dishes. Most of the recipes in this chapter are suitable for freezing and reheating in a microwave. Some will need a topping or garnish added after reheating.

61 | Beef in Beer

Preparation time
20 minutes

Cooking time
1 hour 45 minutes

Oven temperature
160 C, 325 F, gas 3

Serves 4

Calories
525 per portion

You will need
8 button onions
100 g/ 4 oz baby carrots
2 celery sticks, cut in chunks
1 green pepper, deseeded and sliced into rings
100 g/ 4 oz button mushrooms
2 tablespoons oil
575 g/ 1¼ lb lean braising steak, cut into cubes
40 g/ 1½ oz plain flour
¼ teaspoon mustard powder
salt and pepper
300 ml/½ pint beer
300 ml/½ pint beef stock
100 g/ 4 oz rindless streaky bacon
1 bay leaf

Garnish
1 tablespoon chopped parsley
bay leaves

Cook the vegetables in the oil for 5 minutes, then transfer to a casserole, reserving the oil. Coat the meat cubes in a mixture of the flour, mustard and seasoning. Fry a few pieces at a time in the reserved oil until just starting to brown. Add to the casserole. Stir any remaining flour into the fat in the pan. Gradually add the beer and stock and bring to the boil. Pour into the casserole. Cut the bacon rashers in half, roll up each half rasher and add to the casserole. Add the bay leaf and stir well. Cover the casserole and cook in a moderate oven for 1½ hours or until the meat is tender. Garnish as shown and serve.

62 | Boeuf Bourguignonne

Preparation time
20 minutes

Cooking time
1 hour 45 minutes

Oven temperature
180 C, 350 F, gas 4

Serves 4

Calories
515 per portion

You will need
575 g/ 1¼ lb chuck steak, cut into cubes
25 g/ 1 oz plain flour
2–3 tablespoons oil
100 g/ 4 oz rindless streaky bacon, diced
1 onion, sliced
1 clove garlic, crushed
100 g/ 4 oz mushrooms, sliced
300 ml/½ pint dry red wine
600 ml/1 pint beef stock
bouquet garni
salt and pepper
1 tablespoon chopped parsley to garnish

Coat the meat cubes in the flour. Heat the oil in a frying pan, brown the meat and transfer to a casserole.

Cook the diced bacon in the oil, until golden in colour and add to the meat. Gently cook the onion and garlic in the frying pan until soft, add the mushrooms and continue cooking for 2–3 minutes. Put all the vegetables in the casserole and pour in the red wine and beef stock. Add the bouquet garni and seasoning and stir well. Cover the casserole and cook in a moderate oven for 1½ hours or until the meat is tender.

Serve with parslied boiled rice and a green salad. Garnish with chopped parsley, and any fresh herbs.

Cook's Tip

To coat meat cubes, or similar items in flour, put the flour in a polythene bag. Add the meat and, holding the end of the bag firmly closed, shake well.

Cook's Tip

To crush garlic, without a crusher, place a peeled clove on a chopping board and sprinkle with a little salt. Then crush with the flat, wide blade of a knife, pressing hard with the palm of your hand.

63 | Beef Cobbler

Preparation time
20 minutes

Cooking time
2 hours 25 minutes

Oven temperature
160 C, 325 F, gas 3 and
220 C, 425 F, gas 7

Serves 4

Calories
750 per portion

You will need
575 g/ 1¼ lb stewing or braising
    steak, cut into cubes
25 g/ 1 oz plain flour
1 teaspoon dried mixed herbs
salt and pepper
1 onion, chopped
3 tablespoons oil
100 g/ 4 oz baby carrots
2 parsnips, quartered and sliced
600 ml/ 1 pint beef stock
100 g/ 4 oz frozen peas

For the topping
225 g/ 8 oz self-raising flour
pinch of salt
50 g/ 2 oz butter or margarine
1 egg, beaten plus extra to glaze
3 tablespoons milk

Toss the meat in a mixture of the flour, herbs and seasoning. Cook in the oil until browned. Transfer to a casserole. Cook the onion in the oil until soft and add to the casserole with the carrots, parsnips and beef stock. Season to taste. Cover and cook in a moderate oven for 2 hours until the meat is cooked. Stir in the peas.

Sift the flour and salt into a bowl, rub in the fat until the mixture resembles fine breadcrumbs. Stir in the beaten egg and enough milk to make a soft dough. Roll out on a lightly floured work surface to about 2.5 cm/1 in thick. Cut into rounds using a 5-cm/2-in scone cutter. Place the cobblers on top of the meat in the casserole, increase the oven heat and bake for 15 minutes.

Freezer Tip

If you intend freezing the cooked cobbler, then first line the casserole dish with double-thick cooking foil, making sure there are no cracks or gaps and allowing plenty of overlap round the rim.

Cook the casserole and cobbler in the lined dish, then cool and lightly cover. Freeze until hard. When solid, the cobbler in foil can be removed from the dish, packed in extra foil, labelled and stored.

64 | Lancashire Hot Pot

Preparation time
10 minutes

Cooking time
2 hours

Oven temperature
160 C, 325 F, gas 3 and
200 C, 400 F, gas 6

Serves 4

Calories
705 per portion

You will need
675–1 kg/ 1½–2 lb middle or best
    end neck of lamb
4 lambs' kidneys, skinned and
    cored
2 carrots, sliced
1 small turnip, diced
2 onions, chopped
salt and pepper
450 g/ 1 lb potatoes, sliced
300 ml/ ½ pint lamb or beef stock
25 g/ 1 oz butter or margarine
1 teaspoon chopped parsley to
    garnish

Cut the lamb and the kidneys into neat pieces and place in alternate layers with the carrot, turnip and onion in a casserole. Season with salt and pepper.

Finish the hot pot with layers of sliced potatoes. Pour over the stock and dot the top with small pieces of butter or margarine. Cover the casserole with a lid and place in a moderate oven for about 2 hours until the meat is cooked. Uncover the casserole for the last half an hour and increase the oven temperature to moderately hot to brown the top layer of potatoes.

Serve immediately garnished with chopped parsley.

Cook's Tip

To core kidneys, cut them in half, then use kitchen scissors to snip out the white cores.

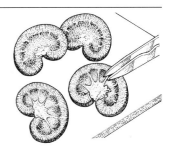

65 | Irish Stew

Preparation time
20 minutes

Cooking time
2 hours

Serves 4

Calories
685 per portion

You will need
2 tablespoons oil
450 g/ 1 lb potatoes, thinly sliced
675–1 kg/ 1½–2 lb middle or scrag
   end neck of lamb or mutton
3 onions, thinly sliced
salt and pepper
900 ml/ 1½ pints lamb stock
chopped parsley to garnish

Heat the oil in a large saucepan and brown the sliced potatoes. Remove the potatoes and reserve. Cut the lamb or mutton into neat joints, then layer the lamb, onion and potato in the saucepan, seasoning each layer well. Pour over the stock and bring the stew slowly to the boil. Reduce the heat, cover with a lid and simmer gently for 2 hours or until the meat is cooked.

   Garnish the stew with parsley and serve with seasonal vegetables.

66 | Hungarian Goulash

Preparation time
15 minutes

Cooking time
2½–3 hours

Oven temperature
160 C, 325 F, gas 3

Serves 4

Calories
495 per portion

You will need
25 g/ 1 oz plain flour
¼ teaspoon mustard powder
1 tablespoon paprika
salt and pepper
575 g/ 1¼ lb stewing or braising
   steak, cut into cubes
3 tablespoons oil
2 onions, sliced into rings
1 red pepper, deseeded and
   sliced
1 green pepper, deseeded and
   sliced
450 g/ 1 lb tomatoes, peeled and
   quartered
600 ml/ 1 pint beef stock
150 ml/¼ pint soured cream
1 tablespoon chopped parsley to
   garnish

Mix together the flour, mustard, paprika, salt and pepper and toss the meat cubes in the mixture. Heat the oil in a frying pan and cook the cubes of meat until brown on all sides. Transfer to a casserole. Gently fry the onions and peppers in the remaining fat until soft, and add to the casserole with the tomatoes and beef stock.

   Mix the ingredients together well. Cover the casserole with a lid and cook in a moderate oven for 2–2½ hours or until the meat is tender.

   Pour the soured cream over the meat and serve immediately, garnished with chopped parsley.

Cook's Tip

Always trim excess fat from lamb before casseroling. If the casserole looks greasy, leave to stand for 5 minutes, then use a large flattish spoon to skim off the fat.

Microwave Tip

Only tender meats microwave well. Use rump steak, cut across the grain into small thin slices. Flour the meat, then mix in all ingredients. Microwave on full power for 20 minutes.

67 | *Cassoulet*

Preparation time
*10 minutes, plus
overnight soaking*

Cooking time
2½ hours

Oven temperature
160 C, 325 F, gas 3

Serves 4

Calories
605 per portion

You will need
*350 g/ 12 oz haricot beans
2 onions, chopped
100 g/ 4 oz rindless streaky
   bacon, chopped
100 g/ 4 oz cervelat sausage,
   sliced
4 chicken drumsticks
225 g/ 8 oz tomatoes, peeled and
   quartered
3 tablespoons tomato purée
900 ml/ 1½ pints chicken stock
bouquet garni
salt and pepper
1 teaspoon chopped parsley to
   garnish*

Soak the haricot beans in cold water overnight, then drain well. Mix the beans, onion, bacon, sausage, chicken and tomatoes in a casserole. Add the tomato purée, chicken stock, bouquet garni, season well and mix together.

Cover the casserole with a lid and cook in a moderate oven for about 2½ hours until the haricot beans are cooked.

Serve immediately, garnished with chopped parsley.

68 | *Sweet 'n' Sour Pork Casserole*

Preparation time
20 minutes

Cooking time
1 hour 45 minutes

Oven temperature
160 C, 325 F, gas 3

Serves 4

Calories
435 per portion

You will need
*25 g/ 1 oz plain flour
1 teaspoon ground ginger
salt and pepper
575 g/ 1¼ lb lean pork, cut into
   2.5-cm/ 1-in cubes
1 onion, finely chopped
1 green pepper, deseeded and
   sliced
2 tablespoons oil
150 ml/¼ pint chicken stock
1 (454-g/ l-lb) can pineapple
   chunks
2 tablespoons soy sauce
3 tablespoons vinegar
50 g/ 2 oz no-need-to-soak dried
   apricots*

Garnish
*tomato rose
cucumber leaves*

Mix the flour, ground ginger, salt and pepper together and toss the pork in the mixture. Fry the onion and pepper in the oil for 2–3 minutes. Transfer to a casserole.

Brown the pork cubes in the oil, then add to the casserole. Stir any remaining flour into the pan, blend in the stock and the juice from the pineapple. Bring to the boil, then add to the casserole with the remaining ingredients. Cover and cook in a moderate oven for 1½ hours. Serve with boiled rice, garnished as shown.

Cook's Tip

Cervelat is a smoked, moist sausage, usually containing finely minced beef and pork. It is made in various European countries, including France and Germany. Cervelat is matured for a shorter time than the Italian salami sausage, and as a result is more pliable. It is also less highly seasoned. Select from a delicatessen.

Microwave Tip

Lean pork microwaves well. Mix all the ingredients, coating meat in flour and omitting oil. Microwave on full power for 15–20 minutes.

69 | Pork and Dumplings

Preparation time
20 minutes

Cooking time
2 hours 45 minutes

Oven temperature
180 C, 350 F, gas 4

Serves 4

Calories
570 per portion

You will need
575 g/ 1¼ lb lean boneless pork, cut
  into cubes
25 g/ 1 oz butter or margarine
2 onions, chopped
100 g/ 4 oz no-need-to-soak
  dried apricots
25 g/ 1 oz plain flour
600 ml/ 1 pint chicken stock
300 ml/½ pint dry cider
salt and pepper
100 g/ 4 oz self-raising flour
1 tablespoon chopped parsley
50 g/ 2 oz suet
2 tablespoons water

Garnish
halved orange slices
rosemary sprigs

Cook the pork cubes in the butter or margarine until golden, then transfer to a casserole. Cook the onion in the remaining fat until soft and add to the casserole with the apricots. Stir the flour into the fat in the pan and pour in the stock. Bring to the boil and add to the casserole with the cider. Mix all the ingredients together, season, cover, and cook in a moderate oven for 2 hours.

Sift the flour and a pinch of salt into a bowl, add the parsley and suet and mix well. Stir in the water and blend to make a soft dough. Divide and roll into small balls on a lightly floured surface. Add the dumplings to the casserole and cook for a further 30 minutes, or until the dumplings are cooked. Garnish as shown.

Cook's Tip

A flameproof casserole is
useful for this type of dish.
The ingredients can be
browned and casseroled in
the one pan.

70 | Coq au Vin

Preparation time
10 minutes

Cooking time
1 hour 15 minutes

Oven temperature
180 C, 350 F, gas 4

Serves 4

Calories
345 per portion

You will need
2 cloves garlic, crushed
½ teaspoon salt
4 chicken joints
25 g/ 1 oz butter or margarine
2 tablespoons oil
12 button onions
100 g/ 4 oz button mushrooms
25 g/ 1 oz plain flour
300 ml/½ pint dry red wine
150 ml/¼ pint chicken stock
bouquet garni
1 teaspoon brown sugar
salt and pepper
chopped parsley to garnish

Rub the crushed garlic and salt into each chicken joint. Heat the butter or margarine and oil in a frying pan and cook the chicken joints until golden on all sides. Transfer the joints to a casserole.

Fry the onions and mushrooms in the remaining fat until golden and add to the casserole.

Stir the flour into the pan, add the wine and bring to the boil. Pour over the chicken joints. Add the stock, bouquet garni and sugar to the casserole, then season well. Cover the casserole with a lid or foil and cook in a moderate oven for about 1 hour. Remove the bouquet garni.

Serve garnished with chopped parsley.

Cook's Tip

For an excellent flavour,
marinate the chicken joints
in the wine overnight.
Drain, reserving the wine
and cook as above.

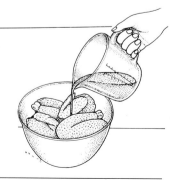

71 | *Turkey with Peaches*

Preparation time
15 minutes

Cooking time
30 minutes

Serves 4

Calories
315 per portion

You will need
25 g/1 oz plain flour
½ teaspoon grated nutmeg
salt and pepper
4 turkey fillets, cut into fine strips
2 tablespoons oil
1 onion, thinly sliced
1 (227-g/8-oz) can peach slices,
    drained
300 ml/½ pint chicken or turkey
    stock
150 ml/¼ pint soured cream

Garnish
chopped parsley
peach slices
bay leaves

Mix together the flour, nutmeg, salt and pepper and toss the turkey strips in the seasoned flour. Heat the oil in a frying pan and brown the turkey strips all over. Add the onion and cook for a further 2–3 minutes until soft. Add the peach slices, reserving a few for garnish, and chicken stock to the pan and bring to the boil. Reduce the heat and simmer gently for 20 minutes.

Remove the pan from the heat and add the soured cream. Reheat without boiling. Garnish with chopped parsley, reserved peach slices and bay leaves, and serve with a mixed salad.

72 | *Chicken Fricassee*

Preparation time
15 minutes

Cooking time
30 minutes

Serves 4

Calories
335 per portion

You will need
4 boneless breasts of chicken, cut
    into 1-cm/½-in wide strips
25 g/1 oz plain flour
50 g/2 oz butter or margarine
1 onion, chopped
100 g/4 oz mushrooms, sliced
½ teaspoon dried thyme
salt and pepper
150 ml/¼ pint chicken stock
150 ml/¼ pint dry white wine
150 ml/¼ pint soured cream
zested lemon rind to garnish

Toss the chicken strips in the flour. Heat the butter or margarine in a frying pan and cook the chopped onion until soft. Add the mushrooms and cook for another 2 minutes. Add the chicken strips and cook until they are golden all over. Sprinkle over the thyme, and season to taste.

Mix in the stock and wine and bring to the boil, then reduce the heat and simmer gently for 20 minutes. Reduce the heat further, stir in the soured cream and cook until the sauce is warmed through, but do not allow the sauce to boil.

Garnish with lemon rind and serve the chicken with parslied boiled rice and buttered carrots.

Cook's Tip

Serve fresh spinach noodles with this dish. Cook fresh pasta in boiling salted water for about 5 minutes. Drain, butter and serve.

Cook's Tip

If your eyes run very badly when peeling onions, then hold the onions under a slow running cold tap.

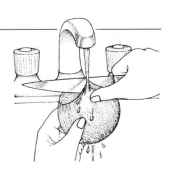

73 | Chicken Curry

Preparation time
20 minutes

Cooking time
50 minutes

Serves 4

Calories
480 per portion

You will need
3 tablespoons oil
575 g/1¼ lb boneless chicken
   breast, cut into cubes
2 onions, chopped
2 cloves garlic, crushed
1 green pepper, deseeded and
   chopped
2 tablespoons garam masala
1–2 teaspoons chilli powder
25 g/1 oz plain flour
50 g/2 oz desiccated coconut
50 g/2 oz ground almonds
450 ml/¾ pint chicken stock
450 g/1 lb tomatoes, peeled and
   quartered
2 tablespoons lemon juice
salt and pepper
chopped fresh coriander to
   garnish

Heat the oil in a large frying pan and brown the chicken cubes on all sides. Remove from the pan. Cook the onion, garlic and pepper in the oil until soft. Stir in the garam masala, chilli powder and flour and cook gently for 5 minutes. Add the coconut, almonds, chicken stock and tomatoes. Bring the mixture to the boil, reduce the heat and simmer gently for 20 minutes.

Add the chicken and lemon juice to the pan, season to taste and continue cooking for a further 20 minutes.

Garnish the curry with coriander and serve with rice and a tomato and onion salad.

74 | Rabbit Casserole

Preparation time
20 minutes, plus 2–3
hours to marinate

Cooking time
3 hours

Oven temperature
160 C, 325 F, gas 3

Serves 4

Calories
340 per portion

You will need
4 rabbit portions
300 ml/½ pint dry red wine
3 tablespoons vinegar
4 tablespoons oil
salt and pepper
1 bay leaf
25 g/1 oz plain flour
8–12 button onions
1 red pepper, deseeded and sliced
   into rings
100 g/4 oz baby carrots
300 ml/½ pint water
1 teaspoon wholegrain mustard
1 tablespoon redcurrant jelly
parsley sprigs to garnish

Place the rabbit joints in a bowl. Mix together the wine, vinegar, 1 tablespoon of the oil, salt and pepper. Pour over the rabbit and add the bay leaf. Marinate the rabbit for 2–3 hours, turning occasionally.

Remove the rabbit joints from the marinade, drain on absorbent kitchen paper and coat with the flour.

Heat the remaining oil in a frying pan, fry the rabbit joints until just golden and transfer to a casserole. Cook the onions in the oil until golden and add to the casserole. Fry the pepper rings in the pan for a few minutes and add to the casserole with the remaining ingredients, seasoning to taste. Pour in the marinade and mix all the ingredients together well. Cover with a lid and cook in a moderate oven for 2½ hours until the rabbit is tender.

Garnish with parsley sprigs.

Cook's Tip

Fresh coriander leaves look similar to flat-leaved parsley, but taste completely different. When buying, look for roots which are left on coriander, not on parsley.

Cook's Tip

To deseed a pepper, cut off the top with a sharp knife, then use the point of the knife to cut through the pith round the inside. Remove core and seeds which should come out as a whole.

75 | Kidney and Sausage Casserole

Preparation time
15 minutes

Cooking time
50 minutes

Oven temperature
160 C, 325 F, gas 3

Serves 4

Calories
615 per portion

You will need
2 tablespoons oil
1 onion, sliced into rings
1 green pepper, deseeded and
  sliced into rings
25 g/ 1 oz plain flour
pinch of mustard powder
salt and pepper
8 lamb's kidneys, cored and
  halved
450 g/ 1 lb cocktail sausages, or
  skinless chipolatas, cut into
  chunks
1 (400-g/ 14-oz) can chopped
  tomatoes
300 ml/½ pint beef stock
chopped parsley to garnish

Heat the oil in a frying pan and cook the onion and pepper in the oil for a few minutes. Transfer to a casserole. Mix together the flour, mustard, salt and pepper and toss the kidneys and sausages in the seasoned flour.

Cook the kidneys and sausages in the remaining oil until brown on all sides and transfer to the casserole. Mix in the tomatoes and beef stock, cover the casserole with a lid and cook in a moderate oven for 30–40 minutes.

Garnish with parsley and serve the casserole with boiled rice, or mashed potato, piped and browned in the oven if liked.

76 | Liver and Watercress

Preparation time
15 minutes

Cooking time
25–30 minutes

Serves 4

Calories
400 per portion

You will need
2 onions, sliced into rings
2 tablespoons oil
25 g/ 1 oz plain flour
pinch of mustard powder
salt and pepper
450 g/ 1 lb lamb's liver, sliced into
  strips
150 ml/¼ pint chicken stock
150 ml/¼ pint orange juice
bunch of watercress, trimmed
  and chopped
150 ml/¼ pint single cream

Garnish
orange slices
parsley sprigs

Cook the onion rings in the oil until soft. Remove from the pan and set aside. Mix the flour with the mustard, salt and pepper and toss the liver strips in it. Reserving the flour, fry the liver in the oil for 2–3 minutes, then add to the cooked onions. Stir the remaining flour into the oil in the pan, blend in the chicken stock and orange juice and bring to the boil. Reduce the heat, add the watercress, onion and liver and simmer for 15 minutes or until the liver is cooked through.

Stir in the cream and seasoning to taste and cook over a gentle heat until the sauce is hot. Do not allow it to boil or the cream will curdle. Serve the liver garnished with orange slices and parsley sprigs and accompanied by Duchesse Potatoes (see recipe 106) and green beans.

Cook's Tip

**Vary the flavour of plain
rice by adding a pinch of
turmeric, herbs, lemon rind
or chopped spring onions.**

Cook's Tip

**To segment an orange, peel
and remove pith. Hold
orange over a bowl (to
catch juice) and cut in
between each membrane to
free and remove the
segments.**

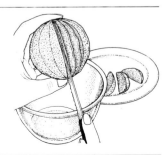

77 | Chilli con Carne

Preparation time
10 minutes

Cooking time
30–35 minutes

Serves 4

Calories
435 per portion

You will need
1 tablespoon oil
1 onion, chopped
2 cloves garlic, crushed
450 g/ 1 lb minced beef
15 g/½ oz plain flour
salt
2 teaspoons chilli powder
1 (400- g/ 14- oz) can tomatoes
300 ml/½ pint beef stock
1 (425- g/ 15- oz) can red kidney
    beans
chopped parsley to garnish

Heat the oil in a frying pan and cook the onion and garlic until soft. Add the minced beef and cook until brown all over. Mix in the flour, salt to taste, chilli powder, tomatoes and beef stock. Stir the mixture well and bring to the boil. Reduce the heat and simmer gently for 30 minutes, stirring occasionally.

Drain the kidney beans, add to the chilli and cook for a further 5–10 minutes or until the kidney beans are heated through.

Serve the chilli on a bed of boiled rice. Garnish with parsley.

78 | Moussaka

Preparation time
30 minutes

Cooking time
1 hour 40 minutes

Oven temperature
180 C, 350 F, gas 4

Serves 4

Calories
630 per portion

You will need
2 aubergines, thinly sliced
salt and pepper
3 tablespoons oil
3 onions, thinly sliced
6 tomatoes, peeled
450 g/ 1 lb minced beef or lamb
1 tablespoon plain flour
1 tablespoon tomato purée
300 ml/½ pint beef stock
1 teaspoon dried mixed herbs
40 g/ 1½ oz butter or margarine
40 g/ 1½ oz plain flour
600 ml/ 1 pint milk
75 g/ 3 oz Cheddar cheese, grated
chopped parsley to garnish

Sprinkle the aubergines with salt to remove bitter juices and leave covered while preparing the other vegetables. Heat the oil in a frying pan and cook the onion until soft. Remove from the pan and set aside. Slice the tomatoes.

Rinse the aubergine, then dry on absorbent kitchen paper and fry in the pan, a few slices at a time, until golden on each side. Drain.

Fry the meat until browned. Stir in the flour, tomato purée, stock, herbs and seasoning. Bring to the boil, then simmer for 15 minutes. Make a cheese sauce with the remaining ingredients, as instructed in recipe 110. Layer the meat and vegetables in an ovenproof dish, then top with the cheese sauce. Bake in a moderately hot oven for 1 hour.

Garnish the moussaka with chopped parsley and serve, accompanied by a mixed salad.

Cook's Tip

Dried red kidney beans need overnight soaking and rapid boiling for 3–5 minutes, then about 1 hour's simmering. They can be used half-cooked in chilli. Add extra liquid and cook until tender.

Cook's Tip

A quick way to make cheese sauce: put all ingredients, except cheese, in a saucepan and heat slowly to boiling point, whisking continuously. Stir in cheese.

79 | *Chicken and Lemon Casserole*

Preparation time
10 minutes

Cooking time
1 hour 15 minutes

Oven temperature
180 C, 350 F, gas 4

Serves 4

Calories
330 per portion

You will need
4 chicken joints
salt and pepper
1 tablespoon chopped lemon
　thyme or thyme
grated rind and juice of 1 lemon
600 ml/ 1 pint chicken stock
3 teaspoons cornflour
150 ml/¼ pint double cream

Garnish
lemon twists
chopped lemon thyme

Place the chicken joints in a casserole, rub in a little salt and pepper and the lemon thyme or thyme. Sprinkle over the rind and juice of the lemon and the chicken stock.

Cook, covered, in a moderate oven for 1 hour. Carefully drain the liquid from the casserole into a saucepan. Return the chicken to the oven to keep warm. Mix the cornflour with a little cold water to a smooth paste, stir into the cooking liquid. Bring the liquid to the boil, stirring all the time. Reduce the heat and add the cream. Season to taste.

Pour the sauce over the joints and garnish with lemon twists and lemon thyme. Serve immediately with boiled rice and Brussels Sprouts with Chestnuts (see recipe 113).

80 | *Shepherd's Pie*

Preparation time
20 minutes

Cooking time
45 minutes

Oven temperature
180 C, 350 F, gas 4

Serves 4

Calories
525 per portion

You will need
1½ tablespoons oil
1 onion, chopped
1 green pepper, deseeded and
　chopped
450 g/ 1 lb minced beef
100 g/ 4 oz mushrooms, sliced
2 tablespoons tomato purée
1 teaspoon Worcestershire sauce
300 ml/½ pint beef stock
salt and pepper
675 g/ 1½ lb potatoes
25 g/ 1 oz butter or margarine
2–3 tablespoons milk

Heat the oil in a frying pan and cook the onion and pepper for a few minutes. Stir in the minced beef and cook until it is evenly browned. Add the mushrooms and cook until soft. Mix in the tomato purée, Worcestershire sauce, beef stock and seasoning and slowly bring the mixture to the boil. Reduce the heat and simmer gently for 20 minutes.

Meanwhile, cook the potatoes in a pan of boiling salted water for 20 minutes or until tender. Drain, mash with a fork, add the butter or margarine and the milk and beat until smooth.

Place the meat mixture in an ovenproof dish and cover with the mashed potato, forking it neatly or piping it. Bake in a moderate oven for 20 minutes or until the top is crisp and golden.

Serve the shepherd's pie immediately.

Cook's Tip

If you prefer, skin the chicken joints for this dish. Trim off leg and wing ends, then pull off the skin from the cut side of the joint.

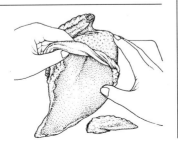

Freezer Tip

Make individual pies, freeze until hard, then pack neatly in a large bag. Microwave on high for 10–20 minutes for one or two pies.

Roasts and Grills

Roasting and grilling are comparatively quick cooking methods, but only suitable for prime cuts of meat and tender poultry. There are many ways of adding flavour to the meat and in this section you will find recipes using stuffings, marinades, sauces and flavoured butters, all of which add taste and appetite appeal to poultry, beef, lamb, pork and bacon.

81 | Roast Chicken

Preparation time
20 minutes

Oven temperature
200 C, 400 F, gas 6

Serves 6

Calories
230 per portion

You will need
1 (1.5-kg/3-lb) oven-ready
  chicken
1–2 tablespoons oil

For the stuffing
1 tablespoon oil
1 onion, chopped
100 g/4 oz fresh white
  breadcrumbs
1 tablespoon dried or 3
  tablespoons chopped
  tresh tarragon
grated rind and juice of 1 lemon
1 small egg, lightly beaten
salt and pepper

Garnish
lemon wedges
parsley sprigs

Weigh the chicken and calculate the cooking time. Allow 20 minutes per 450 g/1 lb plus an extra 20 minutes. Remove and reserve the giblets for gravy, then wash the chicken. Brush the chicken with the oil.

Heat the oil and cook the onion until soft. Mix with the breadcrumbs, tarragon, lemon rind and juice, egg and seasoning. Stuff the neck end of the chicken and secure with a skewer. Place the bird in a roasting tin and roast in a moderately hot oven for the calculated time.

Garnish the chicken as shown and serve with gravy (see Cook's Tip 86) and vegetables of your choice.

82 | Chicken with Honey

Preparation time
10 minutes

Cooking time
25–30 minutes

Serves 4

Calories
320 per portion

You will need
50 g/2 oz butter or margarine
2 tablespoons honey
grated rind of 1 lemon
50 g/2 oz flaked almonds
1 teaspoon wholegrain mustard
salt and pepper
4 chicken joints

Mix together the butter or margarine, honey, lemon rind, almonds, mustard and seasoning.

Spread the mixture all over the chicken joints. Cook under a moderate grill for 25–30 minutes, turning the joints once and basting occasionally.

Serve the chicken with boiled parslied rice and a crisp green salad.

Freezer Tip

Fresh herbs such as tarragon freeze well. Chop finely and open freeze on a metal tray. Store in small plastic pots. Measure out amount needed from frozen.

Microwave Tip

To measure honey easily remove lid and heat pot in the microwave for a few seconds to thin.

83 | *Easy Chicken Kiev*

Preparation time
20 minutes, plus 30 minutes to freeze

Cooking time
30–40 minutes

Oven temperature
190 C, 375 F, gas 5

Serves 4

Calories
435 per portion

You will need
4 boneless breasts of chicken
2 cloves garlic, crushed
grated rind of 1 lemon
100 g/4 oz butter
1 tablespoon chopped parsley
salt and pepper
25 g/1 oz plain flour
1 egg, lightly beaten
100 g/4 oz fresh white breadcrumbs

Beat the chicken breasts flat with a meat mallet or a rolling pin. Mix together the garlic, lemon rind, butter, parsley and seasoning to form a paste. Divide the butter evenly between the chicken breasts and carefully roll up. Secure with string.

Freeze for 15 minutes, or until the butter is firm. Coat the chicken in the flour, dip in the beaten egg and coat in the breadcrumbs, pressing firmly to make sure they stick. Return to the freezer for a further 15 minutes.

Bake the chicken Kiev in a moderately hot oven for 30–40 minutes or until the outside is golden and crisp.

Serve with boiled vegetables.

84 | *Tandoori Chicken*

Preparation time
15 minutes, plus overnight marinating

Cooking time
25–30 minutes

Serves 4

Calories
240 per portion

You will need
4 chicken joints
1 teaspoon chilli powder
1 teaspoon ground coriander
1 teaspoon ground cumin
2 teaspoons garam masala
$\frac{1}{2}$ teaspoon ground ginger
2 cloves garlic, crushed
juice of 1 lemon
2 tablespoons tomato purée
salt and pepper
150 ml/$\frac{1}{4}$ pint natural yogurt
50 g/2 oz butter or margarine

Remove the skin from the chicken joints. Place the chicken in a glass or earthenware dish. Mix together the remaining ingredients, except for the butter or margarine. Pour the marinade over the chicken, cover and chill overnight.

Remove the chicken from the marinade and dot with the butter or margarine. Grill the chicken, turning and basting with the marinade frequently, for 25–30 minutes or until the chicken juices run clear when the joints are pierced with the point of a sharp knife.

Serve immediately with boiled rice, garnished with lemon wedges and a parsley sprig, and a mixed salad.

Cook's Tip

Use a pastry brush to remove grated lemon rind from grater.

Cook's Tip

Line the base of the grill pan with kitchen foil before putting the chicken on the rack for easy cleaning of grill.

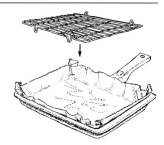

85 | Roast Turkey with Chestnut Stuffing

Preparation time
20 minutes

Oven temperature
220 C, 425 F, gas 7,
OR 160 C, 325 F, gas 3

Serves 10

Calories
355 per portion

You will need
100 g / 4 oz butter or lard
1 (3.5-kg / 8-lb) turkey
4 rashers rindless streaky bacon,
   chopped and fried
1 small onion, chopped
50 g / 2 oz fresh white
   breadcrumbs
grated rind of 1 lemon
225 g / 8 oz unsweetened canned
   chestnut purée
25 g / 1 oz butter, melted
1 egg, lightly beaten
salt and pepper
parsley sprigs to garnish

Spread the fat over the turkey. Combine the remaining ingredients, stuff the neck end and secure with a skewer.

Weigh the stuffed turkey and calculate the cooking time. For quick roasting method (at 220 C, 425 F, gas 7), allow 15 minutes per 450 g / 1 lb, up to 5.5 kg / 12 lb weight, and 12 minutes per 450 g / 1 lb over 5.5 kg / 12 lb weight. For slow roasting method (at 160 C, 325 F, gas 3), allow 25 minutes per 450 g / 1 lb, plus 25 minutes, up to 5.5 kg / 12 lb weight and 20 minutes per 450 g / 1 lb, plus 20 minutes, over 5.5 kg / 12 lb weight.

Roast the turkey for the calculated time. Garnish with parsley and serve with thin gravy (see Cook's Tip 86), bread sauce (see Microwave Tip below), cranberry sauce, Brussels sprouts, cocktail sausages and bacon rolls.

Microwave Tip

Bread sauce: microwave a small peeled onion stuck with 4 cloves for 1 minute. Add 300 ml / ½ pint milk, cook for 3 minutes. Add 50 g / 2 oz breadcrumbs and cook for 2 minutes. Season and add a pinch of nutmeg.

86 | Roast Duck with Pear Stuffing

Preparation time
10 minutes

Cooking time
2–2½ hours

Oven temperature
190 C, 375 F, gas 5

Serves 4

Calories
300 per portion

You will need
1 (1.75-kg / 4-lb) duck
salt

For the stuffing
225 g / 8 oz pears, peeled, cored
   and chopped
1 onion, grated
100 g / 4 oz fresh brown
   breadcrumbs
juice and rind of 1 lemon
2 teaspoons dried sage
salt and pepper
1 egg, lightly beaten

Garnish
parsley sprigs
lemon twists
chopped pears

Rinse the inside and outside of the duck and pat dry. Rub the salt over the duck. Mix the remaining ingredients together thoroughly, binding with the egg and stuff the neck end of the duck. Secure with a skewer.

Weigh the bird and calculate the cooking time. Allow 30 minutes per 450 g / 1 lb. Place the duck on a wire rack in a roasting tin, prick skin with a sharp fork and roast in a moderate oven for the calculated time.

Transfer the duck to a serving plate and garnish as illustrated. Serve the duck with a thin gravy (see Cook's Tip below), roast potatoes, buttered carrots and peas.

Cook's Tip

To make gravy: cover giblets and a sliced onion with water. Simmer for 1 hour. Strain. Pour off fat from roasting tin, leaving about 2 tablespoons juices. Stir in 1–2 tablespoons plain flour, depending on thickness required. Cook, stirring, for 2 minutes. Blend in 450 ml / ¾ pint giblet, meat or vegetable stock. Bring to the boil. Cook 3 minutes. Season and add gravy browning if liked.

87 | Roast Duck with Orange Sauce

Preparation time
20 minutes

Cooking time
2–2½ hours

Oven temperature
190 C, 375 F, gas 6

Serves 6

Calories
200 per portion

You will need
1 (1.75-2.25-kg/4-5 lb) duck
salt
300 ml/½ pint chicken stock

For the sauce
1 onion, finely chopped
1 tablespoon oil
25 g/1 oz plain flour
150 ml/¼ pint orange juice
2 tablespoons brandy (optional)
salt and pepper

Garnish
orange slices
watercress sprigs

Weigh the duck and calculate the cooking time. Allow 30 minutes per 450 g/1 lb. Rub the salt over the duck. Place the duck on a wire rack in a roasting tin and roast in a moderately hot oven for the calculated time.

Remove the duck from the oven and place on a hot serving dish to keep warm. Pour off the fat and reserve any juices from the tin.

To make the sauce: fry the onion in the oil until soft, add the flour and gradually blend in the orange juice, stock and reserved juices. Bring the sauce to the boil, reduce the heat and simmer gently for 2 minutes, then add the brandy, if using, and seasoning.

Serve the duck garnished with orange slices and watercress sprigs and serve the sauce separately.

Microwave Tip

For a really crisp skin and moist, tender flesh, cook duck in microwave oven for 25 minutes, turning dish once. Remove from dish and cook on rack in roasting tin in a very hot oven for a further 25 minutes.

88 | Roast Beef

Preparation time
5 minutes

Oven temperature
220 C, 425 F, gas 7
OR 160 C, 325 F, gas 3

Calories
200 per 100 g/4 oz
portion lean roast beef

You will need
1 joint of beef (see notes below)
50 g/2 oz lard or dripping, if needed
salt and pepper

Beef can be either quick roasted at a high temperature of 220 C, 425 F, gas 7, or slow roasted at 160 C, 325 F, gas 3. Quick roasting should only be used for prime cuts of beef such as fillet, rib, topside or sirloin. Slow roasting can be used for prime cuts, aitchbone and best brisket. When quick roasting beef, allow 15 minutes per 450 g/1 lb plus 15 minutes for a rare joint, 20 minutes per 450 g/1 lb plus 20 minutes for medium rare and 25 minutes per 450 g/ 1 lb plus 25 minutes for a well done joint. When slow roasting beef, allow 25 minutes per 450 g/1 lb plus 25 minutes for a rare joint, 30 minutes per 450 g/1 lb plus 30 minutes for medium rare and 35 minutes per 450 g/1 lb plus 35 minutes for a well done joint. Allow 100–175 g/ 4–6 oz beef from a boneless joint per person and 175– 225 g/6–8 oz of beef from a joint on the bone. Weigh the joint and calculate the cooking time.

Spread fat over all surfaces of lean joints. Place the joint in a roasting tin and season. Roast for the calculated time, basting regularly. Transfer the meat to a hot serving plate and keep warm. Serve with gravy, Yorkshire pudding (see Cook's Tip below) and vegetables.

Cook's Tip

To make Yorkshire pudding: blend 100 g/4 oz plain flour, 1 egg and 150 ml/¼ pint milk until smooth. Stir in 150 ml/ ¼ pint milk and water mixed. Heat a little of the fat from roasting tin in 1 large tin or 12 bun tins.

Pour in batter and cook in hot oven for 20–40 minutes until risen and brown. For extra light and crisp Yorkshire puddings use 2 eggs.

89 | Roast Lamb

Preparation time
10 minutes

Oven temperature
190 C, 375 F, gas 5

Calories
190 per 100 g/4 oz
portion lean roast lamb

You will need
1 leg or shoulder of lamb
salt and pepper
3 cloves garlic, thinly sliced
    (optional)
a few rosemary sprigs, plus
    extra to garnish (optional)

To roast a leg or shoulder of lamb medium rare allow 20 minutes per 450 g/1 lb, plus 20 minutes, or for a well done joint allow 25 minutes per 450 g/1 lb, plus 25 minutes. Weigh the joint and calculate the cooking time.

Rub the joint with salt and pepper, cut small incisions in the skin and insert the slices of garlic, if liked. Place the joint on a wire rack in a roasting tin in the oven. Insert a few rosemary sprigs in the joint, if liked and roast in a moderate oven. When the lamb is cooked remove the rosemary and transfer to a hot serving dish to keep warm.

Make the gravy for lamb as described in Cook's Tip 86.

Garnish the lamb with rosemary sprigs, and serve with mint sauce, roast potatoes, carrots and a green vegetable, such as broccoli.

90 | Stuffed Shoulder of Lamb

Preparation time
15 minutes

Oven temperature
190 C, 375 F, gas 5

Serves 6

Calories
360 per 100 g/4 oz
portion lean roast lamb
with stuffing

You will need
1 (1.5-1.75 - kg/ 3½–4 - lb) shoulder
    of lamb, boned
salt and pepper
50 g/ 2 oz white rice, cooked
1 small onion, finely chopped
50 g/ 2 oz sultanas
50 g/ 2 oz no-need-to-soak dried
    apricots, finely chopped
50 g/ 2 oz peanuts, finely
    chopped
1 teaspoon dried rosemary,
    crushed
salt and pepper
1 egg, lightly beaten
1–2 tablespoons oil

Spread out the lamb and season well with salt and pepper.

To make the stuffing: mix together the rice, onion, fruit, peanuts, rosemary and salt and pepper in a large mixing bowl. Bind well with the egg, then spread the stuffing over the lamb. Carefully roll up the lamb and secure with string. Weigh the lamb and calculate the cooking time, allowing 25 minutes per 450 g/1 lb plus an extra 25 minutes. Place the joint in a roasting tin and brush the outside with oil. Roast in a moderately hot oven for the calculated time.

Remove the string, slice and serve the lamb with gravy, baked potatoes and tomato halves filled with peas.

Cook's Tip

To make mint sauce: chop 6 sprigs of mint with 1 tablespoon sugar. Place in a bowl, add 2 tablespoons boiling water and 4 tablespoons vinegar.

Microwave Tip

Neatly shaped joints cook well in a microwave. For a 1.75 kg/4 lb joint, cook for 30 minutes on full power, turning 3 times. Transfer to a conventional oven and cook for a further 30 minutes.

91 | Stuffed Breast of Lamb

Preparation time
15 minutes

Oven temperature
180 C, 350 F, gas 4

Serves 4

Calories
450 per 100 g/4 oz portion lean roast lamb with stuffing

You will need
1 boned breast of lamb
salt and pepper
¼ teaspoon tarragon
1 onion, grated
100 g/4 oz fresh brown breadcrumbs
100 g/4 oz dried prunes, finely chopped
grated rind and juice of 1 orange
grated rind of 1 lemon
50 g/2 oz blanched almonds, chopped
1 egg, lightly beaten

Spread out the breast of lamb on a board and rub in the salt, pepper and tarragon.

Mix the onion, breadcrumbs, prunes, orange rind and juice, lemon rind, almonds and salt and pepper and bind well with the egg. Spread the stuffing over the meat. Carefully roll up the lamb. Do not roll too tightly as the stuffing tends to expand slightly during cooking. Tie the joint securely with string. Weigh the stuffed lamb to calculate the cooking time. Allow 25 minutes per 450 g/ 1 lb plus an extra 25 minutes. Place on a wire rack in a roasting tin and cook in a moderate oven for the calculated time.

When cooked, carefully remove the string, slice and serve with gravy (see Cook's Tip 86) and a selection of vegetables, such as peas and Duchesse Potatoes (see recipe 106).

Cook's Tip

Blanched almonds are much easier to chop or cut into slivers if covered with boiling water for 30 seconds then drained.

92 | Noisettes of Lamb with Savoury Butter

Preparation time
20 minutes, plus
30 minutes to freeze

Cooking time
10 minutes

Serves 4

Calories
340 per portion

You will need
1 boned best end of lamb
salt and pepper
a few rosemary sprigs, plus extra to garnish
50 g/2 oz butter
1 clove garlic, crushed
1 tablespoon chopped parsley

Season the lamb with salt and pepper on the boned surface. Break the rosemary between your fingers and sprinkle over the lamb. Starting at one end roll up the lamb to form a Swiss roll shape. Tie the roll securely with string at 2.5-cm/1-in intervals. With a sharp knife cut the noisettes between each piece of string.

To make the savoury butter: beat the butter until pale and creamy, then work in the garlic, parsley and seasoning to taste. Turn out the butter on to a sheet of greaseproof paper and with wet hands rock the butter back and forth to form a roll. Freeze for about 30 minutes.

Cook the noisettes under a hot grill for 5 minutes, then remove the pan from the heat, turn the noisettes over, add a slice of savoury butter and grill for a further 5 minutes.

Garnish the noisettes with rosemary sprigs and serve with a selection of vegetables.

Cook's Tip

Flavoured butters perk up all grilled meats and fish. Try butter with chopped anchovies or grated onion with steak, fresh fennel or dill butter with white fish and mustard butter with mackerel.

93 | *Roast Pork*

Preparation time
15 minutes

Oven temperature
190 C, 375 F, gas 5

Calories
*185 per 100 g / 4 oz
portion lean roast pork*

You will need
*1 leg, loin or shoulder of pork
salt and pepper
1 tablespoon oil*

The cooking time for a leg or loin of pork is 30 minutes per 450 g / 1 lb plus 35 minutes, or for part of a leg or a shoulder 30 minutes per 450 g / 1 lb plus 35 minutes. Weigh the joint and calculate the cooking time.

Score the rind of the joint with a sharp knife at 5-mm/ $\frac{1}{4}$ in intervals. Rub salt and pepper into the rind and then brush the oil over. Place the meat, rind side up, on a wire rack standing in a roasting tin and roast in a moderate oven for the time calculated. Check the meat is cooked by inserting a skewer into the centre – the juices that emerge should be colourless.

Transfer the meat to a hot serving dish and keep warm whilst making the gravy (see Cook's Tip 86), but using half vegetable water and half cider, if liked.

Serve the pork with apple sauce and roast and boiled vegetables as accompaniments.

94 | *Stuffed Pork Roll*

Preparation time
15 minutes

Oven temperature
180 C, 350 F, gas 4

Calories
*285 per 100 g / 4 oz
portion lean roast pork
with stuffing*

You will need
*1 hand of pork, skinned and
    boned
salt and pepper*

For the stuffing
*225 g / 8 oz cooking apples,
    peeled, cored and sliced
100 g / 4 oz fresh white
    breadcrumbs
juice and rind of 1 lemon
$\frac{1}{2}$ teaspoon sage
salt and pepper
1 egg, lightly beaten*

Place the pork joint on a work surface and rub in the seasoning.

To make the stuffing: mix together the apples, breadcrumbs, lemon juice and rind, sage and seasoning. Bind the mixture together well with the egg. Spread the stuffing over the joint. Roll up and secure with string. Sprinkle salt and pepper over the top of the joint.

Weigh the pork to calculate the cooking time. Allow 30 minutes per 450 g / 1 lb plus 30 minutes. Wrap the joint in foil, place in a tin and bake in a moderate oven for the calculated time.

When cooked, remove the foil and string and serve sliced with gravy (see Cook's Tip 86), potato croquettes and green beans.

Microwave Tip

To make apple sauce, put sliced apples in a large basin with sugar. Cover and cook on full power for 7 minutes. Beat well and serve in a small dish.

Cook's Tip

To make breadcrumbs quickly, use a blender or food processor. Cut bread in cubes and drop into running machine through hole in lid or tube.

95 | *Pork Chops with Orange and Cashew Nut Stuffing*

Preparation time
15 minutes

Cooking time
16–20 minutes

Serves 4

Calories
370 per portion

You will need
4 loin pork chops
salt and pepper

For the stuffing
1 onion, grated
grated rind of 1 orange
50 g/2 oz cashew nuts, chopped
½ teaspoon sage
1 teaspoon Dijon mustard
50 g/2 oz fresh brown
    breadcrumbs
salt and pepper
1 egg, lightly beaten
1–2 tablespoons oil

Garnish
orange slices
parsley sprigs

Cut the rind and excess fat off the chops and season the chops with salt and pepper. Carefully cut each chop horizontally, leaving joined at the bone.

Mix together the onion, orange rind, cashew nuts, sage, mustard, breadcrumbs, seasoning and bind with the egg. Place the stuffing inside the chops. Brush with the oil and cook under a medium grill for 8–10 minutes on each side or until the chops are golden and the stuffing is cooked. Serve garnished with orange slices and parsley sprigs.

Cook's Tip

For a change, substitute lemon rind and almonds for the orange rind and cashew nuts in this stuffing.

96 | *Spiced Glazed Ham*

Preparation time
10 minutes, plus
overnight soaking

Oven temperature
220 C, 425 F, gas 7

Calories
165 per 100 g/4 oz
portion lean cooked
gammon

You will need
1 joint middle or corner of
    gammon
1.15 litres/2 pints water
1 onion
1 bay leaf
salt and pepper
100 g/4 oz soft brown sugar
grated rind of 1 orange
½ teaspoon grated nutmeg
½ teaspoon ground cinnamon

To serve
3 dessert apples
cloves
zested orange rind
orange slices to garnish

Weigh the gammon and calculate the cooking time, allowing 30 minutes per 450 g/1 lb. Soak the gammon in cold water overnight. Drain.

Put the gammon in a saucepan with the water, onion, bay leaf and seasoning. Cover, bring to the boil, then reduce the heat and simmer for 1½ hours. Drain the gammon and peel off the skin, marking the fat into diamond shapes with a sharp knife. Mix together the sugar, orange rind, nutmeg and cinnamon for the glaze and rub into the gammon fat. Place joint in a roasting tin.

Bake the gammon in a hot oven for the remainder of the calculated cooking time, or until the fat is crisp and golden. Stick the cloves in the apples and place them in the roasting tin for the final 15 minutes cooking time, basting with any meat juices. Garnish with orange slices.

Cook's Tip

For a delicious sauce with the gammon, pour a small bottle of ginger ale around the joint before roasting and if liked substitute ground ginger for the spices.

97 | Gammon Steak with Apricot and Walnut Sauce

Preparation time
15 minutes

Cooking time
12–16 minutes

Serves 4

Calories
330 per portion

You will need
4 gammon steaks
grated rind of 1 lemon
2 tablespoons oil
salt and pepper
100 g/ 4 oz no-need-to-soak
  dried apricots
150 ml/¼ pint dry cider
150 ml/¼ pint water
50 g/ 2 oz walnuts, chopped
¼ teaspoon grated nutmeg
a little grated orange rind to
  garnish

With a sharp knife trim the rind from the gammon and score the fat so that the steaks lie flat. Mix together the lemon rind, oil, salt and pepper. Brush this mixture over both sides of the gammon and cook the steaks under a hot grill for 6–8 minutes on each side.

Blend the apricots and cider in a liquidiser, then pour into a saucepan. Add the water, walnuts, nutmeg and seasoning to taste to the fruit mixture and bring the sauce to the boil. Reduce the heat and simmer gently for 5–10 minutes or until the sauce has thickened.

Arrange the gammon steaks on a serving plate, and garnish with grated orange rind. Pour over the sauce, and serve with broccoli and parslied boiled potatoes.

Cook's Tip

The sauce is equally good with pork chops or roast pork. If liked, substitute 225 g/ 8 oz sliced apple for the apricots.

98 | Meat Loaf

Preparation time
15 minutes

Cooking time
1–1¼ hours

Oven temperature
180 C, 350 F, gas 4

Serves 4

Calories
525 per portion

You will need
675 g/ 1½ lb minced beef
1 onion, finely chopped
1 tablespoon chopped parsley
100 g/ 4 oz fresh white
  breadcrumbs
1 egg, lightly beaten
2–3 tablespoons dry red wine
salt and pepper
1 tablespoon oil
1 onion, finely chopped
2 cloves garlic, crushed
1 (400-g/ 14-oz) can chopped
  tomatoes
150 ml/¼ pint beef stock
1 tablespoon chopped parsley
sliced pickled cucumber to
  garnish (optional)

Grease a 1-kg/2-lb loaf tin. Mix the mince, onion, parsley, breadcrumbs, egg, red wine and seasoning together thoroughly. Pack firmly into the tin and cover with a sheet of greased foil. Bake in a moderate oven for 1–1¼ hours or until the loaf begins to shrink from the tin.

Heat the oil in a saucepan and cook the onion and garlic until soft. Blend the tomatoes in a liquidiser and add to the onion mixture with the stock, parsley and seasoning to taste. Bring the sauce to the boil, reduce the heat, and simmer for 10–15 minutes, stirring occasionally, until the sauce has thickened.

Tip the meat loaf out of the tin and arrange on a serving dish, then pour over the hot tomato sauce. Garnish with sliced pickled cucumber, if liked.

Microwave Tip

Tomato sauce is easily made in the microwave. Cook onion and garlic for 4 minutes. Add remaining ingredients and cook for 7 minutes.

99 | Grilled Steak

Preparation time
10 minutes

Cooking time
6–10 minutes

Serves 4

Calories
300 per portion

You will need
4 medium rump steaks
50 g/2 oz butter, melted
1 teaspoon prepared English
  mustard
2 cloves garlic, crushed
salt and pepper

Garnish
4 firm tomatoes
100 g/4 oz mushrooms
1 tablespoon chopped parsley,
  plus a few sprigs

Place the steaks on a rack in the grill pan. Mix together the butter, mustard, garlic and seasoning and brush half of the mixture over the steaks.

Cook under a hot grill for 1–2 minutes, then remove the pan from the heat, turn the steaks over, brush with more butter (reserving some for the garnish ingredients) and cook for a further 1–2 minutes.

Turn the grill down to a medium heat. Cut a small cross on the top of the tomatoes and arrange the tomatoes and mushrooms around the steaks. Brush the vegetables with the remaining butter. Continue cooking for 2 minutes on each side for a rare steak, 3 minutes for medium rare, and 4 minutes for well-done steak.

Transfer the steaks to a warmed serving plate and sprinkle over the chopped parsley. Add the vegetable garnishes and a few sprigs of parsley to the plate.

Serve the steaks immediately, accompanied by Duchesse Potatoes (see recipe 106), broccoli and carrots.

100 | Honey-Glazed Lamb Chops

Preparation time
10 minutes,
plus 1 hour to chill

Cooking time
10 minutes

Serves 4

Calories
355 per portion

You will need
salt and pepper
4 lamb chump chops
50 g/2 oz butter or margarine
2 tablespoons honey
2 teaspoons wholegrain mustard

Garnish
chopped parsley
watercress sprigs

Season the chops well and beat the butter or margarine until pale and creamy. Blend in the honey, mustard and seasoning to taste to form a smooth paste. Brush the honey mixture over the chops, cover and chill for about an hour.

Grill the chops under a hot grill for 5 minutes on each side.

Serve the chops, garnished with a little chopped parsley and sprigs of watercress and accompanied by boiled broccoli and jacket potatoes.

Cook's Tip

Rump is usually the cheapest grilling or frying steak. It should have a good layer of fat along the edge. Sirloin is dearer and leaner. Fillet steak is very lean and tender but expensive.

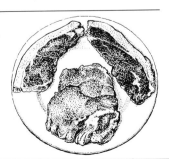

Cook's Tip

Lamb chops are very good cooked on a barbecue, but trim off excess fat to prevent it dripping on charcoal and flaring.

101 | Mixed Kebabs

Preparation time
10 minutes

Cooking time
10–15 minutes

Serves 4

Calories
255 per portion

You will need
4 rashers rindless, streaky bacon
4 kidneys
1–2 tablespoons oil
1 red pepper, deseeded and cut into triangles
1 green pepper, deseeded and cut into triangles
8 bay leaves
8 cocktail sausages
1 (227-g 8-oz) can pineapple slices, drained and cut into chunks
4 tomatoes, halved
salt and pepper

Cut the bacon rashers in half. Halve the kidneys and snip out the cores. Wrap a piece of bacon round each piece of kidney. Brush four skewers with oil, then thread each one, rotating the ingredients as shown in the photograph. Brush lightly with oil and sprinkle over the salt and pepper.

Cook the kebabs under a hot grill for 10–15 minutes, or until cooked, turning and brushing with extra oil occasionally.

Serve the kebabs hot with boiled potatoes, garnished with chopped parsley, or boiled white rice and a crisp green salad.

102 | Meatballs and Peanut Sauce

Preparation time
15 minutes

Cooking time
8–10 minutes

Serves 4

Calories
490 per portion

You will need
450 g/1 lb minced beef
1 onion, grated
salt and pepper
50 g/2 oz fresh white breadcrumbs
1 egg, lightly beaten
1 tablespoon chopped parsley
2 tablespoons plain flour
2 tablespoons oil
1 clove garlic, crushed
2 tablespoons crunchy peanut butter
150 ml/¼ pint natural yogurt
1 teaspoon chilli powder
pinch of cayenne
1 teaspoon chopped parsley to garnish

Mix together the meat, onion, seasoning, breadcrumbs, egg and parsley. Form the mixture into 18 small balls the size of marbles and roll in the flour. Combine the oil and the crushed garlic and brush the mixture over the meatballs. Thread the meatballs on to oiled skewers and grill for 2–3 minutes, turn the skewers and grill for a further 2–3 minutes.

Melt the peanut butter over a gentle heat, add the remaining ingredients and cook gently until hot, but do not let the sauce boil. Serve the meatballs on a bed of mixed salad. Serve the sauce separately, garnished with chopped parsley.

Cook's Tip

For a change, serve the kebabs with hot lemon and herb bread. Work 2 teaspoons grated lemon rind, 2 teaspoons lemon juice and 1 tablespoon chopped parsley into 100 g/ 4 oz butter. Slice a stick of French bread almost through. Spread the butter on both sides of each slice, and press together. Bake in a moderately hot oven (200 C, 400 F, gas 6) for 20 minutes.

Cook's Tip

A food processor 'minces' meat well. Use lean stewing or braising beef and cut into cubes before placing in machine. A mixture of beef and pork makes an interesting change.

103 | *Spicy Burgers*

Preparation time
10 minutes

Cooking time
4–6 minutes

Serves 4

Calories
300 per portion

You will need
*450 g/1 lb minced beef, lamb or
  pork
1 onion, grated
2 cloves garlic, crushed
1 green chilli, deseeded and finely
  chopped (optional)
salt and pepper
oil for frying*

Mix together the meat, onion, garlic, the chilli, if using, and seasoning to taste. Shape the mixture into eight burgers. Heat the oil in a frying pan and cook the burgers for 2–3 minutes on either side.

Serve the burgers in baps with lettuce, tomato slices and sweetcorn relish, garnished with tomato wedges, baby gherkins and lettuce. Alternatively, serve with mashed potatoes and Ratatouille (see recipe 115).

104 | *Kebabs*

Preparation time
*15 minutes, plus 2
hours to marinate*

Cooking time
10–12 minutes

Serves 4

Calories
310 per portion

You will need
*450 g/1 lb boned leg, fillet or
  shoulder of lamb
2 tablespoons olive oil
juice of 1 lemon
1 teaspoon dried marjoram
salt and pepper
4 button onions
8 cherry tomatoes, or 4 quartered
  tomatoes
8 button mushrooms
1 green pepper, deseeded and
  cut into squares
8 bay leaves*

Cut the lamb into 2.5-cm/1-in cubes and place in a glass or earthenware dish.

To make the marinade: mix together the oil, lemon juice, marjoram and salt and pepper. Pour the marinade over the lamb, cover and chill for about 2 hours, basting the lamb with the marinade occasionally.

Drain the meat, reserving the marinade. Thread the meat and vegetables on to four oiled skewers alternating the ingredients.

Brush the kebabs with the reserved marinade and grill for about 10–12 minutes. Turn two or three times during cooking and brush with extra marinade if necessary.

Serve the kebabs immediately, accompanied by parslied boiled rice and a crisp mixed salad.

Cook's Tip

**For a low-calorie meal use
lean minced beef and serve
burgers on thick slices of
Iceberg or Webb's lettuce.
Top with low-calorie salad
dressing.**

Cook's Tip

**These kebabs are excellent
cooked on a barbecue. You
can use any lean meat or
even cubes of firm white
fish such as monkfish.**

Vegetables and Salads

Vegetables add colour, flavour and texture to the main course of a meal and should be chosen with this in mind to complement the meat or fish dish. Braised or saucy vegetables go well with grills, brightly coloured peppers or tomatoes look attractive with white fish and a crunchy salad adds texture to minced meat dishes. Some of the recipes in this chapter make a complete meal.

105 | Baked Potatoes

Preparation time
15 minutes

Cooking time
1½ hours

Oven temperature
200 C, 400 F, gas 6

Serves 4

Calories
355 per portion

You will need
4 large baking potatoes
1–2 tablespoons oil
½ teaspoon salt

For topping 1
175 g / 6 oz cottage cheese
2 tablespoons chopped chives
salt and pepper

For topping 2
100 g / 4 oz peeled, cooked
    prawns
salt and pepper
50 g / 2 oz Cheddar cheese, grated
parsley sprigs to garnish

Wash the potatoes and prick them with a fork. Brush the oil all over the potatoes and sprinkle a pinch of salt on each. Bake in a moderately hot oven for about 1½ hours or until soft right through to the centre.

Mix the cottage cheese and chives with seasoning to taste. Mix the prawns with seasoning to taste.

When the potatoes are cooked, slit them almost in half and spoon the chosen filling into the cut. Sprinkle the Cheddar over the prawns and heat quickly under the grill. Serve at once.

106 | Duchesse Potatoes

Preparation time
15 minutes

Cooking time
45 minutes

Oven temperature
200 C, 400 F, gas 6

Serves 4

Calories
255 per portion

You will need
675 g / 1½ lb potatoes
salt and pepper
50 g / 2 oz butter or margarine
1 egg, plus beaten egg to glaze
parsley sprigs to garnish

Peel and quarter the potatoes. Cook the potatoes in boiling salted water for 20 minutes or until tender. Drain and mash. Beat in the butter or margarine, egg and seasoning. Set aside until cool enough to pipe.

Fit a piping bag with a large star nozzle. Place the potato mixture in the piping bag and pipe rosettes on to a greased baking tray.

Brush the rosettes with the beaten egg and bake in a moderately hot oven for 25 minutes or until golden. Arrange in a warmed serving dish and garnish with parsley sprigs. Serve immediately.

Microwave Tip

One to four whole potatoes microwave well. Place them on a double piece of absorbent kitchen paper. Allow about 5, 10, 15 or 20 minutes for 1–4 potatoes.

Freezer Tip

These can be frozen uncooked. Pipe on greaseproof paper. Freeze on the trays until solid, then pack in rigid containers.

107 | Fantail Potatoes

Preparation time
15 minutes, plus 2
hours for soaking

Cooking time
1 hour

Oven temperature
190 C, 375 F, gas 5

Serves 4

Calories
280 per portion

You will need
4 medium potatoes
2 tablespoons lemon juice
50 g/ 2 oz butter or margarine,
  melted
1 onion, finely chopped
1 clove garlic, crushed (optional)
salt and pepper
50 g/ 2 oz Cheddar cheese, finely
  grated
parsley sprig to garnish

Peel the potatoes and slice thinly into vertical slices, leaving them attached at the base. Soak the potatoes in a bowl of water with the lemon juice for 2 hours or until the potatoes have fanned out. Drain.

Mix together the melted butter or margarine, the onion, garlic, if using, and seasoning. Place the potatoes in a baking tin, pour over the butter mixture and bake in a moderately hot oven for 50 minutes, basting occasionally. Sprinkle the Cheddar on each potato and bake for a further 10–15 minutes or until the potatoes are crisp and golden. Serve immediately, garnished with a sprig of parsley.

108 | Lyonnaise Potatoes

Preparation time
15 minutes

Cooking time
25 minutes

Serves 4

Calories
235 per portion

You will need
675 g/ 1½ lb potatoes
salt
50 g/ 2 oz butter or margarine
2–3 small onions, sliced into
  rings
chopped parsley to garnish

Peel and cook the potatoes whole in plenty of boiling salted water for 15 minutes. Drain and cool. Slice the potatoes evenly. Fry the potato slices in the butter or margarine until crisp and golden. When two-thirds cooked, add the onion rings and continue cooking until they are softened.

Garnish with chopped parsley and serve immediately.

Microwave Tip

Microwave these for about 10–12 minutes on full power. Cook the butter, onion and garlic separately for 5 minutes, pour over potatoes, sprinkle with cheese and grill to brown.

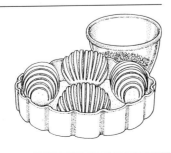

Microwave Tip

This recipe can be microwaved. Put the raw sliced potatoes in a serving dish with the onions. Cover with cling film. Cook on high for about 30 minutes, stirring several times.

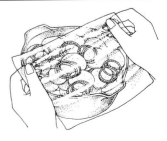

109 | Buttered Carrots

Preparation time
10 minutes

Cooking time
15–20 minutes

Serves 4

Calories
150 per portion

You will need
1 kg / 2 lb carrots
salt and pepper
50 g / 2 oz butter
chopped parsley to garnish

Peel the carrots and cut into four lengthways, then cut each quarter into 5-cm/2-in strips. Bring a saucepan of salted water to the boil and cook the carrots for 10 minutes. Drain well.

Heat the butter gently in a large frying pan. Cook the carrots in the butter for 5 minutes until tender. Season to taste and garnish with chopped parsley.

110 | Cauliflower Cheese

Preparation time
15 minutes

Cooking time
40 minutes

Serves 4

Calories
215 per portion

You will need
1 medium cauliflower

For the cheese sauce
25 g / 1 oz butter or margarine
25 g / 1 oz plain flour
300 ml / ½ pint milk
75 g / 3 oz Cheddar cheese, grated
¼ teaspoon mustard powder (optional)
salt and pepper
¼ teaspoon grated nutmeg to garnish (optional)

Trim the cauliflower, cut a cross in the stem and cook in boiling salted water for about 15 minutes. Drain thoroughly, place on a serving plate and keep hot.

To make the sauce, melt the butter or margarine over a gentle heat, stir in the flour and cook for 2 minutes. Gradually add the milk, stirring all the time. Bring the sauce to the boil, reduce the heat and simmer gently for a few minutes. Remove the saucepan from the heat. Stir the Cheddar into the sauce with the mustard, if using and seasoning until smooth. Pour the sauce over the cauliflower.

Sprinkle the nutmeg over the top, if liked, and serve immediately.

Microwave Tip

Put the prepared carrots and butter in a dish with a sprinkling of water. Cover and microwave on high for about 15 minutes stirring once.

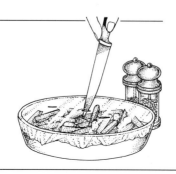

Microwave Tip

All sauces cook well in the microwave. Put all the ingredients in a bowl, whisk well and microwave for 8–10 minutes. Whisk thoroughly.

111 | *Leeks in Sauce*

Preparation time
10 minutes

Cooking time
20 minutes

Serves 4

Calories
215 per portion

You will need
8 medium leeks
salt

For the cheese sauce
25 g / 1 oz butter or margarine
25 g / 1 oz plain flour
150 ml / ¼ pint milk
75 g / 3 oz Cheddar cheese,
  grated
salt and pepper
pinch of mustard powder

Trim, wash and slice the leeks in half lengthways. Put the leeks in a large saucepan, add a little salt, then pour in enough water to just cover the vegetables. Bring to the boil, then simmer for 10 minutes. Drain the leeks well and reserve 150 ml / ¼ pint of the cooking water for the sauce. Place in a serving dish and keep hot.

To make the sauce, melt the butter or margarine over a gentle heat, then stir in the flour and cook for 2 minutes. Gradually add the milk and leek water, stirring the mixture all the time. Bring the sauce to the boil and simmer gently for a few minutes. Remove from the heat, stir in the Cheddar, seasoning and mustard. Mix until smooth and pour the sauce over the leeks. Serve at once.

112 | *Celery with Walnuts*

Preparation time
5–10 minutes

Cooking time
25–30 minutes

Serves 4

Calories
195 per portion

You will need
1 large head of celery
1 large onion, chopped
50 g / 2 oz butter or margarine
50 g / 2 oz walnut halves
300 ml / ½ pint chicken stock
few drops of soy sauce

Trim and wash the celery. Cut the sticks in 5-cm / 2-in lengths.

Fry the onion in the butter or margarine in a large pan. Add the celery and walnuts. Cook for a few minutes, then pour in the stock. Simmer uncovered for 25–30 minutes until softened. Season with soy sauce. Serve immediately.

Cook's Tip

Substitute dry white wine for cooking water and use half the quantity of cheese to make a wine sauce. Or use all milk to make a creamy sauce.

Cook's Tips

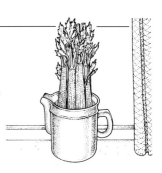

To keep a head of celery fresh, store it on a cool windowsill with root end in a jug of water.

113 | *Brussels Sprouts with Chestnuts*

Preparation time
20 minutes

Cooking time
20 minutes

Serves 4

Calories
290 per portion

You will need
1 kg/2 lb Brussels sprouts
450 g/1 lb chestnuts
50 g/2 oz butter or margarine

Trim the sprouts, removing any damaged outer leaves and cut a cross in the stalks. Slit the chestnut skins, put in cold water in a saucepan and bring to the boil. Boil for 2 minutes, then drain and remove outer and inner skins. (Dried, frozen or canned chestnuts may be used, following the instructions on the packet or can.) Cook the sprouts and chestnuts in boiling salted water for 15 minutes. Drain well.

Heat the butter or margarine in a large frying pan and fry the sprouts and chestnuts together for 5 minutes, tossing well. Serve immediately. This dish is a good accompaniment for Roast Turkey (see recipe 85).

114 | *Courgette Fritters*

Preparation time
15 minutes

Cooking time
5–10 minutes

Serves 4

Calories
385 per portion

You will need
450 g/1 lb courgettes
flour to dust
1 quantity tomato sauce (recipe 161)
chopped parsley to garnish

For the batter
100 g/4 oz plain flour
pinch of salt
1 egg yolk
300 ml/½ pint milk or water (to make a crisper batter)
1 tablespoon oil
oil for deep frying

Trim and slice the courgettes and dust with flour. For the batter sift the flour and salt into a bowl. Make a well in the centre. Add the egg yolk, then gradually beat in the milk and 1 tablespoon oil. Beat until smooth.

Heat the oil for deep frying to 190 C/375 F; test the temperature by dropping a cube of bread into the oil; it should turn golden in 30 seconds. Dip the courgette slices in the batter and drop into the hot oil a few at a time. Fry the fritters for 5 minutes or until golden. Drain on absorbent kitchen paper and keep warm while cooking the remaining courgettes. Serve immediately with tomato sauce and garnish with chopped parsley.

Microwave Tip

Brussels sprouts microwave well – prepare and wash them. Cook the wetted sprouts in a roasting bag for about 15 minutes.

Cook's Tip

To make aubergine fritters, trim and slice two large aubergines. Salt them for 30 minutes, then rinse and dry well. Dust with flour and cook as above.

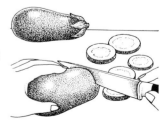

115 | *Ratatouille*

Preparation time	**You will need**
15 minutes	*1 aubergine*
	salt and pepper
Cooking time	*2 medium onions*
20–25 minutes	*2 courgettes*
	1 red pepper
Serves 4	*1 green pepper*
	675 g / 1½ lb tomatoes
Calories	*4–6 tablespoons oil*
235 per portion	*2 cloves garlic, crushed*
	¼ teaspoon dried mixed herbs

Thinly slice the aubergine, place in a colander and sprinkle generously with salt to remove the bitter flavour. Leave to drain while preparing the other vegetables. Thinly slice the onions and courgettes. Core, deseed and slice the peppers. Peel, quarter and deseed the tomatoes.

Heat the oil in a large saucepan. Cook the onion with the garlic until softened. Rinse and dry the aubergine slices and add to the pan with the remaining vegetables, herbs and seasoning. Bring the mixture to the boil, reduce the heat and simmer gently, covered, for 15–20 minutes. Stir the vegetables from time to time during cooking to ensure that the juices are evenly mixed.

116 | *Chilli-Stuffed Peppers*

Preparation time	**You will need**
15 minutes	*4 green peppers, tops reserved and deseeded*
Cooking time	
50 minutes	For the filling
	1 onion, chopped
Oven temperature	*1 clove garlic, crushed*
180 C, 350 F, gas 4	*350 g / 12 oz minced beef*
	1 tablespoon oil
Serves 4	*100 g / 4 oz mushrooms, sliced*
	2 teaspoons chilli powder
	1 tablespoon tomato purée
Calories	*150 ml / ¼ pint beef stock*
375 per portion	*salt and pepper*
	1 (425-g / 15-oz) can kidney beans

Blanch the peppers in boiling salted water for 1–2 minutes and drain. Place in an ovenproof dish.

Fry the onion, garlic and minced beef in the oil until browned. Stir in the mushrooms, chilli powder, tomato purée, stock and seasoning and simmer gently for 10 minutes. Drain the kidney beans and add to the meat.

Fill the peppers with the chilli mixture, cover the dish and bake in a moderate oven for 30 minutes.

Cook's Tip

Ratatouille makes a refreshing starter – cut the vegetables into chunks instead of slices. Cook and cool, then chill and serve with warm French bread.

Cook's Tip

If you find a whole pepper too much for 1 serving, then cut 2 peppers in half lengthways to make boat shapes. Place in a baking dish and pile the filling in. Cook as above.

117 | Stuffed Marrow Rings

Preparation time
5–10 minutes

Cooking time
55 minutes

Oven temperature
190C, 375F, gas 5

Serves 4

Calories
440 per portion

You will need
1 onion, chopped
1 tablespoon oil
450 g/ 1 lb minced beef
1 (400-g/ 14-oz) can chopped
 tomatoes
50 g/ 2 oz flaked almonds
50 g/ 2 oz sultanas
1 teaspoon ground cinnamon
1 teaspoon grated nutmeg
salt and pepper
4 (5-cm/ 2-in) thick slices
 marrow, peeled
parsley sprig to garnish

Fry the onion in the oil until softened and transparent. Add the minced beef and cook until browned, stirring briskly. Add the remaining ingredients, except the marrow slices, bring the mixture to the boil and simmer until thickened, about 15 minutes.

Meanwhile, scoop out the seeds from the marrow slices, leaving a hole in the centre of each slice. Arrange the rings in a baking dish.

Pour the meat mixture into the centre of each marrow slice and pile the remainder on top. Cover the dish with foil and bake in a moderately hot oven for 30 minutes or until the marrow is tender.

Transfer to a serving plate, garnish with a sprig of parsley, and serve immediately with baked potatoes.

118 | Hot Spring Salad

Preparation time
10 minutes

Cooking time
15 minutes

Serves 4

Calories
370 per portion

You will need
675 g/ 1½ lb fresh spinach
4 slices bread, crusts removed,
 cut into cubes
50 g/ 2 oz butter, or 15 g/½ oz
 butter and 2 tablespoons oil
8 rashers rindless streaky bacon,
 diced
100 g/ 4 oz button mushrooms,
 whole
3 tablespoons oil
2 cloves garlic, crushed
1 tablespoon wine vinegar
¼ teaspoon mustard powder
salt and pepper

Wash and shred the spinach. Place in a large salad bowl. Fry the bread cubes in the butter, or butter and oil mixture, until golden. Remove, drain on absorbent kitchen paper, then sprinkle the cubes over the spinach. Fry the bacon in any remaining fat until really crispy. Add the mushrooms and continue cooking for a few minutes.

Mix the remaining ingredients together and pour over the mushrooms and bacon. Bring the mixture quickly to the boil, pour over the spinach and toss gently. Serve at once.

Cook's Tip

Use the meat mixture to stuff courgettes. Cut 4 large courgettes in half lengthways. Scoop out the middle and fill with the mixture. Bake as above.

Cook's Tip

Prepare flavoured vinegars for use in salads. Put herb sprigs – tarragon, thyme, basil, rosemary – into bottles of white wine vinegar and leave for 1 month before use.

119 | Chicken and Rice Salad

Preparation time
35 minutes

Cooking time
25 minutes

Serves 4

Calories
400 per portion

You will need
225 g / 8 oz long-grain rice
600 ml / 1 pint water
salt and pepper
450 g / 1 lb cooked chicken
2 tablespoons mayonnaise
150 ml / ¼ pint soured cream
1 tablespoon curry powder
1 tablespoon oil
1 tablespoon chutney
coriander leaves to garnish

Put the rice in a saucepan with the water, and a little salt. Bring to the boil, cover and reduce the heat. Simmer for about 20 minutes or until the rice is cooked and all the water has been absorbed. Fluff up the grains with a fork and leave to cool.

Arrange the rice in the base and to form a border round the rim of a serving dish. Dice the chicken and place in a bowl. Cook the curry powder in the oil for 2–3 minutes, cool and mix with the remaining ingredients, seasoning with salt and pepper to taste. Toss with the chicken and spoon over the rice.

Garnish with fresh coriander leaves just before serving. Accompany with a green salad.

120 | Cheese and Salami Salad

Preparation time
15 minutes, plus 30 minutes to chill

Serves 4

Calories
330 per portion

You will need
100 g / 4 oz Gruyère cheese
100 g / 4 oz Edam cheese
100 g / 4 oz salami, sliced
6–8 black olives
50 g / 2 oz cocktail gherkins
chopped chives to garnish

Dice the Gruyère and Edam cheeses into 1-cm/½-in cubes. Cut a slit in each piece of salami from the centre to the edge and roll to form a cone. Arrange the cheeses and salami cones on a serving dish. Halve and stone the black olives and add them to the dish with the cocktail gherkins.

Chill for about 30 minutes. Serve garnished with chopped fresh chives.

Microwave Tip

Rice cooks well in the microwave. Put 225 g / 8 oz rice, 600 ml / 1 pint water and ½ teaspoon salt in a large bowl. Cook for 15 minutes. Stand for 5 minutes then fluff up with a fork.

Cook's Tip

Flavour bottled mayonnaise with tomato purée, Worcestershire sauce, garlic salt and paprika. Thin with cream or yogurt to serve with this salad.

121 | Cheese and Fruit Salad

Preparation time
15 minutes, plus time
to chill

Serves 4

Calories
290 per portion

You will need
small head of Chinese leaves,
   shredded
1 (227-g/8-oz) can pineapple
   chunks
100 g/4 oz cottage cheese
100 g/4 oz Cheddar cheese,
   diced
100 g/4 oz cooked ham, diced
salt and pepper
1 avocado
1 tablespoon lemon juice

Arrange the Chinese leaves in the bottom of a serving dish. Drain the pineapple chunks. Mix with the cottage cheese, Cheddar and ham. Season well and spoon the mixture on top of the leaves.

Halve the avocado. Scoop out the stone, then peel and thinly slice. Sprinkle with lemon juice and arrange the slices on top of the cheese mixture. Chill before serving.

122 | Smoked Mackerel and Egg Salad

Preparation time
15 minutes

Serves 4

Calories
335 per portion

You will need
1 lettuce, shredded
2 smoked mackerel fillets
4 hard-boiled eggs
4 tomatoes, peeled and quartered

For the dressing
1 tablespoon wine vinegar
2 tablespoons oil
1 teaspoon prepared French
   mustard
salt and pepper
1 tablespoon chopped parsley

Put the lettuce in a serving bowl. Skin and flake the mackerel. Roughly chop the hard-boiled eggs. Mix together the mackerel, eggs and tomatoes and arrange on top of the lettuce.

Combine the ingredients for the dressing and pour over the fish. Serve immediately.

Cook's Tip

If you're counting the calories, omit the avocado. Use fruit canned in unsweetened juice, low-fat Cheddar and lean ham.

Cook's Tip

In Spring thin out young lettuce plants to use in this salad. Use horseradish sauce instead of the mustard to pep up the salad.

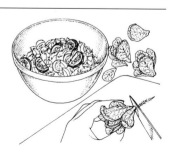

123 | Waldorf Salad

Preparation time
10–15 minutes

Serves 4

Calories
140 per portion

You will need
1 lettuce
2 red dessert apples
2 tart green dessert apples
4 celery sticks
50 g/2 oz walnut halves
150 ml/¼ pint natural yogurt
½ teaspoon sugar
1 teaspoon prepared mustard
salt and pepper

Shred the lettuce and place in a salad bowl. Halve, core and cut the apples into triangles or cubes, cutting and reserving a few slices for garnish. Chop the celery.

Mix together the apples, celery, walnuts, yogurt, sugar, mustard and seasoning and turn into the salad bowl on top of the lettuce. Top with a walnut and apple slices and serve to accompany cold meats.

124 | Peanut Coleslaw

Preparation time
15 minutes

Serves 4

Calories
370 per portion

You will need
½ small white cabbage
1 onion
4 carrots
2 tart dessert apples
50 g/2 oz salted peanuts
150 ml/¼ pint mayonnaise
1 tablespoon lemon juice
salt and pepper

Core and finely shred the cabbage. Halve and thinly slice the onion. Peel and coarsely grate the carrots. Peel, core and coarsely grate the apples. Place all the ingredients in a mixing bowl and toss well.

Turn the coleslaw into a serving dish and serve to accompany cold meats and flans.

Cook's Tip

Nuts add texture interest as well as flavour to salads. Used in adequate proportions they also provide protein to make a main dish. Try hazelnuts, pecans, brazils, peanuts and almonds in salads.

Cook's Tip

Make a delicious supper with coleslaw and grilled bacon rolls in buttered French bread.

125 | Green Salad

Preparation time
10–15 minutes

Serves 4

Calories
120 per portion

You will need
1 lettuce
¼ cucumber
1 green pepper

Possible additions
4 spring onions
bunch of watercress

For the French dressing
1 tablespoon wine vinegar
3 tablespoons olive oil
1 teaspoon mustard powder
½ teaspoon sugar
salt and pepper

Separate the lettuce into leaves and arrange in a large salad bowl. Thinly slice the cucumber. Core, deseed and slice the pepper into rings. Chop the spring onions, if using, and remove the stalks from the watercress; separate into small sprigs. Scatter the salad vegetables over the lettuce.

To make the dressing, put all the ingredients in a screw-topped jar, shake well and pour over the salad. Serve immediately.

126 | Mushroom Salad

Preparation time
10 minutes, plus 30 minutes to chill

Serves 4

Calories
115 per portion

You will need
450 g / 1 lb button mushrooms

For the dressing
2 cloves garlic, crushed
3 tablespoons oil
1 tablespoon lemon juice
salt and pepper
2 tablespoons chopped fresh mint

Wipe the mushrooms and place in a serving bowl. Mix the dressing ingredients together well. Pour over and toss the mushrooms in the dressing.

Chill for at least 30 minutes before serving.

Cook's Tip

If the variety of green salad ingredients is limited add lots of coarsely chopped parsley for a fresh taste.

Cook's Tip

Scoop out bread rolls, brush all over with melted butter or margarine and bake until crisp. Serve the salad in the cooled rolls to make a delicious starter.

127 | *Tomato and Onion Salad*

Preparation time
10 minutes

Serves 4

Calories
170 per portion

You will need
8 tomatoes
2 onions
coriander or parsley sprig to garnish

For the dressing
4 tablespoons olive oil
1 tablespoon wine vinegar
pinch of mustard powder
1 teaspoon sugar
1 tablespoon chopped fresh herbs, for example, coriander, parsley, and basil
salt and pepper

Thinly slice the tomatoes and onions, and arrange in a serving dish.

To make the dressing, put all the ingredients in a screw-topped jar and shake well. Pour the dressing over the tomato and onion. Garnish with a sprig of coriander or parsley.

128 | *Potato Salad*

Preparation time
10 minutes

Cooking time
15 minutes

Serves 4

Calories
345 per portion

You will need
675 g/ 1½ lb potatoes
150 ml/¼ pint mayonnaise
2 tablespoons single cream
2–3 tablespoons chopped chives
salt and pepper

Use small, whole new potatoes when in season; leave the skins on and scrub clean. If using old potatoes, peel and cut into chunks. Cook in a pan of boiling salted water for 15 minutes, or until tender. Drain and allow to cool.

Mix together the remaining ingredients; pour over the potatoes and mix well. Place the potato salad in a serving bowl and serve with cold meats or a quiche.

Cook's Tip

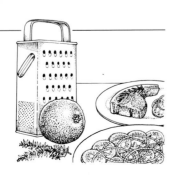

Alternative idea: add grated orange rind to the dressing and use finely chopped fresh rosemary instead of the basil. Good with grilled lamb or pork sausages.

Cook's Tips

Flavour a simple potato salad with chopped black olives, garlic and marjoram. Dress with olive oil and lemon juice for a mediterranean flavour.

Vegetarian Recipes

Many people are finding that they feel healthier if they cut down on the amount of meat they eat each week and are looking for alternative forms of protein. The recipes in this chapter are for delicious and nutritious meals and snacks using beans, pulses, nuts and seeds. There is a wide variety of dishes suitable for all occasions, from family meals to dinner parties.

129 | Vegetable Pancakes

Preparation time
30 minutes

Cooking time
35–40 minutes

Oven temperature
220 C, 425 F, gas 7

Serves 4

Calories
425 per portion

You will need
100 g/4 oz plain flour
salt and pepper
1 egg
300 ml/½ pint milk
oil for frying
1 onion, chopped
1 green pepper, deseeded and diced
4 courgettes, diced
1 (400-g/14-oz) can tomatoes
½ teaspoon oregano
1 quantity cheese sauce (recipe 110)
chopped parsley to garnish

Sift the flour and pinch of salt into a bowl. Make a well in the centre, add the egg and gradually beat in the milk to make a smooth batter. Lightly oil a crêpe pan or small frying pan. Place over a moderate heat. Pour in about 2 tablespoons of the batter, tilting the pan to coat the base. Cook until golden, turn and cook the second side. Repeat to make about eight large pancakes.

Cook the onion, and pepper in a little oil until softened. Add the courgettes, tomatoes, oregano and seasoning and simmer for 10–15 minutes. Fill the pancakes, roll up and place in an ovenproof dish. Pour over the cheese sauce and bake in a hot oven for 15 minutes. Garnish with parsley and serve with a green salad.

130 | Vegetable Lasagne

Preparation time
55 minutes

Cooking time
1 hour

Oven temperature
200 C, 400 F, gas 6

Serves 4

Calories
650 per portion

You will need
1 aubergine
salt and pepper
1 onion, chopped
1 green pepper, deseeded and cut into rings
2 cloves garlic, crushed
oil for frying
4 courgettes, sliced
100 g/4 oz mushrooms, sliced
1 (400-g/14-oz) can tomatoes
½ teaspoon dried basil
225 g/8 oz no-need-to-cook wholewheat lasagne
double quantity cheese sauce (recipe 110)

Slice the aubergine, place in a colander, sprinkle generously with salt and leave to drain for 30 minutes. Wash, drain and dry well. Fry the onion, pepper and garlic in oil until softened. Add the aubergine and cook until softened. Stir in the courgettes, mushrooms, tomatoes, basil and seasoning.

Layer the lasagne and vegetable mixture in a greased lasagne dish, ending with pasta on top. Pour the sauce over and bake in a moderately hot oven for 45–50 minutes, or until golden and bubbly.

Cook's Tip

Interleave cooked pancakes with absorbent kitchen paper (separate layers in each piece to give fine sheets) to prevent them sticking together when stacked.

Cook's Tip

To use ordinary dried wholewheat lasagne for this dish, cook in plenty of boiling salted water for 15 minutes. Drain, rinse in cold water then lay the sheets on absorbent kitchen paper to dry.

131 | Sunflower Seed Vegetable Bake

Preparation time
20 minutes

Cooking time
55 minutes

Oven temperature
200 C, 400 F, gas 6

Serves 4

Calories
255 per portion

You will need
450 g/1 lb potatoes, peeled and
  quartered
225 g/8 oz carrots, sliced
salt and pepper
1 onion, chopped
50 g/2 oz sunflower seeds
oil for frying
¼ teaspoon marjoram
2 leeks, sliced into rings
2 cloves garlic, crushed
2 courgettes, sliced
100 g/4 oz mushrooms, sliced
1 tablespoon grated Parmesan
  cheese
1 tablespoon chopped parsley to
  garnish

Cook the potatoes and carrots together in boiling salted water. Drain and mash. Fry the onion and sunflower seeds in the oil until the onion is soft. Stir into the potato mixture, add the marjoram and season to taste.

Fry the leeks and garlic in the oil for about 5 minutes. Season to taste. Add the courgettes and mushrooms and cook for 2–3 minutes.

Put half the leek mixture in an ovenproof dish. Spread half the potato mixture on top. Add the rest of the leek mixture, then top with the remaining potato.

Sprinkle the Parmesan over and bake in a moderately hot oven for 20–25 minutes or until golden. Garnish with parsley and serve immediately.

Microwave Tip

Microwave the potatoes with 2 tablespoons water in a roasting bag for about 15 minutes. Microwave the remaining vegetables together in a covered dish for 8–10 minutes. Layer and brown under a grill.

132 | Aubergine and Tomato Bake

Preparation time
50 minutes

Cooking time
45 minutes

Oven temperature
200 C, 400 F, gas 6

Serves 4

Calories
95 per portion

You will need
2 aubergines, cubed
salt and pepper
1 onion, chopped
2 cloves garlic, crushed
1–2 tablespoons oil
2 courgettes, diced
1 (400-g 14-oz) can plum
  tomatoes
1 teaspoon ground cumin

For the topping
50 g/2 oz butter or margarine
100 g/4 oz plain flour
25 g/1 oz unroasted sesame
  seeds
salt and pepper
knobs of butter

Place the aubergine in a colander, sprinkle with salt and leave to drain for 30 minutes. Rinse, drain and pat dry. Fry the onion and garlic in the oil until soft. Add the aubergine and courgette and fry for a further 5 minutes. Pour in the tomatoes, add the cumin and seasoning and bring to the boil.

Rub the fat into the flour until the mixture resembles fine breadcrumbs. Stir in the sesame seeds and seasoning. Pour the vegetable mixture into an ovenproof dish, spread the crumble mixture on top and dot with the butter. Bake in a moderately hot oven for 30 minutes, or until the top is golden.

Cook's Tip

Try growing your own garlic – divide a bulb and plant plump individual cloves. They grow like onions but put them in the garden or outside in a pot as they can smell strongly.

133 | Savoury Puff

Preparation time
20 minutes

Cooking time
45 minutes

Oven temperature
220 C, 425 F, gas 7
180 C, 350 F, gas 4

Serves 4

Calories
530 per portion

You will need
2 small carrots, diced
100 g / 4 oz broccoli, separated
  into florets
1 small green pepper, deseeded
  and diced
2 leeks, trimmed and sliced into
  rings
salt and pepper
100 g / 4 oz Lancashire cheese
  diced
1 teaspoon dill weed
1 (368-g / 13-oz) packet frozen
  puff pastry, defrosted
beaten egg to glaze
watercress sprig to garnish

Cook the prepared vegetables together in boiling salted water for 5 minutes. Drain and plunge into a basin of cold water. Leave for a few minutes in the water, then drain again thoroughly. Mix the vegetables with the cheese, dill weed and seasoning to taste.

Roll out the pastry thinly to make a 30-cm / 12-in square. Place on a greased baking tray. Spoon the filling into the centre of the square. Brush the edges of the pastry with a little water and bring the four corners to the centre, pinching well to seal. Glaze the pastry with beaten egg and decorate with small pastry shapes.

Bake in a hot oven for 15 minutes, then reduce the heat to moderate and cook for a further 30 minutes until golden. Garnish with a sprig of watercress and serve immediately, accompanied with a salad.

Cook's Tip

Look out for ready-rolled puff pastry, sold frozen in thin sheets, and chilled puff pastry. If you prefer to avoid animal fat in your diet, puff pastry made from vegetable oil is available, and wholemeal puff pastry can also be bought. Any can be used in the above recipe.

134 | Spring Rolls

Preparation time
20 minutes

Cooking time
15–20 minutes

Serves 4

Calories
280 per portion

You will need
50 g / 2 oz plain flour
salt and pepper
1 egg yolk
150 ml / ¼ pint milk
oil for frying, plus extra for deep
  frying
1 onion, thinly sliced
1 red pepper, deseeded and
  thinly sliced
100 g / 4 oz bean sprouts
½ teaspoon ground ginger
1 tablespoon soy sauce
1–2 egg whites
parsley sprigs to garnish

Make the pancake batter as instructed in recipe 129, using the egg yolk. Heat a little oil in a small frying pan. Pour in a little batter and tilt the pan so the batter covers the base. Cook until the underside is golden, then turn and lightly brown the second side. Turn out of the pan and repeat with the remaining batter.

Mix together the vegetables, ginger, soy sauce and seasoning. Place some of this filling in the centre of each pancake. Brush the edges of the pancakes with egg white. Roll up, folding in the sides to enclose the filling completely in a neat package. Seal the join with egg white, then brush egg white all over the pancakes.

Heat the oil for deep frying to 190 C / 375 F. Fry the rolls for 4–5 minutes or until golden. Drain on absorbent kitchen paper and serve, garnished with parsley and accompanied with tomato sauce (see recipe 161) and rice.

Freezer Tip

Make a large batch of these, fill and brush with egg white. Place on cling film on a baking tray and freeze. Deep fry from frozen as required.

135 | *Lentil Loaf*

Preparation time
15 minutes

Cooking time
1½ hours

Oven temperature
180 C, 350 F, gas 4

Serves 4

Calories
390 per portion

You will need
225 g / 8 oz red lentils
600 ml / 1 pint boiling water
1 onion, chopped
2 cloves garlic, crushed
1 tablespoon oil
100 g / 4 oz fresh brown
  breadcrumbs
100 g / 4 oz Cheddar cheese,
  grated
1 tablespoon chopped parsley
½ teaspoon dried mixed herbs
1 egg
salt and pepper
halved hazelnuts to garnish

Line a 1-kg / 2-lb loaf tin with greaseproof paper, grease well.

Cook the lentils in the boiling water for about 30 minutes, or until all the water has been absorbed and the lentils are mushy; stir frequently towards the end of the cooking time.

Cook the onion and garlic in the oil until soft. Mix with the lentils and remaining ingredients and season to taste. Pack the lentil mixture into the prepared tin, cover with a sheet of greaseproof paper and bake in a moderate oven for 1 hour. Serve garnished with hazelnuts.

136 | *Vegetarian Burgers*

Preparation time
15 minutes

Cooking time
15–20 minutes

Serves 4

Calories
330 per portion

You will need
1 onion, grated
675 g / 1½ lb white cabbage, grated
225 g / 8 oz carrots, grated
100 g / 4 oz hazelnuts, coarsely
  chopped
100 g / 4 oz fresh brown
  breadcrumbs
1 large egg
3 tablespoons soy sauce
1 teaspoon marjoram
salt and pepper
25 g / 1 oz plain flour
oil for deep frying
parsley sprig to garnish

Mix together all the ingredients, except the flour, and beat well. Shape the mixture into eight cakes and coat each in the flour.

Heat the oil for deep frying to 190 C / 375 F (until a cube of bread turns golden in 30 seconds). Cook the burgers a few at a time for 5–7 minutes, or until golden, and drain on absorbent kitchen paper. Keep hot while cooking the remaining burgers. Garnish with a sprig of parsley and serve hot with Leeks in Sauce (see recipe 111).

Cook's Tip

Instead of lentils, try chick peas, haricot beans or butter beans.

Freezer Tips

These burgers freeze well. Make a large batch, shape and open freeze on cling film until firm. Pack in bags and label. Cook from frozen.

137 | Potato Cakes

Preparation time
20 minutes, plus 30 minutes to chill

Cooking time
10–15 minutes

Serves 4

Calories
400 per portion

You will need
675 g/ 1½ lb potatoes, cooked
knob of butter or margarine
1 tablespoon milk
salt and pepper
1 onion, grated
50 g/ 2 oz Cheddar cheese, grated
2 tablespoons chopped parsley
1 teaspoon mustard powder
flour to coat
1 egg, lightly beaten
100 g/ 4 oz fresh wholemeal breadcrumbs
oil for frying
parsley sprig to garnish

Mash the potatoes with the butter or margarine, milk and seasoning until smooth. Allow to cool. Mix in the onion, Cheddar, parsley and mustard. Divide the mixture into eight portions, shape into cakes and coat in flour. Dip the cakes in the beaten egg and coat in the breadcrumbs, pressing them on well. Refrigerate for about 30 minutes.

Shallow fry the cakes in oil, a few at a time, for about 2–3 minutes on each side. Drain on absorbent kitchen paper and keep hot while cooking the remaining cakes. Garnish with parsley and serve immediately with a crisp green salad.

138 | Baked Stuffed Courgettes

Preparation time
20 minutes

Cooking time
20 minutes

Oven temperature
200 C, 400 F, gas 6

Serves 4

Calories
250 per portion

You will need
4 large courgettes
1 onion, finely chopped
1 tablespoon oil
50 g/ 2 oz Lancashire cheese, grated
25 g/ 1 oz butter
25 g/ 1 oz plain flour
300 ml/½ pint milk
salt and pepper
2 teaspoons sesame seeds
watercress sprigs to garnish

Cut the courgettes in half lengthways, scoop out the middle and chop finely.

Cook the onion in the oil until soft. Mix with the chopped courgette and cheese. Melt the butter in a saucepan, stir in the flour and cook for 2 minutes. Gradually add the milk, stirring continuously. Add the courgette and cheese mixture, season to taste with salt and pepper. Spoon the filling into the courgette shells and place in an ovenproof dish.

Sprinkle over the sesame seeds and bake in a moderately hot oven for about 20 minutes. Serve hot, garnished with sprigs of watercress.

Cook's Tip

For a quick alternative substitute instant mashed potato. Add 2 tablespoons grated Parmesan cheese for a good cheesy flavour.

Cook's Tip

For an attractive main dish, cook swedes and carrots together, drain and mash. Pipe between the courgettes in the dish, top with grated cheese and bake as above.

139 | Stuffed Cabbage Leaves

Preparation time
20 minutes

Cooking time
50 minutes

Oven temperature
190 C, 375 F, gas 5

Serves 4

Calories
340 per portion

You will need
12 large cabbage leaves
1 onion, grated
2 carrots, grated
100 g/4 oz brown rice, cooked
100 g/4 oz salted peanuts, chopped
1 egg
2 tablespoons soy sauce
salt and pepper
150 ml/¼ pint vegetable stock
1 quantity tomato sauce (recipe 161)

Cut away the stem from each cabbage leaf and blanch the leaves in boiling water. Drain thoroughly and leave to cool.

Mix together the onion, carrot, rice, peanuts, egg, soy sauce and seasoning. Divide the mixture between the cabbage leaves and roll up each leaf, folding in the sides, to enclose the filling in a neat package. Place the stuffed cabbage leaves in an ovenproof dish and pour over the vegetable stock.

Cover and bake in a moderately hot oven for about 45 minutes. Carefully drain off the stock and serve immediately, accompanied with tomato sauce.

140 | Vegetable Terrine

Preparation time
25 minutes, plus 2 hours to chill

Cooking time
1½ hours

Oven temperature
160 C, 325 F, gas 3

Serves 4

Calories
740 per portion

You will need
75 g/3 oz margarine
75 g/3 oz plain flour
600 ml/1 pint milk
2 eggs, lightly beaten
salt and pepper
225 g/8 oz carrots, chopped
1 onion, chopped
1 tablespoon oil
300 g/11 oz Cheddar cheese, grated
bunch of watercress, trimmed
¼ cauliflower, lightly cooked
225 g/8 oz peas, cooked
watercress sprigs to garnish

Line a 1-kg/2-lb loaf tin with greased greaseproof paper.

Melt the margarine, stir in the flour. Add the milk and bring to the boil, stirring. Cool slightly, then beat in the eggs. Season and cool.

Cook the carrots and onion in the oil for 5 minutes. Blend in a liquidiser with a quarter of the sauce, pour into the tin.

Repeat with 225 g/8 oz of the Cheddar, watercress and another quarter of sauce. Blend the cauliflower with the remaining Cheddar and a third quarter of the sauce. Finally blend the peas and remaining sauce in a liquidiser. Pour into the tin.

Cover the tin with foil and stand in a roasting tin half-full of hot water. Cook in a moderate oven for 1½ hours. Leave to cool. Refrigerate for 1–2 hours before turning out to serve. Garnish as above.

Microwave Tip

To microwave, cook the cabbage leaves in a roasting bag with 2 tablespoons water for 5 minutes. Microwave assembled dish, covered, on full power for 15–20 minutes.

Microwave Tip

Layer in a loaf dish (not tin). Cover, microwave on full power for 20 minutes turning occasionally.

141 | Hummus

Preparation time
10 minutes

Serves 4

Calories
340 per portion

You will need
1 (439-g/15½-oz) can chick peas, drained
1–2 cloves garlic, crushed
grated rind and juice of 1 lemon
2 tablespoons tahini
2 tablespoons mayonnaise
salt and pepper

For the crudités
1 green pepper, deseeded and thinly sliced
1 red pepper, deseeded and thinly sliced
2 carrots, thinly sliced lengthways
2 celery sticks, thinly sliced
chunks of nutty brown bread to serve

Blend the chick peas, garlic, lemon rind and juice in a liquidiser or food processor until as smooth as possible. Add the tahini and mayonnaise, 1 tablespoon at a time, blending between each addition. Season well with salt and pepper, pour the hummus into a small bowl and place on a large serving plate.

Prepare the vegetables as instructed and arrange with the bread around the hummus.

142 | Fruit and Vegetable Kebabs

Preparation time
10 minutes

Cooking time
10 minutes

Serves 4

Calories
110 per portion

You will need
1 courgette, sliced
8 canned pineapple chunks
1 small green pepper, deseeded and cut into squares
8 canned apricot halves
8 button mushrooms
1 small onion, quartered
4 cherry tomatoes
1 tablespoon oil
salt and pepper

Divide the prepared kebab ingredients equally between four long skewers and thread on. Mix a little juice from the canned pineapple with the oil and seasoning, and brush over the kebabs.

Cook under a hot grill for about 10 minutes, turning and basting occasionally. Serve hot on a bed of rice and accompany with a green salad.

Cook's Tip

For a simple starter serve hummus in scooped out tomatoes, top each with a black olive. Serve with hot pitta bread.

Cook's Tip

Marinate the ingredients in 2 tablespoons chopped fresh herbs, 4 tablespoons oil, garlic salt and 4 tablespoons orange juice for several hours. Baste generously with marinade during cooking.

143 | Mixed Bean Curry

Preparation time
20 minutes, plus
overnight soaking

Cooking time
1 hour 20 minutes

Serves 4

Calories
235 per portion

You will need
100 g/4 oz dried red kidney
   beans
100 g/4 oz dried black-eye beans
1 onion, chopped
1–2 cloves garlic, crushed
1–2 tablespoons oil
½ teaspoon chilli powder
½ teaspoon ground ginger
1 tablespoon ground cumin
1 tablespoon ground coriander
½ teaspoon turmeric
juice of 1 lemon
1 (400-g/14-oz) can tomatoes
150 ml/¼ pint vegetable stock
salt and pepper
chopped parsley to garnish

Soak the beans in cold water overnight. Drain and put in a large saucepan. Cover with fresh water and bring to the boil. *Boil rapidly for 10 minutes* then reduce the heat and simmer for 30 minutes. Drain.

   Cook the onion and garlic in the oil until soft. Add the spices and cook over a gentle heat for 2–3 minutes. Add the lemon juice, tomatoes and stock and bring to the boil. Reduce the heat, add the beans and cover the pan. Simmer gently for 30–40 minutes, or until the beans are tender and the excess liquid has been absorbed.

   Season to taste, garnish with chopped parsley and serve with brown rice, poppadums and a suitable relish or chutney.

144 | Vegetable Curry

Preparation time
45 minutes

Cooking time
40 minutes

Serves 4

Calories
155 per portion

You will need
1 kg/2 lb mixture of following
   vegetables: aubergines,
   potatoes, carrots and
   cauliflower
1 onion, chopped
1–2 cloves garlic, crushed
1–2 tablespoons oil
1 teaspoon ground ginger
1 teaspoon mustard powder
1 teaspoon ground cumin
1 teaspoon ground coriander
2 teaspoons turmeric
300 ml/½ pint vegetable stock
salt and pepper
1 tablespoon coriander leaves

Prepare the vegetables according to type. Cut the aubergine into chunks and put in a colander. Sprinkle with salt and leave for 30 minutes. Drain, rinse and pat dry. Break the cauliflower into florets, roughly chop the carrots and potatoes.

   Cook the onion and garlic in the oil until soft. Stir in the spices and cook over a gentle heat for 2 minutes. Add the vegetables and stir well to mix with the fried spices. Stir in the vegetable stock and season with plenty of salt and pepper. Bring to the boil, cover and simmer gently for about 30 minutes. Pour into a warmed serving dish and garnish with chopped coriander. Serve the curry with poppadums and rice.

Cook's Tip

A spicy egg side dish tastes good with this curry. Roughly chop 4 hard-boiled eggs, sprinkle with chopped onion, chopped fresh coriander and chilli powder.

Microwave Tip

Microwave onion, garlic, oil and spices on full power for 5 minutes. Add all ingredients, using hot stock, cover and microwave for 15–20 minutes.

Rice and Pasta

Many of the recipes in this chapter have an international flavour. The imaginative use of flavourings and relatively small quantities of meat or fish has made the rice dishes of the Far East famous throughout the world. Italy is renowned for its delicious pasta dishes and with so many different types of pasta readily available, both fresh and dried, it deserves to be included more often in our meals.

145 | Chicken Liver Risotto

Preparation time
15 minutes

Cooking time
30 minutes

Serves 4

Calories
390 per portion

You will need
1 onion, chopped
1 red pepper, deseeded and
   chopped
1 green pepper, deseeded and
   chopped
2 carrots, chopped
2 tablespoons oil
225 g/ 8 oz chicken livers, diced
225 g/ 8 oz long-grain rice
600 ml/ 1 pint chicken stock
salt and pepper
chopped watercress to garnish

In a large frying pan, fry the onion, pepper and carrot in the oil for 5 minutes until soft. Add the chicken livers and cook for a few minutes until browned. Add the rice, stock and seasoning. Bring to the boil and simmer gently for 15–20 minutes, stirring occasionally until cooked.

Serve immediately, garnished with chopped watercress.

146 | Paella

Preparation time
15 minutes

Cooking time
30 minutes

Serves 4

Calories
650 per portion

You will need
1 onion, chopped
2 cloves garlic, crushed
1 red pepper, deseeded and
   chopped
3 tablespoons oil
225 g/ 8 oz long-grain rice
pinch of turmeric
600 ml/ 1 pint chicken stock
salt and pepper
225 g/ 8 oz cooked chicken, cut
   into thick strips
100 g/ 4 oz ham, diced
2 chorizo sausages, thickly sliced
100 g/ 4 oz frozen peas
2 tomatoes, peeled and quartered
100 g/ 4 oz peeled cooked prawns
1 tablespoon chopped parsley to
   garnish

In a large frying pan, fry the onion, garlic and pepper in the oil for a few minutes until soft.

Add the rice and stir until it is lightly fried and the grains are transparent. Stir in the turmeric, stock and seasoning and simmer, covered, for 15 minutes. Add all the remaining ingredients and cook, covered, for a further 5–10 minutes until almost all the liquid has been absorbed. The paella should be moist.

Sprinkle with the chopped parsley and serve immediately.

Cook's Tip

Turkey livers can be substituted for the chicken livers or this is an ideal way of using up cooked chicken or turkey. Add the chopped meat to the risotto when rice is partially cooked.

Cook's Tip

For a delicious and more exotic paella add some firm white fish such as monk fish, haddock or turbot, mussels and squid with the chicken.

147 | Basic Rice

Serves 2

Calories
180 per portion of white, brown, or Basmati rice

You will need
For white rice
100 g / 4 oz long-grain rice
300 ml / ½ pint water
salt

For brown rice
100 g / 4 oz long-grain rice
350 ml / 12 fl oz water
salt

For Basmati rice
100 g / 4 oz Basmati rice
scant 300 ml / ½ pint water
salt

The method is the same for white and brown rice. Easy-cook varieties do not need washing, but other types of rice should be placed in a sieve and thoroughly rinsed. Put the rice in a saucepan and pour in the water. Add a little salt, then bring to the boil. Reduce the heat so that the liquid barely simmers. Give a light stir to make sure the grains are not stuck together and cover the pan.

Simmer very gently, allowing about 15–20 minutes for white rice and about 30–40 minutes for brown rice. At the end of cooking all the liquid should have been absorbed. Fork up the grains and serve.

Basmati rice has a unique and delicate flavour. The grains are quite fragile and starchy. To wash the rice, put it in a basin and pour in cold water to cover. Gently swirl the water with your fingertips, then drain it off. Repeat once or twice until the water runs clear. Cook as white and brown rice, allowing about 25 minutes cooking time.

Cook's Tip

To keep rice hot for up to 30 minutes, place in a metal colander over an open pan of simmering water. Cover with a tea towel and lid.

148 | Pilau Rice

Preparation time
10 minutes

Cooking time
25–30 minutes

Serves 4

Calories
390 per portion

You will need
225 g / 8 oz Basmati rice
1 onion, chopped
50 g / 2 oz butter or margarine
3 cloves
5-cm / 2-in piece cinnamon stick
1 bay leaf
50 g / 2 oz flaked almonds
25 g / 1 oz raisins
600 ml / 1 pint water
salt and pepper

Wash and drain the Basmati rice and set aside. Cook the onion in the butter or margarine in a saucepan until soft. Add the remaining ingredients and bring to the boil. Reduce the heat, cover the pan tightly and simmer gently for 20–25 minutes, or until all the water has been absorbed. Fluff up the rice with a fork and serve immediately.

This is the traditional accompaniment to curry and chicken dishes.

Cook's Tip

Add a little chopped cooked meat, chicken or fish to the pilau for a light lunch or supper dish.

149 | Saffron Rice

Preparation time
5 minutes

Cooking time
15–20 minutes

Serves 4

Calories
200 per portion

You will need
$\frac{1}{4}$ teaspoon saffron strands
600 ml / 1 pint water
225 g / 8 oz long-grain rice
salt

Put the saffron strands in a pestle and pound them with a mortar until reduced almost to a powder. Stir in a little of the measured water to dissolve the saffron.

Put the rice in a saucepan. (Remember to wash Basmati rice first, see recipe 147.) Pour in the saffron liquid, rinse the pestle with a little of the measured water to obtain all the colour and flavour. Pour in the rest of the water. Add a pinch of salt and bring to the boil. Reduce the heat, cover and simmer for 15–25 minutes or until all the water has been absorbed. Fluff up the grains with a fork and serve.

150 | Savoury Rice

Preparation time
10–15 minutes

Cooking time
20–25 minutes

Serves 4

Calories
390 per portion

You will need
225 g / 8 oz long-grain white rice
$\frac{1}{4}$ teaspoon turmeric
600 ml / 1 pint water
salt and pepper
1 onion, chopped
1 red pepper, deseeded and
  chopped
1 green pepper, deseeded and
  chopped
100 g / 4 oz button mushrooms
1 tablespoon oil
2 peperoni sausages, sliced
  (optional)
2 tomatoes, peeled and quartered
6 black olives, stoned

Put the rice and turmeric in a saucepan and pour in the water. Add a little salt, then bring to the boil. Reduce the heat so that the liquid barely simmers. Give the rice a light stir to make sure the grains are not stuck together and cover the pan tightly.

Simmer very gently, allowing about 15–20 minutes. At the end of cooking all the liquid should have been absorbed.

Fry the onion, pepper and mushrooms in the oil for 5 minutes until soft. Mix all the ingredients together.

Arrange the rice attractively on a serving dish and serve hot as an accompaniment, or with a salad as a meal in itself.

Cook's Tip

Add a cinnamon stick or cloves to water or add chopped fresh herbs such as thyme, dill or parsley to the cooked rice.

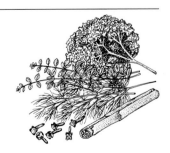

Cook's Tip

The vegetables in this recipe can be varied according to what is available. Aubergines, sweetcorn kernels, peas and courgettes are other good choices.

151 | Brown Rice Ring Mould

Preparation time
5–10 minutes, plus 1½ hours to chill

Cooking time
45 minutes

Serves 4

Calories
400 per portion

You will need
225 g/8 oz long-grain brown rice
350 ml/12 fl oz water
salt
100 g/4 oz walnut halves, roughly chopped
1 (325-g/11.8-oz) can sweetcorn, drained
1 green pepper, deseeded and diced
¼ teaspoon paprika
pinch of salt
watercress sprigs to garnish

Grease a 1.15-litre/2-pint ring mould with oil.

Put the rice in a saucepan and pour in the water. Add a little salt, then bring to the boil. Reduce the heat so that the liquid barely simmers. Give the rice a light stir to make sure the grains are not stuck together and cover the pan tightly.

Simmer very gently for 30–40 minutes. At the end of cooking all the liquid should have been absorbed. Mix all the ingredients together and pack the mixture into the ring mould.

Leave the rice to cool and chill thoroughly. Turn out and serve as an accompaniment to a salad.

152 | Tomato Rice Mould

Preparation time
10 minutes

Cooking time
15–20 minutes

Serves 4

Calories
295 per portion

You will need
2 (400-g/14-oz) cans plum tomatoes
2 onions, chopped
1 clove garlic, crushed
1 teaspoon dried or 2 teaspoons chopped fresh basil
salt and pepper
225 g/8 oz long-grain white rice
450 ml/¾ pint water
50 g/2 oz Parmesan cheese, grated
watercress sprigs to garnish

Grease a 1.15-litre/2-pint ring mould with oil.

For the tomato sauce, blend the tomatoes, onion, garlic, basil and seasoning in a liquidiser until smooth. Cook the rice in the tomato sauce and water for 15–20 minutes or until the liquid has evaporated, stirring occasionally. Stir in the Parmesan cheese.

Press the rice into the mould and leave for 5 minutes. Turn out the rice, and serve with a salad or with grilled meat.

Cook's Tip

For a more colourful dish, add peas or diced, peeled and deseeded tomatoes to the rice.

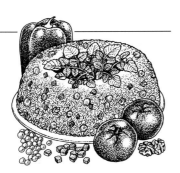

Cook's Tip

For a buffet party dish fill centre of rice ring with lightly cooked cauliflower florets tossed in French dressing.

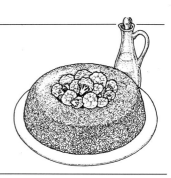

153 | Rice Cakes

Preparation time
10–15 minutes

Cooking time
25 minutes

Makes 8 cakes

Calories
370 per portion

You will need
225 g/8 oz long-grain rice
300 ml/½ pint water
salt and pepper
350 g/12 oz smoked haddock,
  cod or coley
3 tablespoons oil
1 onion, chopped
grated rind and juice of 1 lemon
2 tablespoons tomato ketchup
2 tablespoons chopped parsley
1 egg

Put the rice in a saucepan and pour in the water. Add a little salt, then bring to the boil. Reduce the heat so that the liquid barely simmers. Give the rice a light stir to make sure the grains are not stuck together and cover the pan tightly.

Simmer very gently, allowing about 15–20 minutes for white rice and about 30–40 minutes for brown rice. At the end of cooking all the liquid should have been absorbed.

Place the fish in a frying pan, cover with water and poach for 10 minutes or until the fish is cooked. Skin the fish and remove any bones, then flake the fish.

Heat 1 tablespoon of the oil and cook the onion for a few minutes, then add the rice, fish and remaining ingredients. Mash together well, remove from the heat and form the mixture into cakes. Fry the cakes in the remaining oil until brown, and serve immediately.

154 | Kedgeree

Preparation time
10 minutes

Cooking time
30 minutes

Serves 4

Calories
430 per portion

You will need
1 onion, chopped
2 tablespoons oil or 25 g/1 oz
  butter
175 g/6 oz long-grain rice
¼ teaspoon turmeric
450 ml/¾ pint water
225 g/8 oz smoked haddock
50 g/2 oz raisins
50 g/2 oz salted peanuts
3 hard-boiled eggs, roughly
  chopped
1 tablespoon lemon juice
salt and pepper
1 tablespoon chopped parsley

Cook the onion in the oil or butter until soft but not browned. Add the rice and turmeric, cook for a minute, then pour in the water. Bring to the boil, reduce the heat and cover the pan. Simmer for 15 minutes until the water is absorbed.

Meanwhile, put the smoked haddock in a pan, cover with water and bring to the boil. Reduce the heat and simmer for 5 minutes, or until the fish flakes easily with the point of a knife. Drain and coarsely flake the fish, discarding the skin and any bones.

Add the fish, raisins, peanuts, eggs, lemon juice, seasoning and parsley to the rice. Fork together gently.

Serve the kedgeree immediately.

Cook's Tip

For a quick supper substitute canned pilchards or tuna fish for the smoked fish.

Cook's Tip

For a more spicy kedgeree omit raisins and peanuts and add ¼ teaspoon freshly grated nutmeg.

155 | *Chicken Pilaff with Apricots*

Preparation time
10 minutes

Cooking time
20 minutes

Serves 4

Calories
555 per portion

You will need
1 onion, chopped
25 g/1 oz butter or margarine
225 g/8 oz long-grain rice
1 kg/2 lb cooked chicken, cut into chunks
225 g/8 oz dried apricots, cut in half
600 ml/1 pint chicken stock
$\frac{1}{4}$ teaspoon mixed spice
salt and pepper
natural yogurt to serve

In a large saucepan cook the onion in the butter or margarine for a few minutes until soft and transparent. Add the rice and stir well until evenly coated in the fat. Add the remaining ingredients, bring the mixture to the boil and simmer gently for 15 minutes or until all the liquid has evaporated.

Serve hot with natural yogurt.

156 | *Rice Bake*

Preparation time
25 minutes

Cooking time
45 minutes

Oven temperature
200 C, 400 F, gas 6

Serves 4

Calories
700 per portion

You will need
100 g/4 oz long-grain rice
300 ml/$\frac{1}{2}$ pint water
salt and pepper
225 g/8 oz cooked ham, diced
4 hard-boiled eggs, chopped
225 g/8 oz Cheddar cheese, diced
bunch of parsley, chopped

For the white sauce
50 g/2 oz butter or margarine
50 g/2 oz plain flour
600 ml/1 pint milk
salt and pepper

Cook the rice as instructed in recipe 147.

Mix together the ham, eggs, Cheddar, parsley and seasoning, reserving a little parsley to garnish. For the white sauce, melt the butter or margarine over a low heat. Add the flour, cook for 2 minutes, stirring constantly, then gradually add the milk and stir until the sauce boils and thickens. Reduce the heat and simmer gently for 2 minutes. Add the seasoning.

Pour some of the sauce into a baking dish, followed by a layer of ham mixture, then a layer of rice. Continue layering in this fashion until all the ingredients are used up. Finish with a layer of sauce.

Bake in a moderately hot oven for 30 minutes until golden. Garnish with the reserved parsley, and serve hot with a green salad.

Microwave Tip

Pilaff reheats particularly well in a microwave. Cover with cling film and heat on full power for 4–5 minutes.

Freezer Tip

Left over rice freezes well. Pack into a polythene bag and seal. Defrost in a microwave or empty into a pan of boiling water and bring back to boil.

157 | Macaroni Cheese

Preparation time
15 minutes

Cooking time
15–20 minutes

Serves 4

Calories
615 per portion

You will need
225 g / 8 oz macaroni
pinch of salt

For the cheese sauce
50 g / 2 oz butter or margarine
40 g / 1½ oz plain flour
600 ml / 1 pint milk
salt and pepper
175 g / 6 oz Cheddar cheese,
  grated

Put the macaroni into a large saucepan of salted boiling water and simmer gently for 10–15 minutes, until just tender. Drain and set aside.

Melt the butter or margarine in a saucepan over a low heat, then add the flour. Cook for 2 minutes, stirring. Gradually add the milk, and bring the sauce to the boil, stirring constantly. Simmer gently for 2–3 minutes. Remove from the heat, and season well with salt and pepper.

Add the cooked macaroni and 150 g / 5 oz of the Cheddar to the sauce and combine well. Pour the mixture into a 1.15-litre / 2-pint serving dish and sprinkle the remaining cheese over the top. Brown under a hot grill and serve immediately.

158 | Lasagne Verdi

Preparation time
25 minutes

Cooking time
1 hour

Oven temperature
200 C, 400 F, gas 6

Serves 4

Calories
900 per portion

You will need
1 onion, chopped
2 cloves garlic, crushed
1 tablespoon oil
450 g / 1 lb minced beef
100 g / 4 oz mushrooms, wiped
  and sliced
3 tablespoons tomato purée
150 ml / ¼ pint beef stock
¼ teaspoon dried basil
¼ teaspoon dried oregano
salt and pepper
double quantity cheese sauce
  (recipe 110), using 75 g / 3 oz
  Cheddar and 75 g / 3 oz
  mozzarella cheese
225 g / 8 oz no-need-to-cook
  green lasagne

Fry the onion and garlic in the oil for 5 minutes until soft. Add the minced beef and cook for 5 minutes or until browned. Add the mushrooms, tomato purée, stock, basil, oregano, salt and pepper. Bring the mixture to the boil, reduce the heat and simmer gently for 20 minutes, stirring occasionally.

Spread a layer of the meat mixture over the bottom of a baking dish, followed by a layer of lasagne. Continue in this fashion until the meat mixture and the lasagne have been used up. Top with the cheese sauce.

Bake in a moderately hot oven for 30 minutes or until golden. Serve hot with garlic bread and a green salad.

Freezer Tip

Grate small left over pieces of hard cheese and keep in a polythene bag in the freezer to use in cooking.

Freezer Tip

To freeze lasagne, assemble dish but freeze before baking. Cook from frozen for 50–60 minutes until hot and golden.

159 | Stuffed Cannelloni

Preparation time
15–20 minutes

Cooking time
1 hour

Oven temperature
180 C, 350 F, gas 4

Serves 4

Calories
750 per portion

You will need
8 cannelloni tubes
salt and pepper
2 onions, chopped
2 cloves garlic, crushed
2 green peppers, deseeded and
    chopped
1 tablespoon oil
1 (400-g/14-oz) can chopped
    tomatoes
225 g/8 oz corned beef
½ teaspoon dried or 1 teaspoon
    chopped fresh basil
double quantity cheese sauce
    (recipe 110)
25 g/1 oz Parmesan cheese,
    grated

Cook the cannelloni in a saucepan of boiling salted water for 10 minutes until just tender. Drain and set aside.

For the filling, fry the onion, garlic and peppers in the oil for 5 minutes until soft. Add the tomatoes and simmer gently for 15 minutes until thickened. Cut the corned beef into small cubes and add to the sauce. Add the seasoning and basil and simmer for a further 5 minutes. Allow the meat mixture to cool slightly. Fill the cannelloni tubes with the meat mixture, then arrange the filled cannelloni in a greased ovenproof dish.

Pour the sauce over the cannelloni, sprinkle over the Parmesan and bake uncovered in a moderate oven for 30 minutes or until the top is crisp and golden.

160 | Spaghetti Bolognese

Preparation time
15 minutes

Cooking time
40–50 minutes

Serves 4

Calories
525 per portion

You will need
1 onion, chopped
1 clove garlic, crushed
1 tablespoon oil
450 g/1 lb minced beef
100 g/4 oz mushrooms, sliced
1 (400-g/14-oz) can chopped
    tomatoes
300 ml/½ pint beef stock
¼ teaspoon dried or ½ teaspoon
    finely chopped fresh basil
salt and pepper
225 g/8 oz spaghetti
grated Parmesan cheese to serve

Fry the onion and garlic in the oil for 5 minutes until soft. Add the mince and continue cooking for 5 minutes or until the meat is browned. Add the mushrooms, tomatoes, stock, basil, salt and pepper to the mince. Bring the mixture to the boil, reduce the heat and simmer gently for 30 minutes or until reduced, stirring occasionally.

Meanwhile, cook the spaghetti in a saucepan of boiling salted water for 10–12 minutes until just tender. Drain and pile the spaghetti into a large serving dish. Pour the Bolognese sauce on top, sprinkle with the Parmesan and serve immediately with a green salad.

Cook's Tip

To fill cannelloni tubes easily, put meat mixture into a piping bag fitted with a 1-cm/½-in plain tube and pipe mixture into cannelloni.

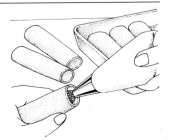

Freezer Tip

Bolognese sauce freezes well. It is worth making double or treble the quantity and storing in two or three portions in the freezer.

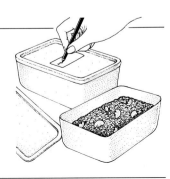

161 | Spaghetti with Tomato Sauce

Preparation time
5 minutes

Cooking time
25 minutes

Serves 4

Calories
480 per portion

You will need
1 onion, finely chopped
2 cloves garlic, crushed
1 tablespoon oil
1 (400-g/14-oz) can chopped
   tomatoes
½ teaspoon dried or 1 teaspoon
   chopped fresh basil
salt and pepper
450 g/1 lb spaghetti

Fry the onion and garlic in the oil for 5 minutes until soft. Add the tomatoes, basil, salt and pepper. Bring to the boil, reduce the heat and simmer gently for 15 minutes or until thickened.

While the sauce is simmering, cook the spaghetti in a large pan of boiling salted water for 10–12 minutes until just tender. Drain, place in a serving bowl and keep hot.

Blend the sauce in a liquidiser. Reheat in a saucepan for a few minutes, pour over the spaghetti and serve immediately.

162 | Spaghetti with Watercress and Walnut Sauce

Preparation time
10 minutes

Cooking time
15 minutes

Serves 4

Calories
615 per portion

You will need
450 g/1 lb wholewheat spaghetti
salt and pepper
1 onion, chopped
1–2 cloves, garlic, crushed
1 tablespoon oil
50 g/2 oz mushrooms, sliced
50 g/2 oz chopped walnuts
bunch of watercress, chopped
300 ml/½ pint soured cream

Cook the spaghetti in a large pan of boiling salted water for 10–12 minutes until just tender.

Meanwhile, make the sauce. Cook the onion and garlic in the oil until transparent. Add the mushrooms and walnuts and cook for a further few minutes. Remove the pan from the heat, stir in the watercress, soured cream and seasoning. Reheat very gently – do not allow the sauce to boil or the cream will curdle.

Drain the spaghetti and place on a serving dish. Pour the sauce over and serve immediately.

Cook's Tip

When fresh tomatoes are cheap and plentiful, use 450 g/1 lb peeled and chopped fresh instead of canned tomatoes and 1 tablespoon tomato purée.

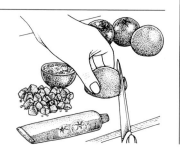

Microwave Tip

To cook sauce in a microwave: cook onion and garlic in oil for 6 minutes. Add mushrooms, walnuts and watercress, cook for 2 minutes. Add cream and cook for 3 minutes.

163 | Tagliatelle alla Carbonara

Preparation time
10–15 minutes

Cooking time
20–25 minutes

Serves 4

Calories
700 per portion

You will need
450 g/1 lb tagliatelle
salt and pepper
100 g/4 oz smoked rindless
   bacon, diced
2 tablespoons oil or 25 g/1 oz
   butter
2 eggs, lightly beaten
150 ml/¼ pint single cream
2 tablespoons chopped parsley
50 g/2 oz Parmesan cheese,
   grated

Cook the tagliatelle in a large saucepan of boiling salted water for 10–12 minutes until just tender. Drain and place in a serving dish. Keep warm.

Fry the bacon in the oil or butter until crispy, reduce the heat, then add the eggs, cream, parsley, seasoning to taste and half of the Parmesan. Heat gently, without boiling, stirring. Pour the sauce over the pasta, then sprinkle the remaining Parmesan cheese on top and serve immediately.

164 | Tagliatelle with Blue Cheese Sauce

Preparation time
5 minutes

Cooking time
15–20 minutes

Serves 4

Calories
665 per portion

You will need
450 g/1 lb green tagliatelle
salt and pepper
300 ml/½ pint single cream
100 g/4 oz Danish Blue cheese
50 g/2 oz chopped walnuts

Cook the tagliatelle in a large saucepan of boiling salted water for 10–12 minutes until just tender. Drain and place in a serving dish. Keep warm. In a saucepan, over a very low heat, heat the cream. Crumble the Danish Blue with your fingers and add to the cream. Add the chopped walnuts and season well.

Heat until the cheese has melted and the sauce is hot – do not let the sauce boil or it will curdle. Pour the sauce over the tagliatelle and serve immediately.

Cook's Tip

For a really quick and easy pasta dish, stir 100 g/4 oz cream cheese with garlic and herbs into the hot drained pasta.

Cook's Tip

Fresh, chilled pasta is available from many supermarkets and delicatessens. Cook for 3–5 minutes according to type.

165 | Quick Ravioli Supper

Preparation time
10 minutes

Cooking time
15–20 minutes

Serves 4

Calories
285 per portion

You will need
1 onion, chopped
2 cloves garlic, crushed
1 tablespoon oil
2 (440-g/15½-oz) cans ravioli in
   tomato sauce
50 g/2 oz Cheddar cheese, grated
50 g/2 oz fresh white
   breadcrumbs

Fry the onion and garlic in the oil for a few minutes until the onion is soft and transparent. Add the ravioli and heat gently for 5 minutes. Pour the mixture into a serving dish, then sprinkle over the Cheddar and breadcrumbs and cook under a hot grill until brown.

Serve immediately with a green salad.

166 | Pork Chow Mein

Preparation time
10 minutes

Cooking time
30 minutes

Serves 4

Calories
345 per portion

You will need
225 g/8 oz Chinese egg noodles
salt and pepper
2 tablespoons oil
225 g/8 oz boneless pork, diced
75 g/3 oz spring onions, chopped
2 cloves garlic, crushed
100 g/4 oz button mushrooms
1 tablespoon soy sauce
2 spring onion curls to garnish

Cook the noodles in a saucepan of boiling salted water for 5–10 minutes until just tender. Drain well and set aside.

Heat the oil in a large frying pan or wok, and fry the pork for 5 minutes. Add the onion, garlic and mushrooms and continue cooking for 2–3 minutes, then add the noodles, seasoning to taste and soy sauce. Mix all the ingredients together well and cook for 5 minutes or until the noodles are crispy. Serve immediately garnished as illustrated.

Cook's Tip

Spaghetti in tomato sauce or other shapes of canned pasta can be used in this dish.

Cook's Tip

For chicken chow mein use boneless shredded chicken in place of pork.

167 | Stuffed Pasta Shells

Preparation time
15 minutes, plus time
to cool the pasta

Cooking time
10–12 minutes

Serves 4

Calories
525 per portion

You will need
1 avocado, peeled and diced
1 tablespoon lemon juice
1 (198-g 7-oz) can tuna, drained
  and flaked
100 g/4 oz cottage cheese
1 onion, chopped
1 green pepper, deseeded and
  chopped
2 tablespoons mayonnaise
salt and pepper
225 g/8 oz large pasta shells
crisp lettuce to serve

Brush or dip the avocado in the lemon juice, then mix with the tuna, cottage cheese, onion, pepper and mayonnaise in a bowl, and season well.

Cook the pasta shells in a large saucepan of boiling salted water for 10–12 minutes until just tender. Drain and leave to cool. Stuff the shells with the filling and serve on a bed of crisp lettuce. This dish can be served either as a starter or a light lunch.

168 | Pasta Salad

Preparation time
15 minutes, plus time
to cool the pasta

Cooking time
10–12 minutes

Serves 4

Calories
495 per portion

You will need
225 g/8 oz pasta bows
salt and pepper
bunch of spring onions, chopped
1 red pepper, deseeded and
  chopped
1 green pepper, deseeded and
  chopped
2 celery sticks, sliced
1 tablespoon chopped parsley
150 ml/¼ pint natural yogurt
150 ml/¼ pint mayonnaise
1 teaspoon honey
¼ teaspoon freshly grated nutmeg

Cook the pasta bows in a large saucepan of boiling salted water for 10–12 minutes until just tender. Drain and leave to cool.

In a large mixing bowl, combine all the salad ingredients. Add the pasta. Mix together the yogurt, mayonnaise, honey and nutmeg. Transfer the salad to a serving bowl, and pour over the dressing. Serve with crisp lettuce leaves.

Cook's Tip

These stuffed pasta shells can be served as a tasty first course, with a light tomato dressing. Arrange the shells on individual plates. Stir 1 tablespoon tomato purée and a generous dash of Worcestershire sauce into 150 ml/¼ pint soured cream. Season to taste with garlic salt and pepper. Spoon this dressing over the pasta shells and serve with crisp toast or French bread.

Cook's Tip

Add cooked or canned fish or meat to this salad for a more substantial lunch or supper dish. If adding fish use small pasta shells instead of bows.

Pies, Pasties and Flans

A pie or flan will suit almost any occasion, from the simple to the sumptuous, depending on how extravagant you are with the filling ingredients. This chapter has recipes using lots of different kinds of pastry from puff and choux to suet and shortcrust.

169 | Sausage Layer Pie

Preparation time
20 minutes

Cooking time
1 hour

Oven temperature
190C, 375F, gas 5

Serves 4

Calories
905 per portion

You will need
1 quantity shortcrust pastry
  (recipe 176)
beaten egg to glaze

For the filling
350 g/12 oz sausagemeat
1 onion, chopped
2 cloves garlic, crushed
100 g/4 oz fresh breadcrumbs
salt and pepper
75 g/3 oz stuffed green olives
3 peperoni sausages

Make the shortcrust pastry as instructed in recipe 176. Roll out two-thirds of the pastry to line a 450-g/1-lb loaf tin.

Combine the sausagemeat, onion, garlic, breadcrumbs and seasoning. Spoon a little into the base of the tin, smooth over and top with a layer of olives and peperoni sausage. Repeat the layers until all the ingredients are used up, finishing with the sausagemeat mixture. Roll out the remaining pastry to form a lid. Dampen the edge of the pastry with water and cover the pie with the pastry lid. Trim and seal the edges and make a small hole in the centre to allow any steam to escape. Use any pastry trimmings to make leaves to decorate the top of the pie. Glaze with beaten egg and cook in a moderately hot oven for about 1 hour. Serve hot or cold with a salad.

Cook's Tip

Peel, core and slice cooking apples to layer in the sausagemeat pie.

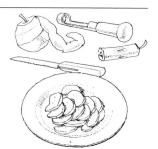

170 | Steak and Kidney Pudding

Preparation time
20 minutes

Cooking time
4 hours

Serves 4

Calories
640 per portion

You will need
225 g/8 oz self-raising flour
salt and pepper
100 g/4 oz shredded suet
6–8 tablespoons cold water, plus
  150 ml/$\frac{1}{4}$ pint
450 g/1 lb stewing steak
100 g/4 oz kidney
1 onion, chopped
25 g/1 oz plain flour
pinch of mustard powder
parsley sprig to garnish

Sift the flour and $\frac{1}{2}$ teaspoon salt into a bowl. Add the suet and mix well, then stir in sufficient water to form a light, elastic dough. Roll out two-thirds of the pastry to a circle large enough to line a 900-ml/1$\frac{1}{2}$-pint pudding basin.

Cut the steak into 2.5-cm/1-in cubes. Remove skin, core and fat from the kidney, then cut into 1-cm/$\frac{1}{2}$-in pieces. Arrange the steak and kidney in layers in the pudding basin. Mix together the onion, flour, mustard, seasoning to taste and the 150 ml/$\frac{1}{4}$ pint water until smooth. Pour over the meat.

Roll out the remaining pastry to form a circle to fit the top of the basin. Brush the rim of the pudding with water, lift the pastry lid over the basin and press down gently around the rim. Trim off surplus pastry.

Cover with a lid of greaseproof paper, then a lid of foil, both pleated to allow for expansion, and tie with string. Steam or boil the pudding for 4 hours, topping up with boiling water as required. Garnish with a sprig of parsley.

Cook's Tip

Traditionally ox kidney is used in this recipe, but if you prefer a milder flavour use lamb's kidneys.

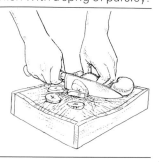

171 | *Spicy Meat Pies*

Preparation time
25 minutes

Cooking time
45–50 minutes

Oven temperature
200 C, 400 F, gas 6

Makes 24

Calories
130 per pie

You will need
1 onion, chopped
1 clove garlic, crushed
1 green pepper, deseeded and
   chopped
1 tablespoon oil
225 g/ 8 oz minced beef
½ teaspoon chilli powder
1 teaspoon Worcestershire sauce
2 tablespoons tomato ketchup
150 ml/¼ pint beef stock
2 teaspoons plain flour
1–2 tablespoons water
salt and pepper
1½ quantities shortcrust pastry
   (recipe 176)
beaten egg to glaze

Fry the vegetables in the oil until soft. Add the minced beef and cook gently for 5 minutes. Stir in the chilli powder, Worcestershire sauce, ketchup and stock, and simmer gently for 15 minutes. Mix the flour with a little cold water to form a smooth paste, add to the pan and simmer for a further 5 minutes. Season and leave to cool.

Make the shortcrust pastry as instructed in recipe 176. Roll out thinly on a lightly floured work surface then, using a floured tartlet cutter, stamp out 24 rounds. Use a slightly smaller cutter to stamp out 24 lids. Place the larger rounds into lightly greased tartlet tins and put a spoonful of the mince mixture in each. Dampen the edges of the pastry with a little water and cover each one with a pastry lid. Seal the edges, brush with beaten egg and bake in a moderately hot oven for about 20 minutes.

172 | *Cornish Pasties*

Preparation time
20 minutes

Cooking time
1 hour

Oven temperature
190 C, 375 F, gas 5

Serves 4

Calories
510 per pasty

You will need
1 quantity shortcrust pastry
   (recipe 176)
beaten egg to glaze

For the filling
225 g/ 8 oz braising steak
1 potato
1 onion
225 g/ 8 oz swede
2 tablespoons beef stock
salt and pepper

Make the shortcrust pastry as instructed in recipe 176 and chill while preparing the filling. Cut the meat and potato into small cubes. Chop the onion and swede. Mix the meat and vegetables with the stock and season generously.

Grease a baking tray. Divide the pastry into four pieces and roll each piece out to a 15-cm 6-in circle. Divide the meat mixture between the pastry circles and dampen the edges with water. Bring the edges together over the middle of the filling and seal, making a fluted pattern with your fingertips, to form an enclosed pasty.

Place on the baking tray and brush with beaten egg. Bake in a moderately hot oven for 1 hour. Serve hot or cold, with a salad and pickles.

Cook's Tip

A quick way of making shortcrust: chill the fat in the freezer, dip in the flour, then grate coarsely. Mix into flour with enough water to bind.

Cook's Tip

For economy, substitute minced beef for the braising steak. Carrots or turnips can be used instead of swedes.

173 | Pizza

Preparation time
20 minutes

Cooking time
25 minutes

Oven temperature
230 C, 450 F, gas 8

Serves 2

Calories
730 per portion

You will need
1 (141-g/5-oz) packet bread or
  pizza mix
1 onion, sliced into rings
1 clove garlic, crushed
50 g/2 oz button mushrooms,
  sliced
25 g/1 oz butter or margarine
4 tomatoes, peeled
1 (190-g/6¾-oz) can pimientos
50 g/2 oz salami
100 g/4 oz mozzarella cheese,
  diced
pinch of oregano
salt and pepper
6–8 black olives
chopped parsley to garnish

Make the dough base as instructed on the packet. Press or roll out to a 20-cm/8-in round on a baking tray and leave to rise for 5 minutes.

Meanwhile cook the onion, garlic and mushrooms in the butter or margarine for a few minutes. Cut the tomatoes into eighths. Drain the pimientos and cut into strips. Thinly slice the salami.

Place the tomatoes and onion mixture on the pizza base, leaving a 5-mm/¼-in border all round. Arrange the pimientos and salami on top, then sprinkle over the mozzarella, oregano, seasoning and olives. Bake in a hot oven for 20 minutes and sprinkle with parsley to serve.

174 | Chicken Pie

Preparation time
25 minutes

Cooking time
2 hours 50 minutes

Oven temperature
190 C, 375 F, gas 5

Serves 4

Calories
675 per portion

You will need
1 small boiling chicken
2 onions
salt and pepper
225 g/8 oz mushrooms
25 g/1 oz butter
1 (298-g/10½-oz) can condensed
  mushroom soup
1 tablespoon lemon juice
½ teaspoon tarragon
1 (368-g/13-oz) packet frozen
  puff pastry, defrosted
beaten egg to glaze

Place the chicken with one onion and seasoning in a large pan. Cover with water. Bring to the boil and simmer for about 2½ hours, or until tender. Drain and reserve the liquid for chicken stock.

Chop the remaining onion and slice the mushrooms. Cook the vegetables in the butter for a few minutes. Dice the chicken meat. Mix together the filling ingredients with 150 ml/¼ pint of the reserved stock and season to taste. Pour into an oval pie dish.

Roll out the pastry to 5 mm/¼ in thick. Dampen the rim of the pie dish and cover with a strip of pastry. Brush the strip with water and cover with the remaining pastry to make a lid. Press the edges together, knock up and flute. Brush with beaten egg and decorate with any pastry trimmings made into leaves. Glaze the decorations and bake in a moderately hot oven for 35–40 minutes. Serve with courgettes or a vegetable of your choice.

Freezer Tip

Make and bake several pizza bases without topping. Remove from the oven when three quarters cooked, cool and freeze. Grill the base, turn and add topping, then grill for a quick meal.

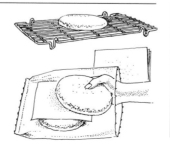

Cook's Tip

Knock up the edges of pies to seal the join. Press the edge of the pastry outwards with the side of your index finger, while knocking it inwards with the blunt edge of a round-bladed knife at a slight angle.

175 | Vegetable Pie

Preparation time
25 minutes

Cooking time
45–55 minutes

Oven temperature
190 C, 375 F, gas 5

Serves 4

Calories
640 per portion

You will need
1 quantity wholemeal pastry
(recipe 185)
beaten egg to glaze

For the filling
225 g/8 oz broccoli
2 celery sticks
2 leeks, trimmed
2 carrots
2 parsnips
1 red pepper, deseeded
1 tablespoon lemon juice
$\frac{1}{4}$ teaspoon grated nutmeg
salt and pepper
1 quantity white sauce (recipe
156), using 40 g/1$\frac{1}{2}$ oz each fat
and flour

Make the wholemeal pastry as instructed in recipe 185 and refrigerate. Break the broccoli into sprigs. Cut the celery into chunks and slice the leeks into rings. Slice the carrots and parsnips. Cut the pepper into strips. Arrange the vegetables in a deep oval pie dish.

Add the lemon juice, nutmeg and seasoning to the white sauce and pour over the vegetables.

Roll out the pastry to 5 mm/$\frac{1}{4}$ in thick, dampen the rim of the pie dish and cover with a strip of pastry cut from the outside of the oval. Brush the strip with water and cover the pie with the remaining pastry. Press the edges together, knock up and flute. Brush with beaten egg and decorate the pie with any pastry trimmings made into leaves. Glaze the decorations and bake in a moderately hot oven for 40–50 minutes.

176 | Pork Parcels

Preparation time
25 minutes

Cooking time
1 hour 5 minutes

Oven temperature
180 C, 350 F, gas 4

Serves 4

Calories
635 per parcel

You will need
350 g/12 oz lean pork
1 onion, chopped
1 tablespoon oil
100 g/4 oz no-need-to-soak
dried apricots
2 tablespoons orange juice
salt and pepper

For the shortcrust pastry
225 g/8 oz plain flour
pinch of salt
100 g/4 oz margarine
2–3 tablespoons cold water
beaten egg to glaze

Cut the pork into small cubes and mix with the onion; fry in the oil for a few minutes. Roughly chop the apricots, add to the pork with the orange juice and seasoning.

Sift the flour and salt into a bowl. Cut the margarine into small pieces and rub into the flour until the mixture resembles fine breadcrumbs. Add enough water to mix to a soft dough.

Divide the pastry into four pieces and roll each piece out to a 15-cm/6-in circle. Divide the pork mixture between the rounds, dampen the edges with water and bring together to one side of the filling. Seal and pinch the edges and place the parcels on a greased baking tray. Brush with beaten egg and bake in a moderate oven for 1 hour. Garnish as illustrated and serve with a salad.

Cook's Tip

Cheese pastry tastes good with vegetable pie. Stir 50 g/2 oz finely grated mature Cheddar cheese into the dry ingredients. Continue as above.

Cook's Tip

If you do not have a rolling pin use a clean empty wine bottle to roll out.

177 | *Crunchy Fish Pie*

Preparation time
15–20 minutes

Cooking time
35–45 minutes

Oven temperature
190 C, 375 F, gas 5

Serves 4

Calories
725 per portion

You will need
50 g/2 oz butter or margarine
50 g/2 oz plain flour
600 ml/1 pint milk
salt and pepper
¼ teaspoon dill weed
1 (198-g/7-oz) can tuna,
   drained and flaked
100 g/4 oz peeled, cooked
   prawns
2 tablespoons lemon juice

For the topping
175 g/6 oz wholemeal flour
50 g/2 oz oatmeal
100 g/4 oz butter
salt and pepper

Garnish
2 whole cooked prawns
parsley sprigs

Melt the butter or margarine over a low heat, stir in the flour, cook for 2 minutes, then gradually add the milk, stirring all the time. Bring the sauce to the boil, simmer gently for a few minutes. Add the seasoning, dill weed, tuna, prawns and lemon juice. Pour into an ovenproof dish.

Place the flour, oatmeal, butter and seasoning in a bowl. Using your fingertips, rub the fat into the dry ingredients until the mixture resembles fine breadcrumbs. Spoon over the fish mixture and bake in a moderately hot oven for 30–40 minutes. Serve hot, garnished with whole prawns and parsley.

Microwave Tip

Whisk the butter, flour and milk and cook in a microwave on full power for 8–10 minutes, whisk again. Add seafood, microwave for 3–5 minutes, then transfer to serving dish, top and grill until brown.

178 | *Fish Envelopes*

Preparation time
15 minutes

Cooking time
20–25 minutes

Oven temperature
220 C, 425 F, gas 7

Serves 4

Calories
585 per envelope

You will need
450 g/1 lb smoked haddock,
   skinned and boned
1 large onion, chopped
50 g/2 oz butter or margarine
2 hard-boiled eggs, chopped
2 tablespoons chopped parsley
2 tablespoons natural yogurt
salt and pepper
1 (368-g/13-oz) packet frozen
   puff pastry, defrosted
beaten egg to glaze

Garnish
watercress sprigs
tomato lily

Grease two baking trays. Cut the fish into small pieces and cook with the onion in the butter or margarine for 5 minutes. Mix the hard-boiled eggs, parsley, yogurt and seasoning with the fish and onion. Leave to cool while preparing the pastry envelopes.

Divide the pastry into four and roll into 18-cm/7-in squares. Divide the fish mixture between the squares, keeping it well in the centre. Dampen the edges of the pastry with a little water and bring the four corners to the centre, pressing well together to seal. Glaze the pastry envelopes with beaten egg, transfer to the baking trays and bake in a hot oven for 15–20 minutes, until golden. Serve immediately, garnished with watercress and a tomato lily.

Microwave Tip

Defrost frozen puff pastry in the microwave. Unwrap and place on double thick absorbent kitchen paper. Allow 1 minute on full power, turning once.

179 | Kipper Flan

Preparation time
20–25 minutes

Cooking time
35 minutes

Oven temperature
180 C, 350 F, gas 4

Serves 4

Calories
570 per portion

You will need
¾ quantity shortcrust pastry
(recipe 176)

For the filling
225 g / 8 oz kipper fillets
40 g / 1½ oz butter or margarine
40 g / 1½ oz plain flour
450 ml / ¾ pint milk
2 tablespoons lemon juice
2 hard-boiled eggs, chopped
½ teaspoon dried sage
salt and pepper

Garnish
parsley sprigs
tomato wedges

Make the shortcrust pastry as instructed in recipe 176. using wholemeal flour if you prefer. Roll out on a lightly floured board to line a 20-cm/8-in flan dish or ring. Bake blind in a moderate oven for 15–20 minutes (see Cook's Tip below).

Meanwhile, simmer the kipper fillets in boiling water for 7–10 minutes. Drain and flake. Melt the butter or margarine over a low heat, add the flour and cook for 2 minutes, stirring continuously, then gradually add the milk, stirring, until the sauce boils and thickens. Reduce the heat and simmer for a few minutes, then add the flaked fish, lemon juice, chopped eggs, sage and seasoning. Pour into the pastry case and bake in the oven for a further 10 minutes. Serve hot, garnished with parsley and tomato.

180 | Rich Salami Flan

Preparation time
20 minutes

Cooking time
35–40 minutes

Oven temperature
180 C, 350 F, gas 4

Serves 4

Calories
610 per portion

You will need
¾ quantity shortcrust pastry
(recipe 176)

For the filling
1 onion
1 red pepper, deseeded
100 g / 4 oz salami, thinly sliced
50 g / 2 oz Cheddar cheese, grated
2 eggs
150 ml / ¼ pint milk
150 ml / ¼ pint single cream
salt and pepper

Garnish
3–4 stuffed green olives
parsley sprigs

Make the shortcrust pastry as instructed in recipe 176. Roll out a lightly floured board and use to line a 20-cm/8-in flan dish or ring.

Finely chop the onion and pepper, spread over the pastry base. Arrange the salami slices on top, reserving a few for garnish, and sprinkle over the Cheddar. Lightly beat together the eggs, milk, cream and seasoning and pour over the salami mixture.

Bake in a moderate oven for 35–40 minutes, until golden. Garnish with the remaining salami slices, rolled into cones, the olives and parsley. Serve hot or cold with a mushroom and tomato salad.

Cook's Tip

To bake blind, place a sheet of greaseproof paper in the pastry case. Sprinkle in baking beans or dried peas. Bake as directed then remove the peas and paper.

Cook's Tip

Instead of rubbing the fat into the flour by hand use a pastry blender. Cut the fat into pieces then use the pastry blender with a bouncing action, mixing the flour and fat.

181 | Onion Flan

Preparation time
20 minutes

Cooking time
35–40 minutes

Oven temperature
180 C, 350 F, gas 4

Serves 4

Calories
620 per portion

You will need
¾ quantity shortcrust pastry
(recipe 176)

For the filling
450 g/1 lb onions, chopped
50 g/2 oz margarine
50 g/2 oz fresh white
breadcrumbs
100 g/4 oz Cheddar cheese,
grated
2 eggs
300 ml/½ pint milk
salt and pepper
paprika to sprinkle
onion rings to garnish

Make the shortcrust pastry as instructed in recipe 176 and roll out to line a 20-cm/8-in flan dish.

Cook the onion in the fat until softened and transparent. Cool slightly. Spoon the onions and breadcrumbs into the flan case, sprinkle over the Cheddar. Lightly beat the eggs, milk and seasoning together, pour over the cheese mixture. Sprinkle with paprika and bake in a moderate oven for 35–40 minutes. Serve hot, garnished with a few raw onion rings.

Cook's Tip

For a satisfactory starter make individual flans and serve freshly cooked.

182 | Quiche Lorraine

Preparation time
25–30 minutes

Cooking time
40–45 minutes

Oven temperature
190 C, 375 F, gas 5

Serves 4

Calories
590 per portion

You will need
¾ quantity shortcrust pastry
(recipe 176)

For the filling
1 onion, chopped
4 rashers rindless streaky bacon,
diced
1 tablespoon oil
100 g/4 oz Cheddar cheese,
grated
2 eggs
300 ml/½ pint milk
salt and pepper
paprika to sprinkle

Make the shortcrust pastry as instructed in recipe 176. Roll out on a lightly floured board to line a 20-cm/8-in fluted flan ring placed on a baking tray.

Fry the onion and bacon in the oil for a few minutes, cool slightly then spread evenly over the pastry. Sprinkle half the Cheddar over the bacon mixture. Beat the eggs, milk and seasoning together and pour into the flan case. Sprinkle the remaining cheese on top and dust with paprika. Bake in a moderately hot oven for 40–45 minutes. Serve hot or cold with a mixed salad.

Cook's Tip

Scissors can be used to dice bacon. First cut the rashers lengthways into thin strips. Holding the strips together snip them across into small pieces.

183 | Sweetcorn Flan

Preparation time
20–25 minutes

Cooking time
25 minutes

Oven temperature
190 C, 375 F, gas 5

Serves 4

Calories
610 per portion

You will need
¾ quantity shortcrust pastry
(recipe 176)

For the filling
1 onion, chopped
1 green pepper, deseeded and
chopped
1 tablespoon oil
1 (326-g/11½-oz) can sweetcorn
100 g/4 oz cooked ham, diced
40 g/1½ oz butter or margarine
40 g/1½ oz plain flour
450 ml/¾ pint milk
salt and pepper

Garnish
3 tomatoes, sliced
parsley sprig

Make the shortcrust pastry as instructed in recipe 176. Roll out and line a 20-cm/8-in flan ring placed on a baking tray. Bake blind (see Cook's Tip 179) for 15 minutes in a moderately hot oven, then remove the paper and beans and return to the oven for a further 10 minutes.

Meanwhile, cook the onion and pepper in the oil for a few minutes until soft. Drain the sweetcorn and add to the mixture with the ham.

Make a white sauce using the butter or margarine, flour and milk as instructed in recipe 156. Add the vegetable mixture and simmer gently for 2 minutes. Season well.

Pour the mixture into the cooked warm flan case, garnish with halved tomato slices and parsley and serve.

184 | Ratatouille Quiche

Preparation time
30 minutes

Cooking time
35–40 minutes

Oven temperature
190 C, 375 F, gas 5

Serves 4

Calories
560 per portion

You will need
¾ quantity shortcrust pastry
(recipe 176)

For the filling
1 red pepper, deseeded and cut
into rings
1 green pepper, deseeded and
cut into rings
1 onion, diced
1 clove garlic, crushed
2 small courgettes, sliced
2 tomatoes, peeled and quartered
50 g/2 oz butter or margarine
3 eggs
300 ml/½ pint milk
salt and pepper
50 g/2 oz Cheddar cheese, grated
chopped parsley to garnish

Make the shortcrust pastry as instructed in recipe 176. Roll out on a lightly floured board and use to line a 20-cm/8-in flan dish or ring placed on a baking tray.

Cook the vegetables in the butter or margarine until soft, arrange in the pastry case. Lightly beat the eggs with the milk and seasoning, pour over the vegetables and sprinkle with the Cheddar. Bake in a moderately hot oven for 35–40 minutes. Garnish with chopped parsley and serve hot with green beans and new potatoes.

Cook's Tip

A quick flan case: melt 100 g/4 oz butter or margarine then stir in 175 g/6 oz crushed savoury biscuits. Press in the base and sides of the dish. Chill, then fill and serve.

Cook's Tip

Flavour the pastry with 2 tablespoons oregano for this flan.

185 | Broccoli Quiche

Preparation time
20 minutes

Cooking time
40–45 minutes

Oven temperature
190 C, 375 F, gas 5

Serves 4

Calories
585 per portion

You will need
For the wholemeal pastry
225 g/8 oz plain wholemeal flour
pinch of salt
pinch of paprika
100 g/4 oz margarine
2–3 tablespoons cold water

For the filling
225 g/8 oz broccoli
2 eggs
300 ml/½ pint milk
salt and pepper
100 g/4 oz Cheddar cheese,
grated

Sift the flour, salt and paprika into a bowl. Cut the margarine into small pieces and rub into the flour until the mixture resembles breadcrumbs. Add enough water to mix to a soft dough. Roll out on a lightly floured surface and use to line a 20-cm/8-in flan dish or ring placed on a baking tray.

Blanch the broccoli in boiling water for 2–3 minutes. Drain very well and cut into neat chunks. Arrange in the flan case. Beat the eggs, milk and seasoning together, pour over the broccoli. Sprinkle with the grated Cheddar.

Bake in a moderately hot oven for 35–40 minutes or until set. Serve hot, with sautéed potatoes.

186 | Courgette Quiche

Preparation time
25–30 minutes

Cooking time
40–45 minutes

Oven temperature
190 C, 375 F, gas 5

Serves 4

Calories
615 per portion

You will need
1 quantity wholemeal pastry
(recipe 185)

For the filling
450 g/1 lb courgettes, sliced
1 clove garlic, crushed
1 onion, chopped
1 tablespoon oil
100 g/4 oz Cheddar cheese,
grated
2 eggs
300 ml/½ pint milk
salt and pepper

Garnish
tomato slices
cress

Make the wholemeal pastry as instructed in recipe 185. Roll out on a lightly floured surface and use to line a 20-cm/8-in flan dish or ring placed on a baking tray.

Cook the courgettes, garlic and onion in the oil until softened. Arrange in the pastry case and sprinkle over the grated Cheddar. Lightly beat the eggs, milk and seasoning together, pour over the cheese mixture.

Bake in a moderately hot oven for 35–40 minutes. Garnish with tomato and cress and accompany with a coleslaw salad.

Microwave Tip

Instead of blanching the broccoli put it in a roasting bag with 2 tablespoons water and microwave on high for 3–4 minutes. Snip the corner off the bag and drain over sink or bowl.

Cook's Tip

To lift pastry into a flan tin, fold it over the rolling pin, then lift it loosely over the tin. Press in with fingertips.

187 | *Samosas*

Preparation time
20–25 minutes

Cooking time
25–30 minutes

Makes 10

Calories
255 per samosa

You will need
225 g / 8 oz minced beef or lamb
1 onion, finely chopped
1 small pepper, deseeded and
finely chopped
1 small carrot, diced
1 small potato, diced
2 cloves garlic, crushed
1½ tablespoons garam masala
salt and pepper
225 g / 8 oz self-raising flour
4 tablespoons oil, plus oil for
deep frying
1 egg
2 tablespoons water

Cook the meat and onion gently until the fat runs. Add the vegetables and seasoning and simmer for 10 minutes, stirring frequently. Leave to cool.

Sift the flour and a pinch of salt into a bowl. Mix in the 4 tablespoons oil, the egg and water to make a dough. Knead gently on a lightly floured surface until smooth. Divide into ten equal portions and roll out each portion to a 13-cm / 5-in square. Place some of the filling in the middle of each square. Dampen the edges with water, fold one top corner over to the opposite corner and seal the edges to form a triangular pasty.

Heat the oil for deep frying and fry the samosas, a few at a time, for about 5 minutes or until golden. Drain on absorbent kitchen paper and keep warm while cooking the remainder. Garnish the samosas as illustrated and serve hot with a cucumber raita. (See Cook's Tip below.)

188 | *Sausage Plait*

Preparation time
10–15 minutes

Cooking time
40–45 minutes

Oven temperature
190 C, 375 F, gas 5

Serves 4

Calories
790 per portion

You will need
1 (368-g / 13-oz) packet frozen
puff pastry, defrosted
beaten egg to glaze

For the filling
450 g / 1 lb sausagemeat
1 onion, finely chopped
1 tablespoon chutney
1 teaspoon dried sage
salt and pepper

Roll out the pastry to an oblong measuring 25 cm × 35 cm / 10 × 14 in. Mix all the filling ingredients together, season well. Arrange the filling down the middle of the pastry. Cut the edges of the pastry diagonally into 2.5-cm / 1-in strips, up to the filling. Fold these strips of pastry over the filling to form a plait, dampening the edges with water in order to hold them in place.

Brush with a little beaten egg and bake in a moderately hot oven for 40–45 minutes. Serve hot or cold, with a salad.

Cook's Tip

To make a raita, coarsely grate ¼ cucumber. Put in a sieve, sprinkle with salt and drain over a bowl. Squeeze out liquid, then mix with 150 ml / ¼ pint chilled natural yogurt and 1 teaspoon chopped mint.

Cook's Tip

Add 100 g / 4 oz finely diced mature Cheddar cheese to the filling. Continue as above.

189 | Chicken and Cheese Puffs

Preparation time
25–30 minutes

Cooking time
35–40 minutes

Oven temperature
200 C, 400 F, gas 6

Makes 6

Calories
410 per puff

You will need
225 g/8 oz cooked chicken
1 onion
1 red pepper
1 green pepper
100 g/4 oz mushrooms
1 tablespoon oil
100 g/4 oz Cheddar cheese
1 tablespoon chopped parsley
salt and pepper
1 (368-g/13-oz) packet frozen
   puff pastry, defrosted
beaten egg to glaze

Dice the chicken. Chop the onion and deseed and dice the peppers. Slice the mushrooms thinly. Cook the vegetables in the oil for a few minutes. Cool.

Dice the Cheddar. Mix together all the ingredients, add the parsley and season to taste.

Roll out the pastry to a 38 × 25-cm/15 × 10-in rectangle and cut into six 13-cm/5-in squares. Spoon the chicken filling into the centre of each, dampen the edges with a little water and fold over to make a triangle. Press the edges well to seal and brush with beaten egg.

Place on a greased baking tray and bake in a moderately hot oven for 35–40 minutes.

190 | Vols-au-Vent

Preparation time
20–25 minutes

Cooking time
25 minutes

Oven temperature
220 C, 425 F, gas 7
200 C, 400 F, gas 6

Makes 12

Calories
340 per vol-au-vent

You will need
2 (368-g/13-oz) packets frozen
   puff pastry, defrosted
beaten egg to glaze

For the fillings
¾ quantity white sauce (recipe
   156)
50 g/2 oz Cheddar cheese, grated
50 g/2 oz cooked ham, diced
100 g/4 oz peeled cooked prawns
1 tablespoon lemon juice
50 g/2 oz sliced cooked
   mushrooms
100 g/4 oz cooked chicken, diced
1 tablespoon dry sherry
salt and pepper

Roll out the pastry to 5 mm/¼ in thickness and stamp out 24 circles using a 7.5-cm/3-in plain cutter. Transfer 12 circles to a greased baking tray, prick with a fork and brush with beaten egg. Using a 5-cm/2-in cutter, cut out the centres of the remaining circles. Lift the rings carefully on to the bases, press down firmly. Glaze the cases and bake in a hot oven for 15 minutes, then reduce to moderately hot for a further 10 minutes.

Divide the sauce into three; add the Cheddar and ham to one third, the prawns and lemon juice to another, and the mushrooms, chicken, sherry and seasoning to the final third. Fill the vol-au-vent cases. Reheat in a hot oven before serving, garnishing as illustrated if you like.

Cook's Tip

If you have a fairly new baking tray, or good non-stick one, there is no need to grease it for puff pastry. Instead dampen the surface with water and the steam during cooking will help the pastry puff.

Cook's Tip

To use pastry cutters successfully for clean shapes, have a small patch of flour near and dip the cutter in it each time it is used.

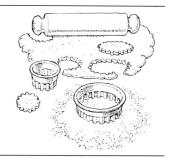

191 | *Savoury Puffs*

Preparation time
20 minutes

Cooking time
25–30 minutes

Oven temperature
220C, 425F, gas 7

Makes 24

Calories
100 per puff

You will need
½ quantity choux pastry (recipe 192)
paprika to sprinkle

For the filling
50 g / 2 oz butter or margarine
50 g / 2 oz plain flour
300 ml / ½ pint milk
150 ml / ¼ pint dry white wine
100 g / 4 oz blue cheese
50 g / 2 oz chopped walnuts
1 tablespoon lemon juice
1 tablespoon chopped parsley
salt and pepper

Make the choux pastry as instructed in recipe 192, omitting the grated cheese. Spoon or pipe 24 small puffs on to a greased baking tray. Bake in a hot oven for 20–25 minutes, then cool on a wire rack. Make a slit in each bun immediately they are removed from the oven to allow any steam to escape.

To make the filling, melt the butter or margarine over a low heat, stir in the flour, then gradually add the milk and wine, stirring continuously. Bring the sauce to the boil, simmer gently for a few minutes. Remove from the heat and crumble in the blue cheese with the walnuts, lemon juice, parsley and seasoning. Using a teaspoon, fill the buns with the sauce. Sprinkle with paprika and serve hot, either as a starter or to have with drinks.

192 | *Gougère*

Preparation time
20 minutes

Cooking time
50 minutes

Oven temperature
200C, 400F, gas 6

Serves 4

Calories
780 per portion

You will need
For the choux pastry
300 ml / ½ pint water
100 g / 4 oz butter or margarine
175 g / 6 oz plain flour
pinch of salt
4 eggs, lightly beaten
50 g / 2 oz Gruyère cheese, grated

For the filling
1 quantity white sauce (recipe 156)
225 g / 8 oz cooked chicken, diced
3 tablespoons lemon juice
pinch of mustard powder
2 teaspoons tarragon
salt and pepper

Place the water in a pan with the fat, heat gently until melted then bring to the boil. Remove from the heat, add the flour and salt and beat quickly to form a smooth paste which comes away from the sides of the pan to form a ball. Cool slightly then gradually beat in the eggs to give a smooth glossy mixture. Fold in the grated Gruyère. Spoon or pipe the mixture around the sides of a buttered oval ovenproof dish.

Mix together all the filling ingredients and simmer gently for 5 minutes. Pour into the centre of the dish and bake in a moderately hot oven for 40 minutes. Serve the gougère hot, sprinkled with paprika.

Cook's Tip

To spoon choux pastry on to a tray, use two teaspoons. Scrape the pastry from spoon to spoon about twice to make even-shaped buns.

Freezer Tip

Line the baking dish with foil and grease well. Pipe the pastry round the edge, then bake empty. Cool, lift out foil and freeze. To use, unpack, put in a dish, fill and heat in the oven for about 15 minutes.

Hot Puddings

Apple charlotte, rhubarb crumble, treacle tart –
no matter how figure conscious we are it is hard
to resist a pudding for 'afters'. Here you will find
all your traditional favourites as well as some
new and different ideas. So even if you don't eat
puddings every day there is lots of choice for a
weekend treat.

193 | Citrus Queen of Puddings

Preparation time
30 minutes

Cooking time
50 minutes

Oven temperature
180 C, 350 F, gas 5

Serves 4

Calories
380 per portion

You will need
300 ml/½ pint milk
25 g/1 oz butter
150 g/5 oz caster sugar
100 g/4 oz fresh white
   breadcrumbs
grated rind and juice of 1 orange
2 eggs, separated
2 tablespoons lemon curd

To decorate
angelica
lemon slices

Gently heat the milk, butter and 25 g/1 oz of the sugar
together until the sugar has dissolved. Remove from the
heat, add the breadcrumbs and orange rind and juice.
Leave the mixture to cool. Beat in the egg yolks. Pour the
custard mixture into a 1.15-litre/2-pint buttered pie dish
and bake in a moderate oven for 30 minutes.

Spread the lemon curd evenly over the top of the
cooked custard. Whisk the egg whites until they stand in
stiff peaks, then gradually whisk in the remaining sugar.
Carefully spoon or pipe the meringue mixture over the
custard. Bake for a further 15 minutes or until the
meringue is set and golden. Decorate with angelica and
lemon slices cut into eighths.

194 | Christmas Pudding

Preparation time
20 minutes, plus at
least 2 months storage
for maturing

Cooking time
8–8½ hours

Serves 8

Calories
530 per portion

You will need
175 g/6 oz currants
175 g/6 oz raisins
175 g/6 oz sultanas
175 g/6 oz shredded suet
100 g/4 oz fresh white
   breadcrumbs
100 g/4 oz plain flour
100 g/4 oz demerara sugar
25 g/1 oz glacé cherries, chopped
25 g/1 oz chopped mixed peel
1 teaspoon grated lemon rind
½ teaspoon mixed spice
½ teaspoon nutmeg
¼ teaspoon salt
1 tablespoon black treacle
2 eggs, lightly beaten
150 ml/¼ pint brown ale
4 tablespoons brandy

Grease and line a 1-litre/2-pint pudding basin. In a large
bowl, mix all the ingredients using a wooden spoon.
Place in the pudding basin and top with a circle of
greaseproof paper. Cover with greaseproof paper and a
piece of greased cooking foil, pleated to allow for
expansion. Secure with string. Steam the pudding in a
saucepan half-full of water for 6 hours, topping up with
boiling water if necessary. Cool, then store in a dry place
for at least two months.

To serve, steam as above for a further 2–2½ hours, then
turn out on to a serving plate. Decorate as illustrated with
lightly whipped cream and a sprig of holly.

Cook's Tip

**To fill a large piping bag,
put it in a large jug and fold
the open end over the rim
of the jug. Spoon in the
meringue.**

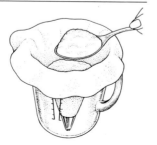

Cook's Tip

**To flame the pudding, warm
3 tablespoons brandy, pour
over the pudding, light, and
carry to the table
immediately.**

195 | Chocolate Pudding

Preparation time
20 minutes

Cooking time
1½ hours

Serves 4

Calories
715 per portion

You will need
100 g/4 oz soft margarine
100 g/4 oz caster sugar
2 eggs, lightly beaten
25 g/1 oz cocoa powder
100 g/4 oz self-raising flour
50 g/2 oz plain chocolate, grated

For the mocha sauce
25 g/1 oz butter
25 g/1 oz plain flour
600 ml/1 pint milk
50 g/2 oz caster sugar
1 tablespoon cocoa powder
1 tablespoon instant coffee

Grease a 1-litre/2-pint pudding basin.

Beat the margarine and sugar until soft and creamy, then gradually beat in the eggs. Fold in the sifted cocoa, flour and chocolate. Pour the mixture into the prepared basin and cover with greased greaseproof paper and a piece of greased cooking foil, pleated to allow for rising. Secure with string. Steam on a trivet or upturned saucer in a saucepan half-full of water for 1½ hours.

To make the sauce, melt the butter over a low heat, add the flour and, stirring continuously, cook for 2 minutes, then gradually add the milk and bring to the boil. Reduce the heat to simmer gently, add the sugar, cocoa and coffee, and cook until dissolved.

Turn out the pudding and pour over the hot sauce to serve.

196 | Baked Ginger Pudding with Lemon Sauce

Preparation time
20 minutes

Cooking time
45–50 minutes

Oven temperature
180 C, 350 F, gas 4

Serves 4

Calories
545 per portion

You will need
100 g/4 oz soft margarine
100 g/4 oz soft brown sugar
2 eggs, lightly beaten
175 g/6 oz self-raising flour, sifted
2 teaspoons ground ginger

For the sauce
grated rind and juice of 2 lemons
25 g/1 oz cornflour
50 g/2 oz sugar
300 ml/½ pint water
25 g/1 oz butter

Grease a deep 15-cm/6-in square cake tin. Beat the margarine and sugar together until creamy, gradually beat in the eggs, then fold in the flour and ginger. Pour into the tin and bake in a moderate oven for 40–45 minutes. Turn out of the tin.

To make the sauce, mix the lemon rind and juice with the cornflour and sugar. Gradually add the water, transfer to the hob and bring to the boil, stirring continuously. Stir in the butter. Cut the pudding into squares and serve hot with the sauce.

Microwave Tip

Steamed puddings microwave well. Cover with cling film instead of foil. Microwave on full power for 5 minutes

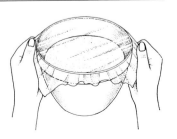

Microwave Tip

To make the lemon sauce in the microwave, mix the ingredients until smooth, adding all the liquid. Microwave on full power for 6 minutes, whisking twice.

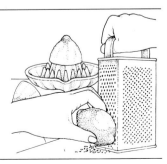

197 | Spiced Bread and Butter Pudding

Preparation time
10 minutes, plus 10 minutes to soak

Cooking time
1 hour

Oven temperature
180 C, 350 F, gas 4

Serves 4

Calories
435 per portion

You will need
50 g / 2 oz butter
8 slices white bread, crusts removed
100 g / 4 oz mixed dried fruit
50 g / 2 oz demerara sugar
600 ml / 1 pint milk
2 eggs, lightly beaten
1 teaspoon mixed spice
grated nutmeg and demerara sugar to sprinkle on the top

Butter each slice of bread generously and cut into four squares. Place a layer of bread over the base of a 1.5-litre / 2½-pint ovenproof dish, overlapping the slices. Sprinkle with mixed fruit and continue to make alternate layers of bread and fruit.

Dissolve the sugar in the milk over a low heat. Remove from the heat, gradually add the egg and mixed spice. Whisk thoroughly. Pour the mixture over the bread and fruit mixture and leave to soak for about 10 minutes. Sprinkle the top with nutmeg and bake in a moderate oven for 1 hour. Sprinkle with sugar and serve immediately.

198 | Marmalade Sponge Pudding

Preparation time
15 minutes

Cooking time
1½–2 hours

Serves 4

Calories
505 per portion

You will need
100 g / 4 oz butter or margarine, softened
100 g / 4 oz soft brown sugar
grated rind of 1 orange
2 eggs, lightly beaten
175 g / 6 oz self-raising flour, sifted
2 tablespoons orange marmalade

Grease a 1-litre / 2-pint pudding basin. Beat the butter or margarine with the sugar until pale and creamy. Beat in the orange rind. Gradually beat in the eggs. Using a metal spoon, fold in the flour.

Spoon the marmalade into the bottom of the pudding basin and spoon the sponge mixture on top. Cover with a double thickness of greased greaseproof paper, folding a pleat to allow the pudding to rise. Tie tightly. Steam on a trivet or upturned saucer in a saucepan half-full of water for 1½–2 hours. Turn out and serve immediately with hot custard.

Cook's Tip

Bread and butter pudding is a good dish in which to use up stale bread. Wholemeal bread can also be used.

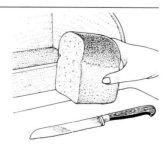

Cook's Tip

For a traditional jam sponge pudding, replace the soft brown sugar with caster sugar, omit the orange rind and replace the marmalade with jam.

To make a plain fruit pudding, use caster sugar **instead of brown sugar then fold in 50 g / 2 oz dried mixed fruit with the flour. Omit the marmalade.**

199 | Pineapple Upside-Down Pudding

Preparation time
15 minutes

Cooking time
50 minutes

Oven temperature
180C, 350F, gas 4

Serves 4

Calories
610 per portion

You will need
25 g/ 1 oz butter
50 g/ 2 oz soft brown sugar
1 (227-g/ 8-oz) can pineapple rings, drained
4 glacé cherries, halved

For the sponge
100 g/ 4 oz butter, softened
100 g/ 4 oz caster sugar
2 eggs, lightly beaten
¼ teaspoon mixed spice
175 g/ 6 oz self-raising flour, sifted

Lightly grease a 15-cm/6-in round cake tin. Melt the butter in a saucepan, add the sugar and pour over the base of the tin. Arrange the pineapple rings and cherries decoratively in the base, placing the cherries rounded side down.

To make the sponge mixture, beat the butter and sugar until soft and creamy. Gradually beat in the eggs and using a metal spoon, fold in the spice and flour. Spoon the mixture over the fruit in the tin, carefully smooth the top and bake in a moderate oven for about 50 minutes or until the sponge is firm and golden.

Turn out the sponge on to a serving plate, and serve immediately with custard or cream.

200 | Prune and Apricot Pudding

Preparation time
10 minutes

Cooking time
1 hour

Oven temperature
180C, 350F, gas 4

Serves 4

Calories
550 per portion

You will need
100 g/ 4 oz no-need-to-soak stoned dried prunes
100 g/ 4 oz no-need-to-soak dried apricots
4 tablespoons water
50 g/ 2 oz chopped walnuts

For the sponge
100 g/ 4 oz soft margarine
100 g/ 4 oz soft brown sugar
2 eggs, lightly beaten
100 g/ 4 oz self-raising wholemeal flour

Arrange the prunes and apricots in the base of a 1.15-litre/2-pint ovenproof dish. Sprinkle over the water and add the walnuts. Beat the margarine and sugar together until creamy. Gradually beat in the eggs, then fold in the flour. The mixture should be a soft dropping consistency. Cover the fruit with the sponge mixture and bake for about an hour in a moderate oven. Serve hot with custard.

Cook's Tip

Other canned fruits can be used in this recipe. Try apricot halves, peach halves or slices, or pear halves.

If you like, make a quick jam sauce to serve with the pudding. Heat 225 g/ 8 oz jam in a saucepan with the *juice from the fruit. Stir to prevent sticking, then strain before serving.*

Microwave Tip

Cover dried fruit with water or fruit juice, cover with cling film and microwave on full power for about 18 minutes instead of soaking.

201 | Apple and Apricot Charlotte

Preparation time
20 minutes

Cooking time
50–60 minutes

Oven temperature
180C, 350F, gas 4

Serves 4

Calories
300 per portion

You will need
7 (1-cm/½in) slices white bread
50 g/2 oz butter
2 large cooking apples
1 (425-g/15-oz) can apricot pie filling
50 g/2 oz soft brown or demerara sugar
½ teaspoon ground cinnamon
knob of butter

Remove the crusts from the bread and use two slices to make breadcrumbs. Butter the remaining slices and use to line a 1.15-litre/2-pint ovenproof dish (buttered sides against the dish), cutting them to fit.

Peel, core and chop the apples. Mix with the apricot pie filling and spoon into the lined dish. Mix together the breadcrumbs, sugar and cinnamon and sprinkle over the top. Dot a knob of butter over the top and bake in a moderate oven for 50–60 minutes. Serve hot with custard or fresh cream.

202 | Rhubarb Crumble

Preparation time
15 minutes

Cooking time
40 minutes

Oven temperature
180C, 350F, gas 4

Serves 4

Calories
445 per portion

You will need
450 g/1 lb rhubarb
75 g/3 oz soft brown sugar
grated rind of 1 orange

For the crumble
75 g/3 oz butter
175 g/6 oz plain flour
75 g/3 oz soft brown sugar

Wash and trim the rhubarb. Cut the stalks into 2.5-cm/1-in lengths and put into a buttered 900-ml/1½-pint pie dish. Sprinkle over the sugar and orange rind.

To make the crumble, rub the butter into the flour until the mixture resembles fine breadcrumbs. Stir in the sugar and spread the crumble over the rhubarb mixture, smoothing it over to cover the fruit completely. Bake in a moderate oven for about 40 minutes or until the crumble is crunchy and golden and the fruit is cooked. Serve hot with vanilla ice cream.

Cook's Tip

Instead of using the apricot pie filling, double the quantity of apples and add 50 g/2 oz raisins to make a simple apple charlotte.

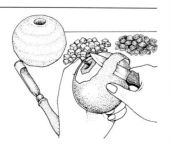

Cook's Tip

Ginger complements rhubarb. Chop about 4 pieces crystallised or preserved stem ginger and add to the rhubarb.

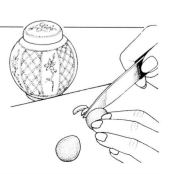

203 | Rice Pudding

Preparation time
5 minutes

Cooking time
1½ hours

Oven temperature
160 C, 325 F, gas 3

Serves 4

Calories
180 per portion

You will need
600 ml/1 pint milk
40 g/1½ oz short-grain rice
few drops vanilla essence
40 g/1½ oz caster sugar
knob of butter

Bring the milk to the boil in a saucepan, then lower the heat, add the rice, vanilla essence and sugar. Simmer gently for a few minutes. Transfer to an ovenproof dish, top with the butter and cook in a moderate oven for 1½ hours. Serve either hot or cold.

There are many variations of rice pudding. For instance you can make a more creamy pudding by adding 150 ml/¼ pint cream, a spicy one by adding ¼ teaspoon each nutmeg and cinnamon, or you can serve the pudding with a spoonful of warmed jam on each portion.

204 | Semolina Swirl Pudding

Preparation time
5 minutes

Cooking time
15 minutes

Serves 4

Calories
265 per portion

You will need
600 ml/1 pint milk
50 g/2 oz caster or granulated
  sugar
50 g/2 oz semolina
4 generous teaspoons chocolate
  hazelnut spread
1 tablespoon chopped mixed
  nuts

Heat the milk and sugar gently, sprinkle in the semolina and bring slowly to the boil. Simmer for 10–15 minutes, stirring constantly until the mixture is thickened and cooked.

Turn out into individual bowls, carefully swirl one teaspoon of chocolate hazelnut spread into each pudding. Sprinkle over the chopped nuts and serve immediately.

Cook's Tip

When time is short, simply stir all the ingredients together in an ovenproof dish and bake, allowing an extra 15 minutes.

Cook's Tip

For a speedy dessert, turn canned semolina pudding into a serving dish. Chill in the freezer, then swirl the chocolate hazelnut spread through and serve.

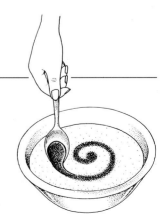

205 | Mince Pies

Preparation time
20 minutes

Cooking time
15–20 minutes

Oven temperature
200 C, 400 F, gas 6

Makes 12

Calories
140 per pie

You will need
225 g / 8 oz plain flour
pinch of salt
100 g / 4 oz margarine
2–3 tablespoons cold water
icing sugar to dust

For the filling
225 g / 8 oz mincemeat
1–2 tablespoons brandy

Sift the flour and salt into a bowl. Cut the margarine into small pieces and rub into the flour until the mixture resembles fine breadcrumbs. Mix to a firm dough with water.

Roll out the pastry thinly on a lightly floured work surface and, using fluted cutters, stamp out 12 7-cm/2¾-in rounds and 12 5.5-cm/2¼-in rounds.

Place the larger rounds in lightly greased tartlet tins. Mix the mincemeat with the brandy and place a teaspoonful in each pastry case. Dampen the edges of the pastry with a little water and cover with a pastry lid. Seal the edges and snip two slits in the top of each pie. Bake in a moderately hot oven for 15–20 minutes or until golden brown. Dust with icing sugar and serve hot or cold with cream.

206 | Blackberry and Apple Pie

Preparation time
20 minutes

Cooking time
45–50 minutes

Oven temperature
180 C, 350 F, gas 4

Serves 4

Calories
485 per portion

You will need
175 g / 6 oz plain flour
pinch of salt
100 g / 4 oz margarine
25 g / 1 oz caster sugar
1 teaspoon grated lemon rind
1 egg yolk
milk to glaze

For the filling
225 g / 8 oz cooking apples,
   peeled, cored and sliced
225 g / 8 oz fresh or frozen
   blackberries, hulled or
   defrosted
75 g / 3 oz caster sugar

Sift the flour and salt into a bowl. Cut the margarine into small pieces and rub in until the mixture resembles fine breadcrumbs. Mix in the sugar, lemon rind and egg yolk to form a dough. Knead lightly.

Spoon the apples and blackberries into a 900-ml/1½-pint pie dish and sprinkle over the sugar. Roll out the pastry to cover the pie. Cut a strip from the outside and place on the dampened rim of the pie dish. Brush the pastry strip with water and lift on the lid to cover the pie. Seal and flute the edges with the blunt edge of a knife. Decorate with any pastry trimmings, glaze with milk and bake in a moderate oven for 45–50 minutes.

Cook's Tip

To make the pies extra special, add the grated rind of 1 orange to the pastry, with the flour.

Cook's Tip

Use cocktail cutters to cut out pastry shapes to decorate the top of the pie.

207 | Treacle Tart

Preparation time
15 minutes

Cooking time
35 minutes

Oven temperature
190 C, 375 F, gas 5

Serves 4

Calories
575 per portion

You will need
225 g / 8 oz plain flour
pinch of salt
100 g / 4 oz margarine
2–3 tablespoons cold water

For the filling
8 tablespoons golden syrup
2 teaspoons grated lemon rind
50 g / 2 oz fresh white
   breadcrumbs

Sift the flour and salt into a bowl. Cut the margarine into small pieces and rub in until the mixture resembles fine breadcrumbs. Sprinkle over the water and mix to form a dough. Knead very lightly, roll out three-quarters of the pastry on a lightly floured surface and use to line a 23-cm/ 9-in ovenproof pie plate. Leave to chill in the refrigerator while preparing the filling.

   Gently heat the syrup and mix in the lemon rind and breadcrumbs. Pour into the pastry shell. Roll out the remaining pastry and cut into thin strips to form a lattice pattern on top of the tart. Bake in a moderately hot oven for about 30 minutes and serve with a custard sauce.

208 | Custard Jam Tart

Preparation time
20 minutes

Cooking time
1 hour 10 minutes

Oven temperature
200 C, 400 F, gas 6
160 C, 325 F, gas 3

Serves 4

Calories
625 per portion

You will need
225 g / 8 oz plain flour
pinch of salt
100 g / 4 oz margarine
2–3 tablespoons cold water

For the filling
2 tablespoons jam
600 ml / 1 pint milk
50 g / 2 oz caster sugar, plus extra
   to sprinkle
4 egg yolks
few drops vanilla essence
$\frac{1}{2}$ teaspoon grated nutmeg

Sift the flour and salt into a bowl. Cut the margarine into small pieces and rub in until the mixture resembles fine breadcrumbs. Add the water and mix to form a dough. Knead very lightly, roll out on a lightly floured surface and use to line a 20-cm/8-in fluted flan ring placed on a baking tray. Prick the base with a fork and bake blind in a moderately hot oven for 10 minutes.

   Spread the jam evenly over the pastry. Heat the milk over a low heat until lukewarm, then beat in the sugar, egg yolks and vanilla. Pour over the jam, sprinkle the nutmeg on top and bake in a moderate oven for about 1 hour until firm. Serve either hot or cold, sprinkled with a little extra caster sugar.

Microwave Tip

Put the syrup in a basin and microwave on full power for 1½–2 minutes, then mix in the lemon rind and breadcrumbs.

Freezer Tip

Open freeze an extra pastry flan case, then pack the middle with crumpled absorbent kitchen paper, put in a polythene bag and freeze. Cook from frozen when required.

209 | Apple Strudel

Preparation time
20 minutes

Cooking time
25–30 minutes

Oven temperature
200 C, 400 F, gas 6

Serves 4

Calories
540 per portion

You will need
1 (212-g/7½-oz) packet frozen
   puff pastry, defrosted
icing sugar to sprinkle

For the filling
50 g/2 oz fresh white
   breadcrumbs
50 g/2 oz chopped walnuts
100 g/4 oz mixed dried fruit
50 g/2 oz caster sugar
450 g/1 lb cooking apples,
   peeled, cored and sliced
1 teaspoon mixed spice
grated rind of 1 orange
50 g/2 oz butter, melted

Roll out the pastry very thinly on a lightly floured board to make an oblong shape.

Mix the breadcrumbs, walnuts, dried fruit, sugar, apples, mixed spice and orange rind together, and spread over one end of the pastry to within 1 cm/½ in of the edges. Brush the edges with the melted butter and roll up like a Swiss roll. Place on a baking tray and brush with the remainder of the butter. Bake in a moderately hot oven for 25–30 minutes or until golden.

Dust with icing sugar, slice and serve hot with custard.

210 | Stuffed Baked Apples

Preparation time
10 minutes

Cooking time
40–50 minutes

Oven temperature
180 C, 350 F, gas 4

Serves 4

Calories
160 per portion

You will need
4 large cooking apples
50 g/2 oz currants or sultanas
25 g/1 oz soft brown sugar
4 teaspoons golden syrup
½ teaspoon ground ginger
25 g/1 oz butter

Remove the cores from the apples using a corer. Slit the skin round the centre of each apple with the tip of a sharp knife to prevent the apples bursting during cooking. Place in an ovenproof dish. Mix together the fruit and sugar, and stuff the apple centres with the mixture. Pour one teaspoon of syrup over each apple, sprinkle over a little ginger and top with a knob of butter.

Bake in a moderate oven for 40–50 minutes. Serve immediately with hot custard.

Cook's Tip

For an authentic strudel, use phyllo instead of puff pastry. Sold frozen in delicatessens, phyllo pastry is in paper-thin sheets. Brush each sheet with melted butter and use two or three sheets thickness.

Cook's Tip

If the apple core does not run straight through the middle, push the corer through from one end first, then from the other to remove all the bits.

211 | Tropical Pancakes

Preparation time
20 minutes

Cooking time
30 minutes

Oven temperature
180 C, 350 F, gas 4

Serves 4

Calories
475 per portion

You will need
100 g/4 oz plain flour
pinch of salt
1 egg, lightly beaten
300 ml/½ pint milk
oil for frying

For the filling
50 g/2 oz butter
25 g/1 oz dark soft brown sugar,
*   plus extra for sprinkling*
6 ripe bananas, roughly chopped
2 tablespoons dark rum
juice of 1 lemon
25 g/1 oz flaked almonds

Sift the flour and salt into a bowl. Add the egg, then gradually add half the milk, beating well to make a smooth batter. Beat in the remaining milk.

Heat a little oil in a frying pan. Pour in a little batter, tilting the pan so the batter covers the base, and cook until the underside is golden. Turn and cook the second side, then remove and keep warm. Repeat with the remaining batter.

Melt the butter in a frying pan with the sugar. Stir in the bananas and cook until softened, add the rum and lemon juice and mix thoroughly. Place one pancake on a greased ovenproof plate. Cover with a little banana mixture and then another pancake. Continue layering in this way, and sprinkle the last pancake with sugar and flaked almonds. Bake in a moderate oven for 12–15 minutes. Serve hot, cut into wedges.

212 | Pineapple and Apricot Fritters

Preparation time
15 minutes

Cooking time
5 minutes

Serves 4

Calories
415 per portion

You will need
1 (425-g/15-oz) can pineapple
*   rings*
1 (410-g/14-oz) can apricot
*   halves*
flour for dusting
oil for deep frying

For the batter
100 g/4 oz plain flour
pinch of mixed spice
pinch of salt
1 large egg, separated
150 ml/¼ pint water
1 tablespoon oil
caster sugar to sprinkle

Drain the pineapple rings and apricot halves, pat dry with absorbent kitchen paper and dust with flour. Sift the flour, mixed spice and salt into a bowl. Gradually beat in the egg yolk, water and oil to form a smooth batter. Whisk the egg white until stiff and fold in.

Heat the oil for deep frying to 180 C/350 F, or until a cube of bread dropped in becomes golden in 30 seconds. Dip the pieces of fruit into the batter to coat well and fry the fritters for 4–5 minutes or until golden. Drain on absorbent kitchen paper. Sprinkle with sugar and serve immediately with cream.

Cook's Tip

If you want to create the pyramid effect in the photograph, cook each pancake slightly smaller than the last, by using a little less batter. When assembling, start with the largest pancake.

Cook's Tip

Use peeled bananas, cut in half, instead of the canned fruit. Serve with a little warmed golden syrup poured over.

213 | Chocolate Fondue with Fresh Fruit

Preparation time
15 minutes

Cooking time
3–5 minutes

Serves 4

Calories
570 per portion

You will need
2 kiwi fruit
225 g / 8 oz fresh strawberries
225 g / 8 oz grapes
100 g / 4 oz fresh or canned
   pineapple segments
100 g / 4 oz fresh or canned
   satsuma segments

For the fondue
225 g / 8 oz plain chocolate
150 ml/¼ pint double cream
2 tablespoons brandy

Peel the kiwi fruit and cut each into four. Hull the strawberries. Arrange all the fruit attractively in serving bowls.

Melt the chocolate gently either in a fondue pan or in a basin over simmering water, and when completely melted gradually add the cream and brandy, stirring well. Transfer the fondue to the table and keep hot over a burner.

Dip the fruit in the fondue, using fondue forks.

214 | Black Cherry Clafouti

Preparation time
15 minutes

Cooking time
50–60 minutes

Oven temperature
190 C, 375 F, gas 5

Serves 4

Calories
545 per portion

You will need
2 (411-g/14.5-oz) cans stoned
   black cherries, well drained
175 g / 6 oz plain flour
100 g / 4 oz caster sugar, plus
   extra to sprinkle
4 eggs
600 ml/1 pint milk

Lightly grease a 1.5-litre/2½-pint shallow ovenproof dish. Spread the drained cherries over the bottom.

Place the flour and sugar in a bowl, make a well in the centre and add the eggs and milk. Gradually work the flour into the liquid to make a smooth batter. Pour over the cherries and bake in a moderately hot oven for 50–60 minutes, or until golden brown and firm to the touch. Sprinkle with caster sugar and serve warm with cream.

Microwave Tip

Melt the chocolate in a basin in the microwave on full power for about 3–4 minutes. Stir in the cream and brandy, microwave for 30 seconds and serve.

Cook's Tip

To make batter in the food processor, put in the flour, eggs and a little milk. Process until smooth, then gradually add the remaining milk as the machine works.

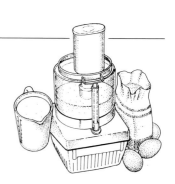

215 | *Pears in Ginger Wine*

Preparation time
5–10 minutes

Cooking time
25–35 minutes

Serves 4

Calories
120 per portion

You will need
450 g / 1 lb cooking pears
juice and rind of 1 lemon
300 ml / ½ pint ginger wine
½ teaspoon ground cinnamon
50 g / 2 oz sugar
angelica to decorate

Peel the pears but leave their stalks in place. Brush the fruit with some of the lemon juice to prevent discolouring. Slowly bring the wine to the boil in a large saucepan, reduce the heat, add the pears, cinnamon and sugar and simmer gently for 20–30 minutes or until the pears are soft. Baste the pears from time to time and turn once during cooking. When the pears are soft, remove them to a serving dish and decorate the top of each with pieces of angelica.

Boil the wine remaining in the saucepan, if necessary, until it is reduced to a syrup consistency. Spoon the syrup over the pears and serve immediately with fresh cream.

216 | *Hot Fruit Salad*

Preparation time
20 minutes

Cooking time
10–12 minutes

Serves 4

Calories
230 per portion

You will need
2 bananas
2 dessert apples
2 oranges
225 g / 8 oz black grapes
100 g / 4 oz seedless grapes
150 ml / ¼ pint apple juice
25 g / 1 oz butter
½ teaspoon ginger
½ teaspoon grated nutmeg
½ teaspoon ground cinnamon
2 tablespoons honey
1 lemon, quartered

Peel and slice the bananas. Core and slice the apples. Peel the oranges, remove the pith and cut oranges into segments. Halve the black grapes and remove the pips. Put all the fruit in a bowl with the apple juice.

Melt the butter in a large saucepan over a gentle heat. Add the spices and honey and mix thoroughly, warming through. Add the fruit salad mixture and the lemon and cook for 8–10 minutes, stirring occasionally. Remove the lemon and serve the fruit salad immediately with clotted or double cream.

Microwave Tip

Pears in wine microwave very well. Place ingredients in a dish, stir, cover and cook on full power for about 10 minutes.

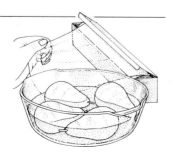

Cook's Tip

Trim the ends off the orange, stand the fruit on a board, then cut downwards to remove strips of peel and pith all at once.

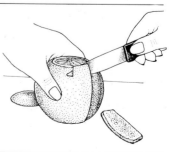

Cool Desserts

Choose a dessert to complement the meal, something light and lemony after a rich pork or duck dish, a crisp pie or tart after fish, or a chocolate dessert after chicken. This chapter includes favourite traditional recipes like trifle, pavlova and a popular Victorian dessert, brown bread ice cream, as well as the more unusual chocolate mint cheesecake and yogurt fool.

217 | Chilled Strawberry Creams

Preparation time
10 minutes, plus 1 hour to chill

Serves 6

Calories
500 per portion

You will need
225 g/8 oz strawberries
600 ml/1 pint double cream
50 g/2 oz caster sugar
1 tablespoon brandy

Slice the strawberries. Whip the cream until thick, fold in the strawberries, sugar and brandy.

Spoon into individual glasses and chill for at least 1 hour.

218 | Pots au Chocolat

Preparation time
15 minutes, plus 1½ hours to chill

Serves 4

Calories
615 per portion

You will need
50 g/2 oz butter
225 g/8 oz plain chocolate
2 eggs
2 tablespoons rum
150 ml/¼ pint double cream

For the decoration
whipped cream
grated chocolate or chocolate caraque

Melt the butter and chocolate in a bowl over a saucepan of simmering water. Remove the bowl from the heat, beat in the eggs and rum, leave to cool. Whip the cream until stiff and fold into the chocolate mixture. Pour the mixture into four ramekin dishes, chill until set.

Decorate with rosettes of piped cream and chocolate caraque (see Cook's Tip below) just before serving.

Cook's Tip

Make creamy banana splits by serving the strawberry cream in split bananas. Top with chopped toasted hazelnuts and grated chocolate.

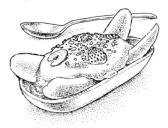

Cook's Tip

To make chocolate caraque (or long curls), take a block of chocolate and a fairly sharp knife. Holding the knife at an acute angle, shave long curls off the chocolate. Turn the block round when you have made a deep groove and work from the opposite end.

An alternative method for making chocolate curls is given in Cook's Tip 236.

219 | Quick Lemon Mousse

Preparation time
10 minutes, plus 1
hour to chill

Cooking time
2–3 minutes

Serves 4

Calories
250 per portion

You will need
2 lemons
1 lemon jelly
150 ml/¼ pint water
1 (410-g/14.5-oz) can
    evaporated milk
angelica to decorate

Reserve four slices of lemon for decoration. Grate the rind from one lemon and extract the juice from both. Melt the jelly in the water over a gentle heat. Remove the pan from the heat, add the lemon rind and juice. Pour into a small bowl and leave to cool.

Whisk the evaporated milk until thick and doubled in volume. Carefully fold in the jelly mixture and pour into a large glass dish. Chill for about an hour or until set. Decorate with the lemon slices and pieces of angelica.

220 | Citrus Syllabub

Preparation time
15 minutes, plus 1
hour to marinate and 1
hour to chill

Serves 6

Calories
290 per portion

You will need
grated rind and juice of 1 orange
grated rind and juice of 1 lemon
4 tablespoons sweet white wine
75 g/3 oz caster sugar
300 ml/½ pint double cream,
    whipped

Place the fruit rinds and juices in a bowl with the wine and marinate for at least 1 hour. Strain the liquid through a fine sieve, reserving a few strands of rind for decoration.

Gently fold the strained liquid and sugar into the cream. Spoon into six glass serving dishes. Decorate with the citrus rind and chill for an hour before serving. Serve with brandy snaps or sweet biscuits of your choice.

Freezer Tip

Double or whipping cream can be frozen in its whipped state. Spoon the whipped cream into a plastic container and label with the quantity of unwhipped cream. Defrost and use as required.

Cook's Tip

Syllabub makes a luscious topping for a traditional trifle. Swirl it over the top of the custard, or it can even be used instead of the custard.

221 | *Rhubarb Fool*

Preparation time
10 minutes, plus 1
hour to chill

Cooking time
10–15 minutes

Serves 4

Calories
345 per portion

You will need
450 g/1 lb rhubarb
50 g/2 oz soft brown sugar
1 (425-g/15-oz) can custard
150 ml/¼ pint double cream
chocolate shavings to decorate

Wash the rhubarb and cut into 2.5-cm/1-in lengths. Place in a saucepan with the sugar, cover and cook gently for 10–15 minutes until the rhubarb is softened. Blend the rhubarb and custard together in a liquidiser or food processor until smooth.

Whip the cream until stiff, fold into the cooled rhubarb mixture and pour into individual glass dishes. Chill for about an hour and decorate with chocolate shavings and biscuits, such as cigarettes russes, shown above.

222 | *Yogurt Fool*

Preparation time
10 minutes, plus 2
hours to chill

Serves 4

Calories
285 per portion

You will need
300 ml/½ pint whipping cream
150 ml/¼ pint natural yogurt
50 g/2 oz soft brown sugar
50 g/2 oz muesli
50 g/2 oz chopped walnuts

Whip the cream until it stands in soft peaks. Fold in the yogurt and carefully spoon into individual glass dishes. Sprinkle generously with the sugar, muesli and walnuts.
  Chill for about 2 hours.

Microwave Tip

**Cook the rhubarb and sugar
in a covered dish in the
microwave. Allow about 8–
10 minutes on full power.**

Cook's Tip

**If you are trying to cut
down on the fat content of
your diet, then simply stir
all the ingredients into
natural yogurt.**

223 | *Frozen Raspberry Delight*

Preparation time
10 minutes, plus 2 hours to freeze

Serves 4

Calories
595 per portion

You will need
1 Swiss roll
3 tablespoons brandy
300 ml/½ pint raspberry yogurt
100 g/4 oz fresh or frozen raspberries, hulled or defrosted
300 ml/½ pint double or whipping cream
whipped cream to decorate

Slice the Swiss roll thinly and use to line the base and sides of a 900-ml/1½-pint pudding basin. Carefully spoon over the brandy.

In a bowl, mix together the yogurt and raspberries. Whip the cream until thick and fold into the yogurt mixture. Pour over the Swiss roll and freeze for 2 hours or until firm.

Dip the basin briefly in warm water to help turn out the pudding. Decorate with piped whipped cream and serve immediately.

224 | *Chocolate Orange Soufflé*

Preparation time
30 minutes, plus 1 hour to chill

Cooking time
5 minutes

Serves 6

Calories
480 per portion

You will need
3 eggs, separated
75 g/3 oz caster sugar
grated rind and juice of 2 oranges
15 g/½ oz gelatine
3 tablespoons hot water
300 ml/½ pint whipping cream
175 g/6 oz plain chocolate, grated

Lightly grease a 600-ml/1-pint soufflé dish. Cut a double strip of greaseproof paper, equal in width to the height of the dish plus 5 cm/2 in and long enough to go right round the outside of the dish. Lightly grease the top 5 cm/2 in and tie securely with string around the dish.

Place the egg yolks and sugar in a bowl over a saucepan of simmering water and whisk until thick and creamy. Whisk in the orange rind and juice. Dissolve the gelatine in the water over simmering water.

Whisk the egg whites until they stand in soft peaks and whip the cream until stiff. Fold the cooled gelatine into the orange mixture, followed by half the cream, the egg whites and two-thirds of the grated chocolate. Pour into the soufflé dish, smooth the top and chill until set.

Peel the paper away from the soufflé using the back of a knife. Press grated chocolate around the sides of the soufflé. With the remaining cream pipe swirls on the top and decorate with a sprinkle of grated chocolate.

Freezer Tip

Pipe swirls of whipped cream on to a cling film lined baking tray. Open freeze, pack carefully in rigid containers and use from frozen to decorate cakes or puddings.

Microwave Tip

Gelatine can be dissolved in the water, in a small basin in the microwave. Allow about 1 minute on full power.

225 | Baked Alaska

Preparation time
15 minutes

Cooking time
3–5 minutes

Oven temperature
230 C, 450 F, gas 8

Serves 4

Calories
695 per portion

You will need
1 bought or home-made 20-cm/
  8-in sponge flan case
1 tablespoon sherry
1 (1-litre/35.2-fl oz) block
  raspberry ripple ice cream
3 egg whites
150 g/5 oz caster sugar

Place the flan case on a baking tray and sprinkle over the sherry. Scoop the ice cream on to the base and smooth over with a knife to make an even round. Freeze to harden again.

Whisk the egg whites until they form stiff peaks. Whisk in the sugar a little at a time. The mixture should be thick and glossy. Quickly spoon or pipe the meringue on to the ice cream and sponge to cover it completely. Bake in a hot oven for 3–5 minutes until the meringue is golden. Serve immediately.

226 | Lemon Meringue Pie

Preparation time
30 minutes

Cooking time
35 minutes

Oven temperature
200 C, 400 F, gas 6
180 C, 350 F, gas 4

Serves 6

Calories
375 per portion

You will need
$\frac{3}{4}$ quantity shortcrust pastry
  (recipe 176)

For the lemon filling
grated rind and juice of 2 lemons
25 g/1 oz cornflour
300 ml/$\frac{1}{2}$ pint water
25 g/1 oz butter
75 g/3 oz caster sugar
2 eggs yolks

For the meringue topping
2 egg whites
100 g/4 oz caster sugar
glacé cherries and angelica to
  decorate

Make the shortcrust pastry as instructed in recipe 176, roll out to line a 20-cm/8-in flan ring placed on a baking tray. Prick with a fork and bake blind (see Cook's Tip 179) in a moderately hot oven for 15 minutes.

Put the lemon rind and juice in a saucepan with the cornflour, add the water and bring slowly to the boil and cook for 2 minutes, stirring all the time. Remove from the heat and add the butter and sugar. Cool slightly, then stir in the egg yolks and spoon into the flan case.

Whisk the egg whites until stiff but not dry, gradually whisk in the sugar. Pipe or spoon the meringue over the lemon filling. Bake in a moderate oven for 15 minutes and serve decorated with pieces of cherry and angelica.

Freezer Tip

For a dinner party, the baked alaska can be prepared in advance, covered with meringue, then open frozen ready to be put in the oven at the last minute.

Cook's Tip

Any citrus fruits or combination of fruits can be used. Substitute 3 limes for the lemons. An orange and lemon mix is delicious, substitute an orange for one of the lemons. When using larger fruits, such as grapefruit use 1 tablespoon of grated rind and reduce the water.

227 | Mandarin Tartlets

Preparation time
20 minutes

Cooking time
20 minutes

Oven temperature
190 C, 375 F, gas 5

Makes 12

Calories
195 per tartlet

You will need
200 g/ 7 oz plain flour
pinch of salt
75 g/ 3 oz butter or margarine
25 g/ 1 oz caster sugar
1 egg

For the topping
150 ml/¼ pint double or whipping
  cream
2 (312-g/ 11-oz) cans
  mandarins, drained
2 tablespoons orange marmalade
1 tablespoon water

Sift the flour and salt into a bowl. Rub in the fat until the mixture resembles fine breadcrumbs. Stir in the sugar and egg and knead lightly to form a smooth soft dough. Roll out on a floured work surface to 3 mm/¼ in thickness and, using a 6-cm/2½-in fluted cutter, stamp out 12 circles. Use to line a tray of 12 tartlet tins, prick the bases with a fork and bake in a moderate oven for 20 minutes or until lightly browned. Leave to cool.

Whip the cream until stiff, place a spoonful in each tartlet and smooth the surface. Arrange the mandarins on each tartlet. Heat the marmalade with the water over a gentle heat until melted. Cool slightly and brush over the mandarins. Place on a pretty plate to serve.

228 | Strawberry Shortbread Creams

Preparation time
20 minutes

Cooking time
45–50 minutes

Oven temperature
160 C, 325 F, gas 3

Serves 4

Calories
570 per portion

You will need
100 g/ 4 oz butter
175 g/ 6 oz plain flour
50 g/ 2 oz caster sugar
grated rind of 1 orange

For the filling
150 ml/¼ pint double or whipping
  cream
225 g/ 8 oz strawberries, halved

Grease a 20-cm/8-in fluted flan ring and a baking tray. Rub the butter into the flour. Add the sugar and orange rind, knead the mixture together until it forms a soft dough.

Turn out on to a lightly floured surface and roll to a circle large enough to fill the flan ring. Place in the flan ring on the baking tray, press into the fluted edges and smooth the top. Prick all over with a fork and mark into eight equal portions. Bake in a moderate oven for 45–50 minutes. Leave the shortbread to cool in the flan ring for 10 minutes then cut into eight.

Whip the cream until stiff. Spoon or pipe the cream on to four pieces of shortbread, add the strawberries to the cream and top with a second piece of shortbread.

Cook's Tip

There is no need to grease baking tins when cooking pastry because of the high fat content of the dough. In some recipes if the filling is likely to stick the tins may be greased.

Dampen baking trays for puff and choux pastry items which are unlikely to stick. The moisture gives a better rise.

Cook's Tip

If you do not have a flan ring, then use a loose-bottomed flan tin or cake tin to cook the shortbread.

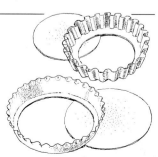

229 | Chocolate Mint Cheesecake

Preparation time
30 minutes, plus 1½ hours to chill

Cooking time
5–10 minutes

Serves 8

Calories
630 per portion

You will need
75 g / 3 oz butter
225 g / 8 oz plain chocolate digestive biscuits, crushed

For the topping
450 g / 1 lb cream cheese
50 g / 2 oz caster sugar
100 g / 4 oz plain chocolate, melted
2 eggs, separated
few drops peppermint essence
3 tablespoons hot water
15 g / ½ oz gelatine
150 ml / ¼ pint double cream to decorate

Lightly grease a 20-cm/8-in loose-bottomed cake tin. Melt the butter in a saucepan, add the crushed biscuits and mix well to coat evenly. Press evenly over the base of the tin and chill until set.

In a mixing bowl beat the cream cheese with the sugar, melted chocolate, egg yolks and peppermint essence. Place the hot water in a small bowl and sprinkle over the gelatine. Stand over a saucepan of simmering water and stir until dissolved. Cool slightly and stir into the cream cheese mixture. Whisk the egg whites until standing in soft peaks and fold in. Pour over the biscuit base and chill until firm.

Remove the cheesecake from the tin. Whip the cream until stiff and pipe around the top of the cheesecake.

230 | Profiteroles

Preparation time
20 minutes

Cooking time
25–30 minutes

Oven temperature
220 C, 425 F, gas 7

Serves 4

Calories
860 per portion

You will need
150 ml / ¼ pint water
50 g / 2 oz butter
75 g / 3 oz plain flour
pinch of salt
2 eggs, lightly beaten

For the filling
300 ml / ½ pint whipping cream

For the chocolate sauce
100 g / 4 oz plain chocolate
75 g / 3 oz butter
3 tablespoons golden syrup

Put the water and butter in a saucepan and heat gently until the butter melts, then bring rapidly to the boil. Remove from the heat and quickly stir in the flour and salt until the mixture leaves the sides of the pan clean. Allow to cool slightly, then beat in the eggs a little at a time. Beat well until the paste is smooth and glossy. Spoon teaspoon-sized balls on to a greased baking tray. Bake in a hot oven for 20–25 minutes until well risen, golden and crisp. Remove from the oven and split each profiterole. Cool on a wire rack.

Whip the cream, then use to fill the profiteroles. Place on a serving plate. Melt the chocolate, butter and syrup over a gentle heat. Pour over the profiteroles and serve immediately.

Cook's Tip

If a loose bottomed tin is not available grease and line a 20-cm/8-in deep cake tin and place double thickness foil strips in a cross to lift out set cheesecake.

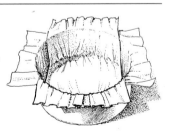

Cook's Tip

Choux pastry items should be cut open immediately they are removed from the oven to allow steam to escape and prevent them becoming soft.

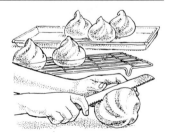

231 | Fresh Fruit Pavlova

Preparation time
30 minutes

Cooking time
1 hour

Oven temperature
150 C, 300 F, gas 2

Serves 6

Calories
410 per portion

You will need
3 egg whites
175 g/ 6 oz caster sugar
1 teaspoon cornflour
1 teaspoon vinegar
½ teaspoon vanilla essence

For the filling
300 ml/ ½ pint double cream
2 bananas, sliced and brushed
   with lemon juice
2 kiwi fruits, peeled and sliced
100 g/ 4 oz green grapes, halved
   and deseeded
2 oranges, peeled and segmented

Mark a 20-cm/8-in circle on a piece of non-stick baking parchment and place on a baking tray. Whisk the egg whites until they stand in stiff peaks. Gradually whisk in half the sugar. Fold in the remaining sugar with the cornflour, vinegar and vanilla. Spoon or pipe the meringue on to the marked circle and bake in the centre of a cool oven for 1 hour. Leave to cool in oven. Remove paper and place on a plate.

Whip the cream until stiff. Spoon over the pavlova base, arrange the prepared fruit on top and chill before serving.

232 | Meringues with Chocolate Sauce

Preparation time
15 minutes

Cooking time
2½ hours

Oven temperature
110 C, 225 F, gas ¼

Serves 6

Calories
265 per portion

You will need
4 egg whites
225 g/ 8 oz caster sugar

For the chocolate sauce
150 ml/ ¼ pint water
50 g/ 2 oz sugar
4 tablespoons golden syrup
4 tablespoons cocoa powder

Grease three baking trays thoroughly or line with non-stick baking parchment. Whisk the egg whites until stiff and standing in peaks. Add the sugar, a tablespoon at a time, whisking continuously. Fit a piping bag with a large star nozzle and fill the bag with the meringue mixture.

Pipe 36 rosettes on to the baking trays or spoon on if preferred. Bake in a very cool oven for 2½ hours or until the meringues are crisp. Remove from the oven and cool on a wire rack.

To make the chocolate sauce, put all the ingredients into a pan and heat very gently. Bring to the boil, reduce the heat and cook for 1 minute, stirring all the time. Spoon over the meringues just before serving.

Cook's Tip

To pipe meringue, use a large piping bag fitted with a large plain nozzle.

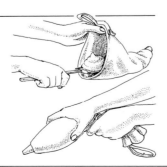

Microwave Tip

To make the chocolate sauce in the microwave, put all the ingredients in a measuring jug and microwave on full power for 5 minutes, stirring once.

233 | Crème Caramel

Preparation time
15 minutes, plus 4
hours to chill

Cooking time
1 hour 10 minutes

Oven temperature
160 C, 325 F, gas 3

Serves 6

Calories
175 per portion

You will need
75 g / 3 oz granulated sugar
3 tablespoons water
600 ml / 1 pint milk
2 eggs plus 2 egg yolks
25 g / 1 oz caster sugar
few drops vanilla essence

Grease six ramekin dishes. Put the granulated sugar and water in a heavy-based saucepan and heat gently until the sugar has dissolved. Bring the syrup to the boil and boil until the sugar caramelises and turns a deep golden colour. Pour the caramel into the ramekins, making sure the bases are evenly covered.

Gently heat the milk to just below boiling point and remove from the heat. Lightly whisk together the eggs, caster sugar and vanilla, and gradually add the hot milk. Strain through a fine sieve and pour the custard into the ramekin dishes. Cover with oiled greaseproof paper and place in a roasting tin half-filled with hot water. Bake in a moderate oven for about 1 hour or until the custard has set. Remove from the oven and allow to cool. Chill the cooked custards for several hours or overnight, then turn out on to individual plates to serve. (Otherwise the caramel will be hard. Do not chill once turned out.)

Cook's Tip

To prevent overheating and curdling delicate dishes, like custards, stand in a roasting tin, then pour in hot water from a kettle to come halfway up the inside of the tin. This is known as a bain-marie.

234 | Traditional Trifle

Preparation time
20 minutes, plus 1
hour to chill

Cooking time
5–10 minutes

Serves 6

Calories
560 per portion

You will need
8 trifle sponge cakes
2 tablespoons raspberry jam
50 g / 2 oz ratafia biscuits
4 tablespoons sweet sherry
225 g / 8 oz fresh or frozen
    raspberries hulled or defrosted
1 tablespoon cornflour
50 g / 2 oz sugar
450 ml / ¾ pint milk
3 eggs
a few drops vanilla essence

For the topping
300 ml / ½ pint double cream
fresh raspberries and angelica

Split the trifle sponge cakes and spread with the jam. Cut up and place in a glass serving dish. Break the ratafias into small pieces and scatter on the trifle sponges. Spoon over the sherry and leave to soak for at least 30 minutes. Top with the raspberries.

Blend cornflour and sugar to a paste with a little of the milk in a saucepan. Blend in remaining milk and bring to the boil, stirring. Cook 2 minutes. Lightly whisk eggs and vanilla essence together, pour on cornflour mixture, whisking. Pour over the trifle and leave until cold then chill in the refrigerator for at least 1 hour.

Whip the cream until thick and spread or pipe on the trifle. Decorate with fresh raspberries and angelica.

Cook's Tip

For a very quick custard for trifle, whip 150 ml / ¼ pint double cream and fold it into a well-chilled 425-g / 15-oz can of custard. Spread over the trifle base and serve.

235 | Summer Pudding

Preparation time
20 minutes, plus overnight chilling

Cooking time
5 minutes

Serves 6

Calories
205 per portion

You will need
225 g / 8 oz blackcurrants, topped and tailed
225 g / 8 oz raspberries
225 g / 8 oz redcurrants, topped and tailed
175 g / 6 oz sugar
3 tablespoons water
8–10 thin slices white bread, crusts removed

Put the prepared fruit in a large saucepan with the sugar and water, bring to the boil and simmer gently for 5 minutes. Leave to cool.

Line a 900-ml/1½-pint pudding basin with slices of bread, cutting the slices to fit and making sure that there are no gaps. Spoon the fruit mixture into the basin, and top with more bread slices cut to fit. Cover the pudding with a plate with a weight on it and chill in the refrigerator overnight so that the juices can penetrate through the bread.

To serve, turn out the pudding and accompany with clotted cream or hot custard.

236 | Black Forest Gâteau

Preparation time
30 minutes

Cooking time
40 minutes

Oven temperature
180 C, 350 F, gas 4

Makes 1 cake

Total calories
4060

You will need
3 eggs
75 g / 3 oz caster sugar
50 g / 2 oz plain flour
25 g / 1 oz cocoa powder
3 tablespoons kirsch
600 ml / 1 pint double or whipping cream
1 (390-g / 13¾-oz) can blackberry pie filling

For the glacé icing
225 g / 8 oz icing sugar, sifted
25 g / 1 oz cocoa powder
2 tablespoons water
chocolate curls to decorate

Line and grease a deep 18-cm/7-in round cake tin. Whisk the eggs and sugar until pale and thick. Fold in the flour and cocoa powder. Pour the mixture into the tin and bake in a moderate oven for about 40 minutes. Cool on a wire rack. Cut into three layers horizontally, and soak each layer with 1 tablespoon kirsch.

Whip the cream until thick. Sandwich the cake together with some of the cream and the pie filling. Pipe the remaining cream on to the side of the cake and a border on the top.

Mix the icing sugar, cocoa powder and water until smooth and pour over the top. Decorate with chocolate curls.

Cook's Tip

When turning out any moulded dish, place a plate over the mould, making sure that it is in exactly the right position. Invert the mould and the plate and give them both a firm jerk.

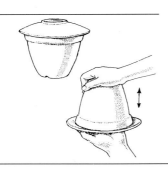

Cook's Tip

To make chocolate curls, spread melted chocolate on a level smooth surface and leave to set. Hold a knife at an angle of 45° and draw across chocolate to make curls.

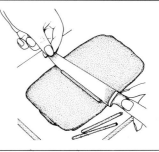

237 | Fresh Fruit Salad

Preparation time
20 minutes

Serves 4

Calories
190 per portion

You will need
2 dessert apples, cored and sliced
2 oranges, peeled, pith removed
  and segmented
1 banana, sliced
225 g/8 oz black grapes,
  deseeded
100 g/4 oz strawberries, sliced
2 tablespoons clear honey
300 ml/½ pint dry cider

Mix all the fruit together in a large serving bowl. Stir the honey into the cider. Pour the liquid over the fruit and leave to cool.

Serve chilled with single or double cream.

238 | Nutty Brown Bread Ice Cream

Preparation time
10 minutes, plus time
to freeze

Serves 6

Calories
640 per portion

You will need
100 g/4 oz fresh brown
  breadcrumbs
100 g/4 oz demerara sugar
600 ml/1 pint double cream
100 g/4 oz walnuts, chopped

Line the grill pan with foil and brush with oil. Sprinkle over the breadcrumbs and sugar and grill until brown and crisp. Leave to cool.

Whip the cream until thick and standing in soft peaks, fold in the breadcrumbs, sugar and walnuts. Pour into a rigid plastic container and freeze until firm.

Cook's Tip

Fresh fruit salad looks particularly splendid served in a scooped-out watermelon or pineapple halves. Add the scooped-out fruit to the salad.

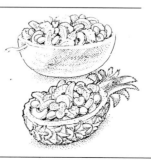

Cook's Tip

Freeze the ice cream in a basin. When hard, dip briefly in hot water and turn out. Decorate with piped whipped cream and serve at once.

239 | Pineapple Ice Cream

Preparation time
15 minutes, plus 4
hours to freeze

Serves 4

Calories
275 per portion

You will need
450 g/1 lb fresh or canned
   pineapple
50 g/2 oz caster sugar
150 ml/¼ pint water
150 ml/¼ pint double or whipping
   cream
2 egg whites

Blend the pineapple in a liquidiser or food processor until smooth. Dissolve the sugar in the water over a gentle heat. Add to the pineapple mixture. When cool, pour into a rigid plastic container and freeze for 1 hour or until half frozen.

Turn out into a large mixing bowl and mash with a fork. Whip the cream until stiff and fold into the pineapple mixture. Finally whisk the egg whites until stiff but not dry and fold in. Pour the ice cream back into the plastic container and freeze for 3 hours, whisking twice more during the freezing process to achieve a really smooth texture.

240 | Creamy Coffee Ice Cream

Preparation time
15 minutes, plus 3–4
hours to freeze

Serves 6

Calories
440 per portion

You will need
300 ml/½ pint milk
2 tablespoons instant coffee
   powder
3 eggs, lightly beaten
50 g/2 oz caster sugar
1 (410-g/14.5-oz) can
   evaporated milk
300 ml/½ pint double or whipping
   cream, whipped

Place the milk, coffee, eggs and sugar in a bowl over a pan of simmering water and cook, stirring continuously, until the mixture coats the back of the spoon. Pour the mixture into a large rigid plastic container, cool and freeze for 1 hour or until half frozen.

Whisk the evaporated milk until doubled in volume. In another bowl whisk the half-frozen coffee mixture until smooth. Whisk the evaporated milk into the coffee mixture. Return to the freezing container and freeze until just firm. Remove from the freezer, whisk the ice cream until smooth, whisk in the whipped cream and freeze again until firm. Accompany with cigarette russes or other sweet biscuits and, if you like, serve with a hot chocolate sauce.

Cook's Tip

If using fresh pineapple, cut off the leafy top and scoop out the inside. Fill the fruit shell with the ice cream, replace the lid and freeze for about 1 hour before serving on a doily-lined cake stand.

Cook's Tip

To make a very quick hot chocolate sauce, melt Mars bars in a basin over a saucepan of hot water, or in the microwave.

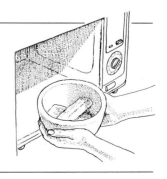

Breads and Scones

Baking bread at home is not difficult and it must be one of the most rewarding pastimes. Not only is there the wonderful aroma which invades the house, but the flavour of home-baked bread is hard to beat. This chapter includes all the most popular recipes for bread, buns and scones, including muffins, teacakes and parkin.

241 | Wholemeal Bread

Preparation time
25 minutes, plus $2\frac{1}{2}$ hours to rise and prove

Cooking time
30–40 minutes

Oven temperature
230 C, 450 F, gas 8

Makes 1 loaf

Total calories
2325

You will need
15 g/$\frac{1}{2}$ oz dried yeast
450 ml/$\frac{3}{4}$ pint warm water
1 teaspoon caster sugar
675 g/1$\frac{1}{2}$ lb plain wholemeal flour
2 teaspoons salt
15 g/$\frac{1}{2}$ oz lard or margarine

Grease a 1-kg/2-lb loaf tin. Sprinkle the yeast over half the water, then stir in the sugar. Leave in a warm place until frothy, about 10 minutes.

Mix the flour and salt in a bowl and rub in the fat. Add the yeast liquid and remaining water and mix to a smooth dough. Turn out on to a lightly floured surface and knead until smooth and elastic, about 10 minutes. Place in an oiled bowl, cover with oiled cling film and leave to rise in a warm place until doubled in size.

Turn the dough on to a lightly floured surface, knock back to release all air bubbles and knead for about 5 minutes. Shape into one large loaf. Place in the tin and cover loosely with oiled cling film. Leave to prove in a warm place until almost doubled in size, about 1 hour.

Remove the cling film and bake in a hot oven for 30–40 minutes. When cooked the loaf should sound hollow when rapped on the bottom. Cool on a wire rack.

Cook's Tip

You may find it easier to measure dried yeast by the teaspoon. Using a proper teaspoon measure, 3 teaspoons equals 15 g/$\frac{1}{2}$ oz.

242 | Basic White Bread

Preparation time
25 minutes, plus $2\frac{1}{2}$ hours to rise and prove

Cooking time
30–40 minutes

Oven temperature
230 C, 450 F, gas 8

Makes 1 loaf

Total calories
2615

You will need
15 g/$\frac{1}{2}$ oz dried yeast
1 teaspoon caster sugar
300 ml/$\frac{1}{2}$ pint warm water
150 ml/$\frac{1}{4}$ pint warm milk
675 g/1$\frac{1}{2}$ lb strong plain white flour
2 teaspoons salt
25 g/1 oz butter
beaten egg to glaze
kibbled wheat to sprinkle

Grease a 1-kg/2-lb loaf tin. Place the yeast, sugar, water and milk in a jug, mixing well. Leave in a warm place until frothy, about 10 minutes.

Sift the flour and salt into a bowl. Rub in the butter. Add the yeast liquid and mix to a smooth dough. Turn out on to a lightly floured surface and knead until smooth and elastic, about 10 minutes. Place in an oiled bowl and cover with cling film. Leave to rise in a warm place until doubled in size, 1–1$\frac{1}{2}$ hours.

Turn the dough on to a lightly floured surface, knock back to release all air bubbles and knead again for 5 minutes. Shape the dough to fit the tin. Place in the tin, glaze the loaf with beaten egg and sprinkle with kibbled wheat. Cover with oiled cling film and leave to prove (the second rising) for about 1 hour. Remove the cling film. Bake in a hot oven for 30–40 minutes. Cook on a wire rack.

Cook's Tip

Easy blend yeast is widely available. This fine-textured, dried yeast is stirred into the dry flour, then the liquid is mixed in and the bread made as for the main recipe.

243 | Grainy Bread

Preparation time
25 minutes, plus 2½ hours to rise and prove

Cooking time
35–40 minutes

Oven temperature
220 C, 425 F, gas 7
190 C, 375 F, gas 5

Makes 2 loaves

Calories
1295 per loaf

You will need
15 g/½ oz dried yeast
1 teaspoon caster sugar
450 ml/¾ pint warm water and milk mixed
275 g/10 oz plain wholewheat flour
275 g/10 oz strong plain white flour
2 teaspoons salt
15 g/½ oz butter or margarine
150 g/5 oz cracked wheat
50 g/2 oz wheatgerm
2 tablespoons malt extract

Grease two 450-g/1-lb loaf tins. Place the yeast, sugar and water and milk mixture in a jug and mix well. Leave in a warm place until frothy, about 10 minutes.

Sift the flours and salt into a bowl. Rub in the butter or margarine, then add 100 g/4 oz of the cracked wheat and the wheatgerm. Mix in the yeast liquid and malt extract.

Turn out on to a lightly floured surface and knead until smooth and elastic, about 10 minutes. Place in an oiled bowl, cover with cling film and leave to rise in a warm place until doubled in size, about 1–1½ hours.

Turn the dough on to a lightly floured surface, knock back and knead again for 2–3 minutes. Shape into two loaves, place in the tins. Cover and leave to rise. Sprinkle with the remaining cracked wheat and bake in a hot oven for 15 minutes. Reduce to moderately hot and bake for a further 20–25 minutes. Cool on a wire rack.

244 | Soda Bread

Preparation time
15 minutes

Cooking time
35 minutes

Oven temperature
220 C, 425 F, gas 7

Makes 1 loaf

Total calories
1805

You will need
450 g/1 lb plain flour
½ teaspoon cream of tartar
1 teaspoon salt
1½ teaspoons bicarbonate of soda
350 ml/12 fl oz milk
flour to sprinkle

Grease a baking tray. Sift the flour, cream of tartar, salt and bicarbonate of soda into a bowl. Add the milk and mix to a smooth soft dough. Knead gently on a lightly floured surface, then shape into a round. Place on the baking tray and mark the top quite deeply into four sections with a sharp knife.

Sprinkle with flour and bake in a hot oven for 35 minutes. Allow to cool on a wire rack. Break into quarters and serve sliced, with butter if liked.

Freezer Tip

Home-made bread freezes well. Put the cold fresh bread in polythene bags and suck out all the air with a pump. Seal, label and store for up to 6 months.

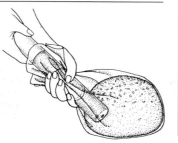

Cook's Tip

For a change, divide the dough into 8 pieces and make round rolls, cutting a cross in each. Bake at the same temperature as the loaf for about 15 minutes. Serve warm.

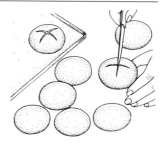

245 | Pitta Bread

Preparation time
25 minutes, plus 2–2½ hours to rise and prove

Cooking time
35–40 minutes

Oven temperature
240 C, 475 F, gas 9

Makes 8

Calories
290 per pitta bread

You will need
15 g/½ oz dried yeast
1 teaspoon caster sugar
about 450 ml/¾ pint warm water
575 g/1¼ lb strong plain white
   flour
½ teaspoon salt
2 tablespoons vegetable oil

Flour four baking trays. Place the yeast, sugar and half the water in a jug. Mix and leave until frothy.

Sift the flour and salt into a bowl. Add the yeast mixture, oil and enough of the remaining water to mix to a firm but pliable dough. Knead and leave to rise as Basic White Bread (recipe 242).

Turn out on to a lightly floured surface. Shape into eight equal-sized balls. Cover and leave to rest for 30 minutes. Roll out each to a 5-mm/¼-in thick oval. Place on the baking trays, cover and leave to prove in a warm place for 30 minutes.

Cook on the lowest shelf of a very hot oven for 5 minutes. Do not open the oven until the time is up. Transfer the tray to a higher shelf and cook for a further 3–5 minutes, until the pittas are puffed and lightly browned.

Split and fill with a salad, if liked.

246 | Naan Bread

Preparation time
25 minutes, plus 1½ hours to rise

Cooking time
15 minutes

Makes 12

Calories
120 per naan

You will need
1½ teaspoons dried yeast
150 ml/¼ pint warm milk
1½ teaspoons caster sugar
350 g/12 oz plain flour
1 teaspoon salt
½ teaspoon baking powder
150 ml/¼ pint natural yogurt
small knob of butter

Place the yeast, milk and sugar in a jug. Mix well, then leave in a warm place until frothy, about 10 minutes.

Sift the flour, salt and baking powder into a bowl. Add the yeast mixture and yogurt and mix well to make a soft dough. Turn out on to a lightly floured surface and knead until smooth and elastic, about 10 minutes. Place in an oiled bowl, cover with cling film and leave to rise in a warm place for 1½ hours.

Turn the dough on to a lightly floured surface, knock back to release all air bubbles and knead for 2–3 minutes. Divide into 12 equal pieces. Roll into balls, then flatten into large oval shapes.

Lightly butter a griddle or large, heavy-based frying pan and heat until very hot. Cook the bread ovals, one or two at a time, until the underside is golden brown and the top begins to bubble. Turn and cook the second side. Repeat with the remaining dough pieces. Serve hot or warm, with Indian or spicy dishes.

Cook's Tip

Make the pitta bread using wholemeal flour. Brush the shaped loaves with a little water and sprinkle with sesame seeds before baking.

Cook's Tip

Naan is an Indian bread which is traditionally baked in a tandoor – a charcoal-fired clay oven. The bread is served with most main dishes or dals to mop up the juices.

247 | *Muffins*

Preparation time
25 minutes, plus 2 hours to rise and prove

Cooking time
15–25 minutes

Makes 10

Calories
205 per muffin

You will need
15 g/½ oz dried yeast
½ teaspoon caster sugar
300 ml/½ pint warm milk
1 egg, beaten
25 g/1 oz butter, melted
450 g/1 lb strong plain white flour
1 teaspoon salt

Flour two baking trays. Whisk together the yeast, sugar and half the milk in a jug. Leave in a warm place until frothy, about 10 minutes.

Mix the egg with the remaining milk and the butter. Sift the flour and salt into a bowl. Add the yeast and egg mixtures and mix to a soft dough. Turn on to a lightly floured surface and knead until smooth and elastic, about 10 minutes. Place in an oiled bowl, cover with cling film and leave to rise in a warm place until doubled in size, about 1½ hours.

Turn out the dough on a lightly floured surface and knead for 2 minutes. Roll and stamp out 10 rounds with a 7.5-cm/3-in plain cutter, re-rolling as necessary. Place on the floured trays, cover with cling film and leave to prove for 30 minutes.

Lightly grease a griddle or heavy frying pan. Cook the muffins a few at a time over a moderate heat for 5–8 minutes each side, until well risen. Leave to cool on a wire rack. Serve split and toasted with butter.

248 | *Croissants*

Preparation time
1 hour, plus 2–2½ hours to rise and time to chill

Cooking time
10–15 minutes

Oven temperature
220 C, 425 F, gas 7

Makes 12

Calories
200 per croissant

You will need
25 g/1 oz fresh yeast
3 tablespoons water
200 g/7 oz butter
2 teaspoons salt
1½ tablespoons sugar
150 ml/¼ pint milk
350 g/12 oz plain flour
beaten egg to glaze

Cream the yeast with water. Put 25 g/1 oz of the butter into a bowl with the salt and sugar and pour over the milk. Cool to lukewarm, then add yeast and flour and knead until smooth. Cover and leave to rise until doubled in size. Knead the dough, wrap in an oiled polythene bag and chill thoroughly. Roll out on a floured board into a rectangle 13 × 38 cm/5 × 15 in. Dot a third of the remaining butter over the top two-thirds of dough. Fold in three and roll out, then fold again. Chill for 30 minutes, then repeat twice more.

Roll out dough to three 30-cm/12-in squares. Cut squares into four triangles. Roll up each and form into crescents. Put on a floured baking tray. Prove for 30 minutes. Brush with glaze and bake in a hot oven for 10–15 minutes.

Freezer Tip

Muffins freeze well. Pack them in a polythene bag when cold. Defrost in the microwave on full power, allowing about 15 seconds for 1, 30 seconds for 2 and 1 minute for 4.

Cook's Tip

When rolling fat into dough for croissants, flaky or puff pastry, do not allow the dough to become greasy during rolling. Chill it frequently between rolling. To do this quickly, put it in the freezer for 10 minutes.

249 | Tea Cakes

Preparation time
25 minutes, plus 1½–2
hours to rise and prove

Cooking time
20–22 minutes

Oven temperature
220 C, 425 F, gas 7

Makes 8

Calories
270 per tea cake

You will need
450 g / 1 lb plain flour
1 teaspoon salt
2 teaspoons sugar
100 g / 4 oz currants
25 g / 1 oz fresh yeast
300 ml / ½ pint warm milk
melted butter to brush

Sift together the flour and salt. Add the sugar and currants. Cream the yeast with a little extra sugar and some of the warm milk. Pour this mixture into a well in the centre of the flour, scatter flour lightly over the yeast and leave in a warm place for 10 minutes. Add the rest of the milk, mix to a light dough and knead well. Cover the bowl with cling film or a cloth, and put in a warm place to rise, until doubled in size, about 1–1½ hours.

Knead again, divide into eight, roll and shape into round tea cakes. Prick each one with a fork. Put on a warmed greased tin, cover with a cloth and stand in a warm place to prove for 30 minutes. Bake in a hot oven for 10–12 minutes, brush with melted butter and return to the oven for 10 minutes. Serve each cake split in half, lightly toasted and spread with butter.

Freezer Tip

Fresh yeast can be frozen. Wrap small pieces in cling film, then pack in a polythene bag. Store for up to 6 months.

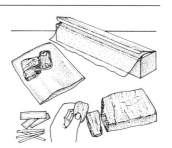

250 | Hot Cross Buns

Preparation time
40 minutes, plus 1½–2
hours to rise and prove

Cooking time
20–25 minutes

Oven temperature
220 C, 425 F, gas 7

Makes 12

Calories
250 per bun

You will need
450 g / 1 lb strong plain flour
1 teaspoon salt
1 teaspoon ground mixed spice
½ teaspoon ground cinnamon
50 g / 2 oz butter
1 sachet easy-blend dried yeast
50 g / 2 oz caster sugar
100 g / 4 oz currants
50 g / 2 oz chopped mixed peel
150 ml / ¼ pint warm milk
4 tablespoons warm water
1 egg, beaten

For the glaze
50 g / 2 oz granulated sugar
3 tablespoons milk

Sift the flour, salt and spices into a bowl. Rub in the butter. Stir in the yeast, sugar, currants and peel. Make a well in centre and add the milk, water and egg. Mix to form a soft dough. Turn out on to a lightly floured surface and knead until smooth and elastic. Place in an oiled bowl, cover with cling film and leave to rise in a warm place until doubled in size, 1–1½ hours.

Knock back the dough, then shape into 12 balls. Place well apart on greased baking trays and flatten slightly. Cover with oiled cling film and leave to prove for 30 minutes. Remove cling film, slash a cross in each bun. Bake in a hot oven for 20–25 minutes.

Bring the sugar and milk to the boil, stirring. Brush over the buns. Cool on a wire rack.

Freezer Tip

Make the buns in advance and freeze them unglazed. When defrosted, put them in a hot oven for 2–3 minutes, then glaze them.

251 | Chelsea Buns

Preparation time
40–45 minutes, plus 1½
hours to rise and prove

Cooking time
30–35 minutes

Oven temperature
190 C, 375 F, gas 5

Makes 9

Calories
185 per bun

You will need
2 teaspoons dried yeast
5 tablespoons warm milk
½ teaspoon sugar
225 g/8 oz strong plain flour
½ teaspoon salt
1 egg, beaten
15 g/½ oz butter, melted
golden syrup to glaze

For the filling
15 g/½ oz butter, melted
50 g/2 oz soft brown sugar
100 g/4 oz mixed dried fruit

Blend the yeast with the warm milk, sugar and 50 g/2 oz of the flour. Leave until frothy, about 20 minutes.

Mix the remaining flour and the salt together. Add to the yeast mixture with the beaten egg and melted butter. Mix well and knead the dough on a lightly floured board for about 10 minutes. Put to rise in a large greased polythene bag, loosely tied, until doubled in size, about 1 hour.

Knead the dough on a lightly floured surface. Roll into a rectangle about 23 × 30 cm/9 × 12 in, brush with the melted butter and sprinkle on the sugar and fruit. Roll up as for a Swiss roll and cut into 9 slices. Place in a greased 23-cm/9-in square cake tin. Leave to rise inside a greased polythene bag until the buns feel springy.

Remove the polythene bag and bake the buns in a moderately hot oven for 30–35 minutes. Place on a wire rack and brush the hot buns with the syrup.

Cook's Tip

Leave yeast doughs to rise in a warm place; near a central heating boiler, radiator or in front of a fire. Alternatively warm the grill compartment of the cooker but make sure that it is not too hot or the dough will dry out on top and begin to cook instead of rise.

252 | Jam Doughnuts

Preparation time
15 minutes, plus 1½
hours to rise and prove

Cooking time
10–15 minutes

Makes 16

Calories
210 per doughnut

You will need
450 g/1 lb strong plain flour
pinch of salt
50 g/2 oz butter or margarine
15 g/½ oz fresh yeast
50 g/2 oz caster sugar
300 ml/½ pint warm milk
2 eggs, beaten
2–3 tablespoons jam
oil for deep frying

Sift the flour and salt into a bowl, then rub in the butter or margarine. Cream the yeast with 15 g/½ oz of the sugar. Make a well in the centre of the flour, pour in the warm milk and beaten eggs. Add the yeast, mix to a light dough, cover and leave to rise in a warm place for 1 hour.

Divide the dough into 16 and shape into rounds. Place a small teaspoonful of jam in the centre of each round and draw up the edges to form a ball, pinching the dough together to seal. Put into oiled tartlet tins to prove in a warm place for 20–30 minutes.

Heat the oil to 180 C/360 F. Deep fry the doughnuts for 3–5 minutes, drain on absorbent kitchen paper and roll in the remaining caster sugar.

Cook's Tip

To make jam and cream doughnuts, shape the unfilled dough into long doughnuts. Deep fry and roll in sugar. Split when cool and fill with jam and whipped cream.

253 | Malt Bread

Preparation time
15 minutes, plus 2
hours to rise

Cooking time
35 minutes

Oven temperature
200 C, 400 F, gas 6
180 C, 350 F, gas 4

Makes 3 loaves

Calories
1060 per loaf

You will need
350 g/ 12 oz strong plain flour
350 g/ 12 oz wholemeal flour
¼ teaspoon salt
25 g/ 1 oz fresh yeast
300 ml/ ½ pint warm water
50 g/ 2 oz black treacle
100 g/ 4 oz malt extract
50 g/ 2 oz butter
100 g/ 4 oz sultanas

For the glaze
2 teaspoons sugar
2 tablespoons boiling water

Grease three 450-g/1-lb loaf tins. Sift the flours and salt into a bowl. Cream the yeast with a little of the water. Add to the flour. Gently heat the treacle, malt extract and butter until the fat has melted. Add to the flour with the remaining water and the sultanas and knead to form a very soft, sticky dough. Beat for 3 minutes. Spoon into the tins and level the top with a floured spoon. Cover with oiled cling film and leave to rise for at least 2 hours.

Bake in a moderately hot oven for 15 minutes, then reduce heat to moderate and bake for a further 20 minutes. Cover loosely with foil during cooking if becoming too brown.

Transfer to a wire rack and glaze with the sugar dissolved in the boiling water. Serve sliced and buttered.

254 | Traditional Teabread

Preparation time
20 minutes

Cooking time
1–1¼ hours

Oven temperature
180 C, 350 F, gas 4

Makes 2 loaves

Calories
1700 per loaf

You will need
450 g/ 1 lb self-raising flour
1 teaspoon ground mixed spice
1 teaspoon baking powder
100 g/ 4 oz butter or margarine
100 g/ 4 oz soft brown sugar
225 g/ 8 oz mixed dried fruit
2 eggs, lightly beaten
250 ml/ 8 fl oz strong cold tea

Base-line and grease two 450-g/1-lb loaf tins. Sift together the flour, mixed spice and baking powder. Rub in the butter or margarine until the mixture resembles fine breadcrumbs. Stir in the sugar and dried fruit. Make a well in the centre and gradually add the eggs and tea to form a soft dropping consistency.

Divide the mixture between the two tins and level the surface with the back of a metal spoon. Bake in a moderate oven for 1–1¼ hours, or until a warmed skewer inserted into the centre comes out clean. Remove from the tins and allow to cool on wire racks. Serve sliced and buttered.

Cook's Tip

The top of the loaf can be brushed with a little warmed clear honey instead of sugar and water.

Freezer Tip

If you want to freeze the loaf sliced, to remove 1 or 2 pieces at a time, then interleave the slices with pieces of plastic or greaseproof paper and reshape the loaf. Pack and freeze.

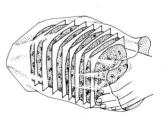

255 | Gingerbread

Preparation time
10 minutes

Cooking time
1½ hours

Oven temperature
180 C, 350 F, gas 4

Makes 1 cake

Total calories
5465

You will need
450 g/ 1 lb plain flour
¼ teaspoon salt
1 tablespoon ground ginger
1 teaspoon ground cinnamon
1 teaspoon ground mixed spice
1 teaspoon ground cloves
1 tablespoon baking powder
1 teaspoon bicarbonate of soda
100 g/ 4 oz walnut halves,
  coarsely chopped
175 g/ 6 oz butter
175 g/ 6 oz molasses or black
  treacle
175 g/ 6 oz golden syrup
200 g/ 7 oz soft dark brown sugar
1 large egg, beaten
300 ml/ ½ pint milk

Line and grease a 23-cm/9-in square cake tin. Sift the flour, salt, spices, baking powder and bicarbonate of soda into a bowl. Stir in the walnuts and make a well in the centre. Heat the butter with the molasses or treacle, syrup and sugar, stirring until smooth. Add to the flour mixture with the egg and milk. Mix thoroughly.

Pour into the prepared cake tin. Bake in a moderate oven for 1½ hours, until a warmed skewer inserted in the centre comes out clean. Cool on a wire rack. Store in an airtight container until required.

256 | Parkin

Preparation time
10 minutes

Cooking time
1–1½ hours

Oven temperature
180 C, 350 F, gas 4

Makes 1 cake

Total calories
3505

You will need
175 g/ 6 oz plain flour
pinch of salt
1 teaspoon ground ginger
2 teaspoons ground cinnamon
1 teaspoon bicarbonate of soda
275 g/ 10 oz medium oatmeal
175 g/ 6 oz black treacle
100 g/ 4 oz butter
100 g/ 4 oz soft brown sugar
150 ml/ ¼ pint milk
1 egg

Line and grease a 23-cm/9-in square cake tin. Sift together the flour, salt, spices and soda. Add the oatmeal and toss lightly to mix. Warm together the treacle, butter, sugar and milk until the butter has melted. Cool slightly, add the egg and beat well. Pour into the centre of the dry ingredients and stir rapidly until smooth.

Pour into the prepared tin and bake in a moderate oven for 1–1½ hours, until a skewer inserted in the centre comes out clean. Cool on a wire rack.

Cook's Tip

To spoon syrup, treacle or honey out of a tin or jar, first warm a metal spoon in a jug of boiling water, or hold over a gas flame for a few seconds. The syrup will slide easily off the hot spoon.

Cook's Tip

Make an interesting apple and raisin parkin by mixing 50 g/ 2 oz raisins and 50 g/ 2 oz dried apple flakes into the dry ingredients. Combine as above.

257 | *Plain Scones*

Preparation time
15 minutes

Cooking time
10–12 minutes

Oven temperature
220C, 425F, gas 7

Makes 8

Calories
170 per scone

You will need
225 g/8 oz plain flour
3 teaspoons baking powder
pinch of salt
50 g/2 oz butter or margarine
25 g/1 oz caster sugar
scant 150 ml/¼ pint milk plus
milk to glaze

Sift the flour, baking powder and salt in a bowl. Rub in the butter or margarine until the mixture resembles fine breadcrumbs, then stir in the sugar. Mix in enough milk to make a soft dough. Turn on to a floured surface and knead very lightly.

Roll out the dough to about 1 cm/½ in thick and cut out 8 rounds using a 6-cm/2½-in cutter, re-rolling the dough as necessary. Place on a greased baking tray and brush with milk. Bake in a hot oven for 10–12 minutes or until well risen and golden brown. Cool on a wire rack. Serve with butter or whipped cream and jam.

258 | *Cheese Scones*

Preparation time
15 minutes

Cooking time
12–15 minutes

Oven temperature
220C, 425F, gas 7

Makes 8

Calories
190 per scone

You will need
225 g/8 oz plain flour
3 teaspoons baking powder
pinch of salt
½ teaspoon mustard powder
40 g/1½ oz butter or margarine
1 onion, finely chopped
75 g/3 oz mature Cheddar
   cheese, grated
scant 150 ml/¼ pint milk
beaten egg or milk to glaze

Sift the flour, baking powder, salt and mustard into a bowl. Rub in the butter or margarine until the mixture resembles fine breadcrumbs. Stir in the onion and Cheddar, then mix in enough milk to make a soft dough. Roll out on a lightly floured surface to about 1 cm/½ in thick. Cut out 8 rounds using a 6-cm/2½-in cutter, re-rolling the dough as necessary. Place on a greased baking tray and brush with a little egg or milk. Bake in a hot oven for 12–15 minutes or until well risen and golden. Cool on a wire rack.

Cook's Tip

To make fruit scones, stir 50 g/2 oz sultanas into the rubbed-in mixture. Combine as above.

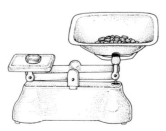

Freezer Tip

For a delicious cobbler topping for casseroles, remove the scones from the oven when they are two-thirds cooked, cool and freeze. Arrange the frozen scones on the casserole and cook for 15–20 minutes.

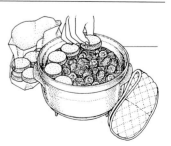

259 | Drop Scones

Preparation time
5 minutes

Cooking time
5–10 minutes

Makes about 30

Calories
40 per scone

You will need
225 g/8 oz plain flour
¼ teaspoon salt
½ teaspoon bicarbonate of soda
1 teaspoon cream of tartar
25 g/1 oz caster sugar
1 egg
300 ml/½ pint milk

Sift together the flour, salt, bicarbonate of soda and cream of tartar. Stir in the sugar and make a well in the centre. Gradually beat in the egg and milk to make a smooth thick batter.

Lightly grease a hot griddle or heavy-based frying pan and drop large spoonsful of the mixture on, allowing plenty of room for spreading. When the surface bubbles and the drop scones are set, turn quickly and cook the other side. Serve wrapped in a clean cloth to keep scones warm and soft.

Cook's Tip

To make savoury drop scones, omit the sugar. Add 4 tablespoons grated Parmesan cheese and 1 teaspoon mixed dried herbs to the batter. Cook as above, then serve hot.

260 | Wholemeal Apple Round

Preparation time
15 minutes

Cooking time
20–25 minutes

Oven temperature
200 C, 400 F, gas 6

Serves 8

Calories
190 per portion

You will need
1 medium cooking apple
225 g/8 oz wholemeal flour
½ teaspoon salt
3 teaspoons baking powder
50 g/2 oz butter or margarine
50 g/2 oz soft brown sugar
about 150 ml/¼ pint milk

For the glaze
a little milk
1 tablespoon demerara sugar

Peel, core and finely chop the apple. Put the flour, salt and baking powder into a bowl. Rub in the butter or margarine, then stir in the sugar and chopped apple. Add the milk and mix to form a soft but not sticky dough.

Roll out on a floured surface to a 5-mm/¼-in thick round. Place on a greased baking tray and mark into eight wedges. Brush the top with milk and sprinkle with demerara sugar. Bake in a moderately hot oven for 20–25 minutes. Serve warm with butter.

Cook's Tip

If you are in a hurry, then prepare the scone dough and flatten it with your hand straight on the greased baking tray to save rolling it out.

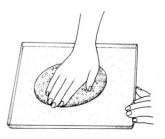

Family Cakes and Biscuits

Making cakes and biscuits at home is doubly rewarding. Not only do they taste much better than the commercial variety, they are more economical too. There is a wonderful selection to choose from in this chapter, from the traditional Victoria sandwich to the crunchy peanut cookie.

261 | Carrot Cake

Preparation time
20 minutes

Cooking time
1½ hours

Oven temperature
160 C, 325 F, gas 3

Makes 1 cake

Total calories
4920

You will need
225 g / 8 oz butter or margarine
225 g / 8 oz soft brown sugar
4 eggs, lightly beaten
225 g / 8 oz self-raising flour, sifted
½ teaspoon salt
1 teaspoon grated nutmeg
3 teaspoons mixed spice
350 g / 12 oz carrots, coarsely grated

For the glacé icing
225 g / 8 oz icing sugar
2 tablespoons water
50 g / 2 oz walnut halves to decorate

Line and grease a deep 20-cm/8-in round cake tin. Cream the butter or margarine and sugar until light and fluffy. Gradually beat in the eggs, adding a little of the flour to prevent curdling. Fold in the remaining flour, salt and spices. Fold in the grated carrot and spoon into the prepared cake tin. Level the top and bake in a moderate oven for 1½ hours or until a skewer inserted in the centre comes out clean. Cool in the tin for 5 minutes before turning out on to a wire rack to cool completely.

Beat the icing ingredients together until smooth, pour over the cake and decorate with walnuts, chopping some to form a border as shown.

262 | Victoria Sandwich Cake

Preparation time
15 minutes

Cooking time
20–25 minutes

Oven temperature
180 C, 350 F, gas 4

Makes 1 cake

Total calories
1910

You will need
100 g / 4 oz butter or margarine
100 g / 4 oz caster sugar
2 eggs, lightly beaten
100 g / 4 oz self-raising flour, sifted
4 tablespoons strawberry jam
sifted icing sugar, for dusting

Grease and flour two 18-cm/7-in sandwich tins. Cream the butter or margarine and sugar until light and fluffy. Gradually beat in the eggs, adding a little of the flour to prevent curdling. Carefully fold in the remaining flour using a metal spoon. Divide the mixture between the two tins and level the tops. Bake in a moderate oven for 20–25 minutes or until the cakes are risen, springy, firm to the touch and golden. Turn out and cool on a wire rack.

When cold, sandwich the two cakes together with the jam and dust with icing sugar.

Cook's Tip

Use a food processor, fitted with a coarse grating disc, to prepare the carrots. Halve any large ones to fit into the feed tube and pack the tube neatly for speed and efficiency.

Cook's Tip

To flour cake tins, put a spoonful of flour in the greased tin. Tilt from side to side, tapping the edge to coat the base and sides evenly in flour. Turn any excess flour into the second tin.

263 | *Dundee Cake*

Preparation time
15 minutes

Cooking time
3½ hours

Oven temperature
150 C, 300 F, gas 2

Makes 1 cake

Total calories
5385

You will need
225 g / 8 oz butter or margarine
225 g / 8 oz caster sugar
5 eggs, lightly beaten
350 g / 12 oz self-raising flour,
*   sifted*
675 g / 1½ lb mixed dried fruit
100 g / 4 oz glacé cherries,
*   washed and quartered*
1 teaspoon mixed spice
50 g / 2 oz whole blanched
*   almonds*

Line and grease a deep 20-cm/8-in round cake tin. Cream the butter or margarine with the sugar until light and fluffy. Gradually beat in the eggs, adding a little flour if necessary to prevent the mixture from curdling. Mix the dried fruit and cherries with a spoonful of the flour. Fold the remaining flour and the mixed spice into the creamed mixture. Stir in the dried fruit and glacé cherries. Spoon the mixture into the prepared tin and level the surface. Top with concentric circles of almonds.

Bake in a cool oven for 3½ hours or until a skewer inserted into the centre of the cake comes out clean. Leave to cool in the tin for about 10 minutes, then turn out on to a wire rack to cool completely.

264 | *Quick Fruit Cake*

Preparation time
15 minutes

Cooking time
1–1¼ hours

Oven temperature
180 C, 350 F, gas 4

Makes 1 cake

Total calories
2410

You will need
100 g / 4 oz butter or margarine
100 g / 4 oz caster sugar
2 eggs, lightly beaten
225 g / 8 oz self-raising flour,
*   sifted*
100 g / 4 oz mixed dried fruit
50 g / 2 oz glacé cherries, washed
*   and sliced*

Line and grease a deep 18-cm/7-in round cake tin. Cream the butter or margarine with the sugar until light and fluffy. Gradually beat in the eggs, adding a little of the flour to prevent curdling. Mix the dried fruit and cherries with a spoonful of the flour. Fold the remaining flour into the creamed mixture, then fold in the fruit. Spoon the mixture into the prepared tin.

Level the top of the cake and bake in a moderate oven for 1–1¼ hours or until a skewer inserted into the centre of the cake comes out clean. Leave to cool in the tin for 5 minutes, then turn out and cool completely on a wire rack.

Cook's Tip

If you have whole almonds with peel on, then cover them with boiling water and leave for 1 minute. Drain and rub off the skins between your thumb and forefinger. Weigh the nuts without skins.

Cook's Tip

To level the surface of a fruit cake mixture, dampen a large metal spoon in hot water, shake off the water and use the rounded side to level the mixture. Dampen the spoon again if the mixture begins to stick.

265 | Chocolate Cake

Preparation time
30 minutes

Cooking time
25–30 minutes

Oven temperature
160 C, 325 F, gas 3

Makes 1 cake

Total calories
4180

You will need
100 g / 4 oz butter or margarine
100 g / 4 oz caster sugar
2 eggs, lightly beaten
100 g / 4 oz self-raising flour,
   sifted
50 g / 2 oz cocoa powder, sifted
2 tablespoons boiling water
100 g / 4 oz butter
450 g / 1 lb icing sugar, sifted
50 g / 2 oz plain chocolate, grated
2–3 tablespoons water
brown food colouring

Base-line and grease two 18-cm/7-in sandwich tins. Cream the butter or margarine with the sugar until light and fluffy. Gradually beat in the eggs. Fold in the flour and 25 g/1 oz cocoa. Divide the mixture between the tins. Bake in a moderate oven for 25–30 minutes. Cool on a wire rack.

Mix the remaining cocoa powder and boiling water together. Beat the butter and 225 g/8 oz icing sugar until pale, beat in the cocoa. Use one-third of the buttercream to sandwich the cakes together. Spread another third over the side of the cake. Press the grated chocolate on the side. Mix the remaining icing sugar and water. Colour a few teaspoons brown and place in a piping bag fitted with a small plain nozzle. Spread the rest over the cake and pipe on parallel rows of brown. Draw the point of a skewer across the rows to give a feathered effect. Pipe a border with the remaining buttercream.

Cook's Tip

For fine piping, fold a 20-cm/8-in paper square in half. Fold the corners of the long side up towards the point and crease the fold lines. Unfold, form into a cone and secure. Snip off corner to take a nozzle.

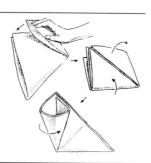

266 | Coffee and Almond Cake

Preparation time
25 minutes

Cooking time
30 minutes

Oven temperature
160 C, 325 F, gas 3

Makes 1 cake

Total calories
3845

You will need
100 g / 4 oz butter or margarine
100 g / 4 oz caster sugar
2 eggs, lightly beaten
100 g / 4 oz self-raising flour
½ teaspoon baking powder
50 g / 2 oz ground almonds
1 tablespoon instant coffee,
   dissolved in 1 tablespoon hot
   water

For the filling and decoration
100 g / 4 oz butter
225 g / 8 oz icing sugar, sifted
1 tablespoon instant coffee,
   dissolved in 1 tablespoon hot
   water
50 g / 2 oz flaked almonds

Base-line and grease two 18-cm/7-in sandwich tins. Cream the fat and sugar until light and fluffy. Gradually beat in the eggs. Fold in the flour, baking powder, ground almonds and coffee. Divide the mixture between the tins. Bake in a moderate oven for 30 minutes or until well risen and firm to the touch. Cool on a wire rack.

Cream the butter and icing sugar until light and fluffy. Stir in the coffee. Use one-third of the mixture to sandwich the cakes together. Use the remainder to spread over the top and sides of the cake and to pipe a border on top of the cake. Press the flaked almonds on the side of the cake.

Cook's Tip

To level out a creamed cake mixture in sandwich tins, tap the base of the tin firmly on the edge of a table or work surface. The mixture will level in the tin.

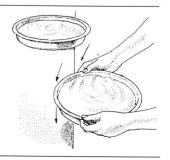

267 | *Nutty Marmalade Cake*

Preparation time
20 minutes

Cooking time
1½ hours

Oven temperature
160 C, 325 F, gas 3

Makes 1 cake

Total calories
5275

You will need
225 g/8 oz butter or margarine
3 tablespoons thick-cut
  marmalade
225 g/8 oz demerara sugar
4 eggs, lightly beaten
225 g/8 oz self-raising flour,
  sifted
2 teaspoons ground cinnamon
a little grated nutmeg
100 g/4 oz chopped walnuts

For the glacé icing
225 g/8 oz icing sugar, sifted
1 tablespoon lemon juice
1 tablespoon orange juice
grated orange rind to decorate

Line and grease a 20-cm/8-in square cake tin. Cream the butter or margarine, marmalade and sugar until light and fluffy. Gradually beat in the eggs, adding a little of the flour to prevent curdling. Fold in the remaining flour, the cinnamon and nutmeg, then fold in the walnuts.

Spoon into the prepared tin, level the top and bake in a moderate oven for 1½ hours or until a skewer inserted into the centre comes out clean. Cool in the tin for 5 minutes before turning out on to a wire rack to cool completely.

Beat the ingredients for the glacé icing together until smooth. Pour the icing over the top of the cake and allow to drizzle down the sides. Decorate with orange rind.

268 | *Banana and Walnut cake*

Preparation time
20 minutes

Cooking time
1¼–1½ hours

Oven temperature
180 C, 350 F, gas 4

Makes 1 cake

Total calories
2720

You will need
100 g/4 oz butter or margarine
100 g/4 oz light soft brown sugar
2 eggs, lightly beaten
225 g/8 oz plain wholemeal flour
1½ teaspoons baking powder
1 teaspoon grated nutmeg
2 bananas, peeled and chopped
100 g/4 oz chopped walnuts
soft brown sugar to decorate

Line and grease a deep 18-cm/7-in round cake tin. Cream the butter or margarine and sugar until light and fluffy. Gradually beat in the eggs. Fold in the flour, baking powder and nutmeg. Carefully fold in the bananas and walnuts.

Spoon into the prepared tin, level the top and bake in a moderate oven for 1¼–1½ hours or until a skewer inserted into the centre comes out clean. Turn out on to a wire rack, sprinkle the top with soft brown sugar and leave to cool.

Cook's Tip

Long strands of orange rind are a useful decoration ingredient. Pare the rind thinly, cut into strips and cook in boiling water for 3–5 minutes. Drain and cool.

Cook's Tip

Freshly grated nutmeg gives a superior flavour to that which is bought ready grated. Miniature nutmeg graters often have a small compartment in the top to store a whole nutmeg.

269 | Madeira Cake

Preparation time
15 minutes

Cooking time
1½ hours

Oven temperature
160 C, 325 F, gas 3

Makes 1 cake

Total calories
3045

You will need
175 g / 6 oz butter
175 g / 6 oz caster sugar
3 eggs, lightly beaten
225 g / 8 oz self-raising flour, sifted
about 3 tablespoons milk
pieces of candied peel

Line and grease a deep 15-cm/6-in round cake tin. Cream the butter and sugar until light and fluffy. Gradually beat in the eggs, adding a little of the flour to prevent curdling. Carefully fold in the remaining flour and add enough milk to make a soft dropping consistency. Spoon the mixture into the prepared tin and lay the candied peel on top.

Bake in a moderate oven for 1¼–1½ hours or until the cake is firm to touch and a skewer inserted into the centre comes out clean. Leave the cake to cool in the tin for about 5 minutes before transferring to a wire rack to cool completely.

270 | Date and Walnut Loaf

Preparation time
15 minutes

Cooking time
about 1 hour

Oven temperature
180 C, 350 F, gas 4

Makes 1 loaf

Total calories
2875

You will need
100 g / 4 oz butter or margarine
100 g / 4 oz caster sugar
2 eggs, lightly beaten
225 g / 8 oz self-raising flour, sifted
1 teaspoon mixed spice
100 g / 4 oz walnuts, roughly chopped
100 g / 4 oz dates, roughly chopped
about 3 tablespoons milk

Line and grease a 1-kg/2-lb loaf tin. Cream the butter or margarine and sugar until pale and fluffy. Gradually beat in the eggs. Fold in the flour, spice, walnuts and dates. Add a little milk to make a dropping consistency.

Bake in a moderate oven for about 1 hour. Insert a skewer in the centre of the cake; if it comes out clean the loaf is cooked. Cool slightly before turning out on to a wire rack to cool completely.

Cook's Tip

To make a cherry cake, halve 225 g / 8 oz glacé cherries and wash them in a sieve under warm water. Dry thoroughly, toss with a little of the flour, then fold in last. Bake as above, omitting the peel.

Cook's Tip

Stand a loaf tin on grease-proof paper big enough to come up 2.5 cm/1 in above edges of the tin. Draw round base; cut in from corners. Line the greased tin, overlapping the cut corners. Grease well.

271 | Swiss Roll

Preparation time
10 minutes

Cooking time
7–10 minutes

Oven temperature
220C, 425F, gas 7

Makes 1

Total calories
1090

You will need
3 eggs
75 g/3 oz caster sugar
75 g/3 oz plain flour, sifted
4 tablespoons raspberry jam
caster sugar for dredging

Line and grease a 23 × 30-cm/9 × 12-in Swiss roll tin. Whisk the eggs and sugar until very pale and thick enough to leave a trail when the whisk is lifted out. Carefully fold in the flour using a metal spoon. Turn the mixture into the prepared tin, spreading it out very lightly. Bake in a hot oven for 7–10 minutes.

Meanwhile place a clean tea-towel on a work surface, cover with greaseproof paper and dredge with sugar. Turn the hot Swiss roll on to the paper. Trim off the edges, spread with jam and, using the cloth and paper as a guide, quickly roll up tightly. Dredge with caster sugar and cool on a wire rack.

272 | Rock Cakes

Preparation time
15 minutes

Cooking time
20 minutes

Oven temperature
190C, 375F, gas 5

Makes 8

Calories
330 per cake

You will need
225 g/8 oz self-raising flour
1 teaspoon mixed spice
½ teaspoon grated nutmeg
150 g/5 oz margarine
75 g/3 oz demerara sugar
150 g/5 oz mixed dried fruit
1 egg, lightly beaten
2 tablespoons milk

Grease 2 baking trays. Sift the flour and spices into a bowl. Rub in the margarine until the mixture resembles fine breadcrumbs. Stir in the sugar and fruit, then mix in the egg and milk to make a fairly stiff mixture. Place eight spoonsful of the mixture well apart on the baking and bake in a moderately hot oven for 20 minutes. Cool on a wire rack. These cakes are best eaten on the same day as baking.

Cook's Tip

Draw round the base of the tin on a sheet of greaseproof paper, snip in from the corners. Place in the greased tin, overlapping corners, then grease. The paper should be 5 cm/2 in higher than the tin.

Cook's Tip

When rubbing fat into flour use only fingertips. Keep fingers spaced apart and lift the ingredients, rubbing quickly and lightly to make a light mixture which is not sticky.

273 | Fruit Buns

Preparation time
15 minutes

Cooking time
15–20 minutes

Oven temperature
190 C, 375 F, gas 5

Makes 18

Calories
100 per bun

You will need
100 g/ 4 oz butter or margarine
100 g/ 4 oz caster sugar
2 eggs, lightly beaten
100 g/ 4 oz self-raising flour
75 g/ 3 oz currants

Place 18 paper cake cases on a baking tray or in two deep bun tin trays.

Cream the butter or margarine with the sugar until light and fluffy. Gradually beat in the eggs. Carefully fold in the flour and currants, using a metal spoon. Divide the mixture between the paper cases.

Bake in a moderately hot oven for 15–20 minutes or until well risen and golden brown. Transfer to a wire rack to cool.

274 | Bakewell Tarts

Preparation time
15 minutes

Cooking time
30 minutes

Oven temperature
190 C, 375 F, gas 5

Makes 18

Calories
155 per tart

You will need
For the shortcrust pastry
225 g/ 8 oz plain flour
pinch of salt
100 g/ 4 oz margarine
2–3 tablespoons cold water

For the filling
4 tablespoons strawberry jam
50 g/ 2 oz butter or margarine
50 g/ 2 oz caster sugar
1 egg, lightly beaten
25 g/ 1 oz ground almonds
50 g/ 2 oz self-raising flour, sifted
few drops of almond essence
1 tablespoon milk

Sift the flour and salt into a bowl. Cut the margarine into small pieces and rub into the flour until the mixture resembles fine breadcrumbs. Add enough water to mix to a soft dough.

Roll out and use to line 18 patty tins. Put half a teaspoon of jam into each pastry case. Beat the butter or margarine with the sugar until pale and creamy. Gradually beat in the egg. Fold in the almonds, flour, almond essence and milk.

Place a small spoonful of this mixture on top of the jam and smooth it to the edge of the pastry. Bake in a moderate oven for 25–30 minutes or until well risen and golden. Cool on wire rack.

Cook's Tip

To cream fat and sugar, make sure they are at room temperature and soft. Use the flat side of a wooden spoon and beat in one direction, keeping the mixture down in the base of the bowl.

Cook's Tip

To fold in dry ingredients use a large metal spoon. Sprinkle some lightly over the surface, then cut and fold in a figure of eight, adding the remaining ingredients. Do not *beat or fold for too long.*

275 | Jam Tarts

Preparation time
15 minutes

Cooking time
15 minutes

Oven temperature
200 C, 400 F, gas 6

Makes 24

Calories
40 per tart

You will need
100 g / 4 oz plain flour
pinch of salt
50 g / 2 oz butter or margarine
1–2 tablespoons water
100 g / 4 oz strawberry jam

Sift the flour and salt into a bowl. Rub in the butter or margarine until the mixture resembles fine breadcrumbs. Stir in just enough water to bind the ingredients, and lightly mix together. Roll out the pastry on a lightly floured surface, then cut out 24 6-cm/2½-in rounds. Use these to line patty tins. Put a small spoonful of jam into each tart. Bake in a moderate oven for 10–15 minutes or until the pastry is golden. Cool on a wire rack. Serve warm or cold.

276 | Lamingtons

Preparation time
25 minutes

Cooking time
45 minutes

Oven temperature
180 C, 350 F, gas 4

Makes 18

Calories
290 per cake

You will need
175 g / 6 oz butter or margarine
225 g / 8 oz caster sugar
1 teaspoon vanilla essence
3 eggs beaten
350 g / 12 oz plain flour
2 teaspoons baking powder
¼ teaspoon salt
150 ml / ¼ pint milk
225 g / 8 oz icing sugar
25 g / 1 oz cocoa powder
about 150 ml / ¼ pint cold water
100 g / 4 oz desiccated coconut

Cream the fat in a bowl and gradually add the sugar. Beat until light and fluffy, then beat in the vanilla essence. Gradually beat the eggs into the creamed mixture until smooth. Sift together the flour, baking powder and salt and add to the mixture, a third at a time, alternating with milk. Beat well after each addition. Pour into a greased 28 × 18-cm/11 × 7-in tin and bake in a moderate oven for 45 minutes. Invert the tin on to a wire rack to cool and leave for 5–10 minutes before removing the tin.

When completely cool, cut the cake into three strips lengthwise, then cut each strip into six pieces. Sift the icing sugar and cocoa into a bowl, pour in the water. Stir over a pan of hot water until the icing is smooth and shiny. Scatter the coconut thickly on a large piece of greaseproof paper. Using a fork, dip each cube of cake into the icing. Allow a moment for the icing to set slightly, then roll each cube in the coconut. Transfer to a wire rack to dry, then store in an airtight container.

Cook's Tip

Use only enough water to bind pastry. Handle the dough lightly, as little as possible. Use a very light sifting of flour for rolling and roll one way only. Do not turn pastry over, lift on the rolling pin if necessary.

Cook's Tip

When coating cakes in dry ingredients, tilt the greaseproof paper from hand to hand to gently rock the piece of cake in the coating ingredient and coat all sides evenly.

277 | Viennese Whirls

Preparation time
15 minutes, plus 15
minutes to chill

Cooking time
12–15 minutes

Oven temperature
190 C, 375 F, gas 5

Makes 18–20

Total calories
2040

You will need
100 g / 4 oz butter or margarine,
   softened
50 g / 2 oz icing sugar, sifted
100 g / 4 oz plain flour, sifted
½ teaspoon vanilla essence

For the filling
50 g / 2 oz butter or margarine
25 g / 1 oz icing sugar, sifted
50 g / 2 oz chocolate, melted
icing sugar to dust

Grease two baking trays. Beat the butter or margarine with the sugar until pale and very soft. Stir in the flour and vanilla essence. Spoon the mixture into a piping bag fitted with a large star nozzle and pipe 18–20 rings on to the baking trays. Chill for 15–20 minutes. Bake in a moderately hot oven for 12–15 minutes. Leave the biscuits on the tray, for a few seconds, then use a palette knife to lift them off. Cool on a wire rack.

For the filling, beat the butter or margarine with the icing sugar. Cool the melted chocolate slightly, then stir into the filling. Pipe a little on half the whirls, top with the remaining halves. Dust with icing sugar.

278 | Shortbread

Preparation time
15 minutes, plus 15
minutes to chill

Cooking time
40 minutes

Oven temperature
160 C, 325 F, gas 3

Makes 8 pieces

Calories
195 per piece

You will need
175 g / 6 oz plain flour, sifted
pinch of salt
100 g / 4 oz butter
50 g / 2 oz caster sugar
grated rind of 1 lemon
icing sugar to dust

Grease and flour a baking tray. Put the flour and salt in a mixing bowl. Rub in the butter, then stir in the sugar and lemon rind. Lightly work the mixture together until it forms a smooth stiff ball of dough. Roll into a 20-cm 8-in circle and place on the baking tray. Pinch the edges, prick the middle all over with a fork and cut the shortbread into eight wedges. Chill for 15 minutes.

Bake in a moderate oven for 40 minutes or until pale golden. Leave on the baking tray for a few minutes, then cool completely on a wire rack.

Cook's Tip

To pipe the biscuits, hold the bag at right angles to the tray, not at a slant. Squeeze the bag evenly and firmly, lift off the nozzle sharply or slide a knife across the nozzle when you have finished.

Cook's Tip

Prick biscuits evenly and decoratively with a fork before cooking to prevent them bubbling up or rising when baked. Chilling first makes a crisp, short biscuit.

279 | Gingerbread Men

Preparation time
15 minutes

Cooking time
10 minutes

Oven temperature
190C, 375F, gas 5

Makes 14

Calories
150 per gingerbread
man

You will need
100 g/ 4 oz butter or margarine
100 g/ 4 oz dark soft brown sugar
2 tablespoons golden syrup
225 g/ 8 oz plain flour, sifted
2 teaspoons ground ginger
currants or raisins to decorate

Grease two baking trays. Cream the butter or margarine with the sugar until light and fluffy. Beat in the syrup. Stir in the flour and ginger. Lightly knead the mixture on a floured surface then roll out.   to 5 mm/$\frac{1}{4}$ in thick.

Cut out 14 gingerbread men. (use gingerbread women cutters too, if you like). Add raisins or currants to represent buttons, eyes, nose and mouth. Transfer to the baking trays and bake in a moderate oven for 10 minutes or until firm and golden. Cool on a wire rack.

280 | Bourbons

Preparation time
20 minutes, plus 1
hour to chill

Cooking time
10–15 minutes

Oven temperature
180C, 350F, gas 4

Makes 16

Calories
200 per biscuit

You will need
175 g/ 6 oz plain flour
25 g/ 1 oz cocoa powder
75 g/ 3 oz butter or margarine
50 g/ 2 oz caster sugar
2 tablespoons golden syrup
1 egg, lightly beaten
granulated sugar for sprinkling

For the filling
100 g/ 4 oz butter
175 g/ 6 oz icing sugar, sifted
25 g/ 1 oz cocoa powder
2 tablespoons boiling water '

Lightly grease two baking trays. Sift the flour and cocoa powder into a bowl. Rub in the fat, then stir in the sugar, syrup and enough beaten egg to make a firm dough. Roll out on a floured work surface to a rectangle 30 × 40 cm/ 12 × 16 in. Cut in half lengthways, then cut each half into 16 evenly sized fingers. Prick all over with a fork. Carefully transfer to the baking trays and chill.

Bake in a moderate oven for 10–15 minutes. Sprinkle the biscuits with the sugar. Leave on the baking trays for 1 minute. Cool completely on a wire rack.

For the filling cream the butter and icing sugar until pale. Dissolve the cocoa in the water, cool, then beat into the filling. Use to sandwich the biscuits in pairs.

Cook's Tip

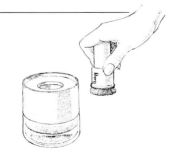

Keep a small lidded jam jar of vegetable oil ready for greasing tins. Alternatively, gadgets known as 'oil wells' have a brush which fits in a neat oil container, spill-proof and ready for use.

Freezer Tip

If you want to chill foods quickly, then place them in the freezer for a few minutes. Do not put unopened cans in the freezer for more than a few minutes.

281 | Chocolate Castles

Preparation time
20 minutes

Cooking time
10–12 minutes

Oven temperature
220C, 425F, gas 7

Makes 18

Calories
145 per cake

You will need
100 g / 4 oz butter or margarine
100 g / 4 oz caster sugar
2 eggs, lightly beaten
75 g / 3 oz self-raising flour, sifted
25 g / 1 oz cocoa powder, sifted
about 6 tablespoons chocolate
    spread
100 g / 4 oz chocolate vermicelli
18 chocolate buttons

Thoroughly grease 18 dariole tins and stand them on a baking tray. Cream the butter or margarine and sugar until light and fluffy. Gradually beat in the eggs. Fold in the flour and cocoa powder using a metal spoon.

Divide the mixture between the tins. Bake in a hot oven for 10–12 minutes. Turn out on to a wire rack and leave to cool.

Smooth the chocolate spread over the top and sides of the castles and roll in the vermicelli. Top with chocolate buttons.

282 | Sesame Flapjacks

Preparation time
10 minutes

Cooking time
45 minutes

Oven temperature
180C, 350F, gas 4

Makes 12

Calories
205 per flapjack

You will need
100 g / 4 oz butter or margarine
50 g / 2 oz demerara sugar
4 tablespoons golden syrup
175 g / 6 oz rolled oats
50 g / 2 oz sesame seeds
100 g / 4 oz dates, chopped

Base-line and grease a 28 × 18-cm / 11 × 7-in Swiss roll tin. Melt the butter or margarine and sugar in a large saucepan over a low heat, then stir in the remaining ingredients. The mixture should be fairly stiff.

Spread the mixture in the prepared tin and bake in a moderate oven for 40 minutes. Cut into 12 equal portions while still hot, and leave to cool in the tin.

Microwave Tip

If the chocolate spread is slightly too thick to spread over the cakes, then warm it in a basin in the microwave. Allow 30 seconds on full power.

Cook's Tip

Muesli flapjacks are delicious and easy. Omit sesame seeds and dates and substitute oats with muesli.

283 | Chocolate Nut Crispies

Preparation time
10 minutes

Cooking time
5 minutes

Makes 18

Calories
60 per cake

You will need
50 g / 2 oz butter or margarine
50 g / 2 oz cocoa powder
2 tablespoons golden syrup
50 g / 2 oz cornflakes
50 g / 2 oz walnuts, roughly
　chopped

Place 18 paper cases on a wire rack. Over a low heat, melt together the butter or margarine, cocoa powder and syrup. Stir in the cornflakes and walnuts, and stir until thoroughly mixed. Spoon into the paper cases and leave to set. These are best eaten the same day as making.

284 | Peanut Cookies

Preparation time
10 minutes

Cooking time
20–25 minutes

Oven temperature
180 C, 350 F, gas 4

Makes 40

Calories
75 per cookie

You will need
100 g / 4 oz crunchy peanut butter
100 g / 4 oz butter or margarine
100 g / 4 oz caster sugar
75 g / 3 oz soft light brown sugar
2 eggs, lightly beaten
225 g / 8 oz self-raising flour,
　sifted
40 salted peanuts

Lightly grease two baking trays. Cream the peanut butter, butter or margarine and sugars until very soft, light and fluffy. Gradually beat in the eggs, then stir in the flour to make a fairly soft dough. Roll the dough into 40 small, evenly sized balls. Place on the prepared baking trays and flatten each ball slightly with the prongs of a fork. Press a peanut in the centre of each biscuit.

　Bake the cookies in a moderate oven for 20–25 minutes or until golden brown. Using a palette knife, carefully remove the cookies from the trays and transfer them to a wire rack to cool completely.

Microwave Tip

Melt the fat, cocoa powder and syrup in a bowl in the microwave oven. Allow 1–2 minutes on full power, stirring once. Add the remaining ingredients, continue as above.

Freezer Tip

For freshly made cookies form half the dough into a roll about 3.5 cm / 1½ in. in diameter, wrap in foil and freeze. Defrost, cut into slices and cook as above.

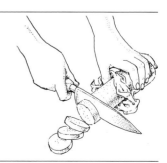

Fancy Cakes

A special occasion calls for a cake to celebrate and you will find a suitable recipe in this chapter. There are cakes for Christmas, Valentine's day and Easter, as well as luscious gâteaux for adult birthdays and a very simple children's birthday cake. There are small cakes suitable for party teas which taste superb but look almost too pretty to eat.

285 | Coffee and Hazelnut Gâteau

Preparation time
25 minutes

Cooking time
40 minutes

Oven temperature
180 C, 350 F, gas 4

Makes 1 cake

Total calories
5000

You will need
3 eggs
175 g/ 6 oz caster sugar
175 g/ 6 oz plain flour
1 tablespoon coffee essence
3 tablespoons brandy
450 ml/¾ pint double or whipping cream
100 g/ 4 oz hazelnuts, chopped

For the glacé icing
225 g/ 8 oz icing sugar
1 tablespoon coffee essence
1 tablespoon water

Line and grease a deep 18-cm/7-in cake tin. Whisk the eggs and sugar until pale and thick. Fold in the flour and coffee essence.

Pour into the tin. Bake in a moderate oven for about 40 minutes. Cool on a wire rack, then cut into three equal layers horizontally. Soak each layer with 1 tablespoon of brandy. Whip the cream until thick. Use a little to sandwich the cake together and coat the sides. Press the hazelnuts on the sides of the cake. For the glacé icing, mix together the icing sugar, coffee essence and water and pour on the top – be careful not to let it go down the sides of the cake. Pipe a border with the remaining cream.

286 | Christmas Cake

Preparation time
30 minutes

Cooking time
3½ hours

Oven temperature
140 C, 275 F, gas 1

Makes 1 cake

Total calories
7120

You will need
225 g/ 8 oz butter
225 g/ 8 oz light soft brown sugar
1 tablespoon black treacle
5 eggs
250 g/ 9 oz plain flour
1 teaspoon ground mixed spice
1 teaspoon grated nutmeg
50 g/ 2 oz ground almonds
grated rind of 1 lemon
grated rind of 1 orange
100 g/ 4 oz almonds, chopped
75 g/ 3 oz glacé cherries, chopped
175 g/ 6 oz raisins
250 g/ 9 oz sultanas
350 g/ 12 oz currants
100 g/ 4 oz chopped mixed peel
2 tablespoons brandy
2 tablespoons orange juice

Line and grease a 23–cm/9-in round cake tin or a 20-cm/8-in square cake tin. Cream the butter and sugar until light and fluffy. Beat in the treacle, then the eggs, adding a little of the flour after the first one. Mix the remaining flour with all the dry ingredients. Fold into the creamed mixture. Stir in the brandy and orange juice. Turn into the tin and level the top. Protect the outside of the tin with newspaper. Bake in a cool oven for 3½ hours or until a metal skewer inserted into the centre of the cake comes out clean. Cool in the tin for 20 minutes, then turn out on to a wire rack and leave to cool completely. Store wrapped in foil.

Cook's Tip

To test whether cake is cooked, press centre gently with fingers. If cooked, cake will spring back.

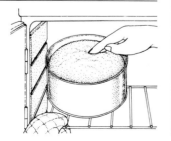

Cook's Tip

To keep cake for 3–4 months and to make it deliciously moist, prick top and bottom of cake with a skewer and spoon 2 tablespoons brandy over it every 2–3 weeks.

287 | Royal Icing

Preparation time
1 hour

Covers 1 cake

Total calories
8650

You will need
For the almond paste
450 g/1 lb ground almonds
225 g/8 oz icing sugar
225 g/8 oz caster sugar
2 teaspoons lemon juice
1 teaspoon almond essence
2 eggs, beaten
4 tablespoons apricot jam, sieved

For the royal icing
4 egg whites
1 kg/2 lb icing sugar, sifted twice
2 teaspoons glycerine
a few drops of rose water

For the almond paste, mix the dry ingredients. Add the lemon juice, almond essence and enough egg to make a stiff, pliable dough. Knead briefly until smooth.

Brush the top of the cake with apricot jam. Roll out a third of the paste large enough to cover the cake top. Lift it on top of the cake, trim the edges. Smooth the top and edges evenly with fingertips. Roll the remaining paste into a strip the width of the side of the cake and long enough to go round the cake. Brush the sides of the cake with jam, then place the almond paste round the cake, smoothing on to the sides. Smooth all edges and joins. Leave for 1–2 weeks.

Lightly whisk the egg whites, then gradually beat in the icing sugar. Beat in the glycerine and rose water to make a smooth thick icing. Spread thickly over the sides of the cake and fork into peaks.

Cook's Tip

To decorate as in the picture, spread the sides with three-quarters of the icing, forking it up and making the top edge higher. Dry overnight. Keep the remaining icing in an airtight container. Thin it by adding water, drop by drop, so that it will only just pour. Spoon this icing on top, teasing it up to the peaked edges with the point of a knife to make a smooth top. Decorate when dry.

288 | Chocolate Log

Preparation time
20 minutes

Cooking time
7–10 minutes

Oven temperature
220 C, 425 F, gas 7

Makes 1

Total calories
2711

You will need
3 eggs
75 g/3 oz caster sugar
2 tablespoons cocoa powder, sifted
65 g/2½ oz plain flour, sifted

For the filling and icing
100 g/4 oz butter or margarine
225 g/8 oz icing sugar
50 g/2 oz plain chocolate
holly leaves and icing sugar to decorate

Line and grease a 23 × 30-cm/9 × 12-in Swiss roll tin. Whisk the eggs and sugar until pale and very thick (see recipe 271). Fold in the cocoa and flour with a metal spoon, then pour the mixture into the tin. Bake in a hot oven for 7–10 minutes.

Place a clean tea-towel on a work surface, cover with greaseproof paper and sprinkle with caster sugar. Turn the Swiss roll out on to the paper. Trim off the crusty edges and lay a sheet of greaseproof paper on top. Roll up tightly to enclose the paper. Cool.

Beat the butter or margarine and icing sugar until pale. Melt the chocolate in a basin over a saucepan of hot water and add it to the mixture. Unroll the cake, remove paper and spread with some buttercream. Roll up and cover with the remaining buttercream. Decorate as shown.

Freezer Tip

Open freeze the cake until firm then place in a polythene box. Remove from box and defrost at room temperature.

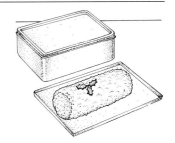

289 | Valentine Cake

Preparation time
30 minutes

Cooking time
35–40 minutes

Oven temperature
180 C, 350 F, gas 4

Makes 1 cake

Total calories
6170

You will need
175 g / 6 oz butter or margarine
175 g / 6 oz caster sugar
3 eggs
175 g / 6 oz self-raising flour

For the filling and icing
600 ml / 1 pint double or
  whipping cream
4 tablespoons redcurrant jelly
100 g / 4 oz icing sugar
1 tablespoon water
a few drops of pink food
  colouring

Grease a 20-cm / 8-in heart-shaped cake tin. Cream the butter or margarine and sugar until light and fluffy. Gradually beat in the eggs, then fold in the flour.

Bake in a moderate oven for 35–40 minutes or until golden and firm. Turn out to cool on a wire rack. Cut the cake horizontally in half.

Whip the cream until thick. Sandwich the cake halves together with half the redcurrant jelly and some of the cream. Dissolve the remaining redcurrant jelly in a saucepan over a low heat, then smooth over the top of the cake. Cool. Pipe cream around the sides of the cake.

Beat the icing sugar with the water and food colouring until smooth. Pour over the jelly on top of the cake. Add a border of cream on the top of the cake.

290 | Easter Cake

Preparation time
30 minutes

Cooking time
2 hours 50 minutes

Oven temperature
160 C, 325 F, gas 3
150 C, 300 F, gas 2

Makes 1 cake

Total calories
8215

You will need
175 g / 6 oz butter or margarine
175 g / 6 oz soft brown sugar
3 large eggs
225 g / 8 oz self-raising flour
2 teaspoons mixed spice
350 g / 12 oz sultanas
225 g / 8 oz raisins
100 g / 4 oz chopped mixed peel
50 g / 2 oz blanched almonds,
  chopped
4–5 tablespoons milk
$\frac{3}{4}$ quantity almond paste (recipe
  287)
2 tablespoons apricot jam, sieved
1 egg white

Line and grease a deep 20-cm / 8-in cake tin. Cream the butter or margarine and sugar until pale and soft. Gradually beat in the eggs adding a little of the flour. Fold in the remaining flour, spice, fruit, peel and nuts. Stir in milk to make a soft consistency. Spread half in the tin.

Roll a third of the almond paste into a 20-cm / 8-in circle. Place on top of the mixture, top with the remaining mixture; hollow out the centre slightly. Bake in a moderate oven 1 hour, reduce to a cool oven for a further 1 hour 15 minutes (approx). Cool in the tin for 15 minutes, then turn out on to a wire rack. Remove paper.

Brush the top of the cake with apricot jam. Roll half the remaining almond paste to fit the top of the cake. Roll the remainder into balls. Press the paste on the cake, adding the balls as shown. Brush with egg white and brown under the grill.

Cook's Tip

Cook this cake in a 20-cm/ 8-in round cake tin and continue as above for a celebration cake for any occasion.

Microwave Tip

To make jam easier to brush on cake, heat in a small bowl in the microwave with 1 teaspoon water for a few seconds, then sieve.

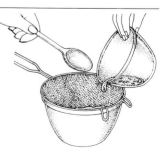

291 | Mocha Gâteau

Preparation time
30 minutes

Cooking time
25–30 minutes

Oven temperature
190 C, 375 F, gas 5

Makes 1 cake

Total calories
3875

You will need
100 g / 4 oz caster sugar
3 eggs
100 g / 4 oz plain flour, sifted
25 g / 1 oz cocoa powder, sifted
2 tablespoons brandy

For the filling and topping
450 ml / ¾ pint double cream
2 tablespoons sweetened strong
　black coffee
1 teaspoon cocoa powder
1 teaspoon instant coffee powder
2–3 teaspoons hot water
175 g / 6 oz icing sugar, sifted
grated chocolate to decorate

Grease a loose-bottomed 20-cm/8-in deep round cake tin. Whisk the sugar and eggs together until pale and thick. Carefully fold in the sifted flour and cocoa powder. Pour into the cake tin and bake in a moderately hot oven for 15–20 minutes. Turn out on to a wire rack. When cool, split in half horizontally and sprinkle over the brandy.

　Whip the cream and black coffee until stiff. Place a star nozzle in a piping bag and fill the bag with the coffee cream. Pipe swirls over one half of the cake, place on a serving plate and top with the other half. Pipe the remainder of the cream around the top of the gâteau.

　Dissolve the cocoa and coffee in the water, then mix with the icing sugar to make glacé icing. Spread on top of the cake up to the piped cream border. Decorate with grated chocolate.

292 | Birthday Cake

Preparation time
20 minutes

Cooking time
1 hour 20 minutes

Oven temperature
180 C, 350 F, gas 4

Makes 1 cake

Total calories
6365

You will need
175 g / 6 oz butter or margarine
175 g / 6 oz caster sugar
3 eggs, lightly beaten
225 g / 8 oz self-raising flour
225 g / 8 oz chocolate chips
a little milk, if necessary

For the topping
75 g / 3 oz butter or margarine
225 g / 8 oz icing sugar, sifted
1–2 tablespoons milk
a few drops of green food
　colouring
1 (150-g / 5.25 oz) packet
　chocolate animals

Decoration
crêpe paper, spotty bow and
　candles

Line and grease a deep 18-cm/7-in cake tin. Cream the butter or margarine and sugar until pale and fluffy. Gradually add the eggs. Fold in the flour and chocolate chips, adding a little milk to make a fairly stiff dropping consistency. Spoon into the tin and bake in a moderate oven for 1 hour 20 minutes. A metal skewer inserted into the cake should come out clean. Leave to cool in the tin for 5 minutes, then turn out to cool completely on a wire rack.

　Beat the butter or margarine, sugar, milk and food colouring together. Spread over the top and sides of the cake and fork up. Decorate as shown. Finally add the candles.

Freezer Tip

This gâteau can be frozen successfully without the glacé icing. Open freeze until firm then wrap carefully in a large polythene bag. Unwrap and place on a serving plate to defrost.

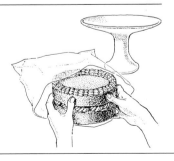

Cook's Tip

To make a very quick, one-stage cake, use soft margarine and add 1 teaspoon baking powder to the ingredients. Beat all together until very soft and light. Stir in the chocolate chips last.

If the chocolate chips are not available, chop a bar of dark plain chocolate.

293 | Battenburg Cake

Preparation time
25 minutes

Cooking time
35–40 minutes

Oven temperature
180 C, 350 F, gas 4

Makes 1 cake

Total calories
4990

You will need
175 g / 6 oz butter or margarine
175 g / 6 oz caster sugar
3 eggs
175 g / 6 oz self-raising flour
grated rind of 1 lemon
a few drops of pink food
   colouring
2 tablespoons lemon curd
450 g / 1 lb marzipan
caster sugar for dredging

Line and grease a deep 18-cm/7-in square cake tin and divide down the middle with a strip of folded greaseproof paper. Cream the fat and sugar until pale and fluffy. Gradually beat in the eggs, then fold in the flour.

Halve the mixture. Add the lemon rind to one portion and colouring to the other. Put mixtures separately in the tin. Bake in a moderate oven for 35–40 minutes or until a skewer inserted into the cake comes out clean. Cool on a wire rack.

Trim the edges, cut each piece of cake in half lengthways, making four strips. Sandwich alternate colours together with lemon curd in two layers. Roll the marzipan to a 20 × 37-cm/8 × 15-in oblong. Spread the outside of the cake with lemon curd. Place in the middle of the marzipan. Ease the marzipan around the cake. With join underneath, pinch the edges and dust with caster sugar.

294 | Devil's Food Cake

Preparation time
20 minutes

Cooking time
2 hours

Oven temperature
150 C, 300 F, gas 2

Makes 1 cake

Total calories
4505

You will need
175 g / 6 oz butter or margarine
175 g / 6 oz caster sugar
3 eggs
4 tablespoons golden syrup
50 g / 2 oz ground almonds
50 g / 2 oz cocoa powder
175 g / 6 oz self-raising flour
150 ml / $\frac{1}{4}$ pint milk
grated chocolate to decorate

For the frosting
1 egg white
175 g / 6 oz icing sugar
1 tablespoon golden syrup
3 tablespoons water

Line and grease a deep 20-cm/8-in round cake tin. Cream the butter or margarine and sugar until light and fluffy. Gradually beat in the eggs, then thoroughly stir in the syrup, almonds and cocoa powder. Carefully fold in the flour and add enough milk to make a mixture with a dropping consistency. Spoon into the tin, smooth the top and bake in a cool oven for about 2 hours. Turn out on to a wire rack to cool.

Make the frosting: place all the ingredients in a basin over boiling water and whisk until the icing stands in soft peaks. Remove from the heat and continue whisking until cool, then quickly spread it over the cake. Decorate with grated chocolate.

Microwave Tip

To make lemon curd: cook the juice of 3 lemons with 100 g / 4 oz butter and 350 g / 12 oz caster sugar on full power for 6 minutes. Meanwhile, whisk 3 eggs and the grated rind of 3 lemons. Whisk in the hot butter. Cook for about 12–14 minutes, whisking every 2 minutes. Strain and pot.

Cook's Tip

To line a cake tin. Cut circles of greaseproof paper the size of base of tin. Cut a double thickness strip of paper 5 cm / 2 in wider than height of tin and the length of circumference. Fold up 1 cm / $\frac{1}{2}$ in along length. Snip at 1 cm / $\frac{1}{2}$ in intervals. Grease tin with melted lard. Place one circle in tin. Place strip around edge with folded edge on bottom of tin. Place second circle in tin. Grease paper.

295 | Marbled Cake

Preparation time
25 minutes

Cooking time
1 hour

Oven temperature
160 C, 325 F, gas 3

Makes 1 cake

Total calories
4635

You will need
175 g/6 oz butter or margarine
175 g/6 oz caster sugar
3 eggs
175 g/6 oz self-raising flour
green food colouring
pink food colouring

For the filling and icing
50 g/2 oz cocoa powder
3 tablespoons boiling water
275 g/10 oz icing sugar
75 g/3 oz butter
chopped pistachio nuts to
   decorate

Line and grease a deep 18-cm/7-in round cake tin. Cream the butter or margarine and sugar until pale and fluffy. Gradually beat in the eggs, then fold in the flour. Divide the mixture into three equal portions. Leave one portion plain, colour one green and the other pink. Drop spoonsful of the mixture in the tin, and carefully smooth the top without mixing the colours.

Bake in a moderate oven for about 1 hour or until a metal skewer inserted into the cake comes out clean. Cool on a wire rack. Dissolve the cocoa in the water; cool. Beat all the icing ingredients together and smooth half over the top and sides of the cake. Pipe a border with the remainder. Decorate with pistachio nuts.

296 | Sachertorte

Preparation time
20 minutes

Cooking time
1 hour

Oven temperature
180 C, 350 F, gas 4

Makes 1 cake

Total calories
3610

You will need
100 g/4 oz plain chocolate
100 g/4 oz butter
4 eggs
100 g/4 oz icing sugar, sifted
50 g/2 oz self-raising flour
50 g/2 oz ground almonds

For the topping
225 g/8 oz plain chocolate

Line and grease a deep 23-cm/9-in round cake tin. Heat the chocolate and butter together in a bowl above a saucepan of hot, not boiling, water until melted. Cool slightly. Stir well and remove from the heat. Whisk together the eggs and icing sugar until pale and very thick. Fold in the chocolate and butter mixture, then fold in the flour and almonds. Pour the mixture into the prepared tin and bake in a moderate oven for about 1 hour, or until a metal skewer inserted into the centre of the cake comes out clean. Turn out on to a wire rack to cool. For the topping, melt the chocolate, and quickly smooth over the cake with a palette knife. Leave to cool. Decorate as shown.

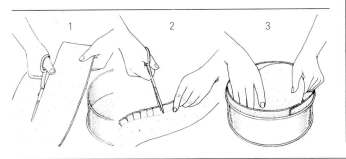

Microwave Tip

To melt chocolate in the microwave, break into squares and place in a bowl. Microwave for 4–6 minutes until soft.

297 | *Treacle Cake*

Preparation time
20 minutes

Cooking time
1 hour

Oven temperature
180 C, 350 F, gas 4

Makes 1 cake

Total calories
4955

You will need
175 g/6 oz butter or margarine
175 g/6 oz caster sugar
3 tablespoons black treacle
3 eggs
350 g/12 oz self-raising flour
2 tablespoons milk

For the icing
50 g/2 oz butter or margarine
1 tablespoon black treacle
1 tablespoon milk
225 g/8 oz icing sugar, sifted

Line and grease a deep 20-cm/8-in square cake tin. Cream the butter or margarine, sugar and treacle together until light and fluffy. Gradually beat in the eggs, adding a tablespoon of flour if necessary to prevent the mixture from curdling. Carefully fold in the flour and milk. Spoon the mixture into the prepared tin and bake in a moderate oven for 1 hour or until a metal skewer inserted into the cake comes out clean. Cool on a wire rack. Beat all icing ingredients together until smooth. Swirl on cake as shown.

298 | *Chocolate Refrigerator Cake*

Preparation time
10 minutes

Cooking time
5 minutes

Makes 1 cake

Total calories
4660

You will need
450 g/1 lb plain chocolate
100 g/4 oz butter or margarine
2 tablespoons brandy
225 g/8 oz chocolate digestive
  biscuits, crushed
100 g/4 oz hazelnuts, chopped

Line and grease a deep 18-cm/7-in square cake tin. Break the chocolate into small pieces and place in a basin with the butter over a saucepan of hot water. Heat gently until the chocolate and butter are melted. Remove from the heat, then stir in the brandy, biscuits and hazelnuts. Mix thoroughly, pour into the prepared tin and leave to cool. When cool, mark into twelve equal squares and refrigerate for 1 hour or until set. Cut into squares to serve.

Cook's Tip

When a cake is cooked in a tin lined with paper, remove paper when cake is turned out to cool unless storing cake for several days, when it can be left on.

Cook's Tip

To crush biscuits, place in a paper bag and roll gently with a rolling pin.

299 | Tipsy Ring

Preparation time
15 minutes

Cooking time
40–50 minutes

Oven temperature
160 C, 325 F, gas 3

Makes 1 cake

Total calories
2600

You will need
100 g/ 4 oz butter or margarine
100 g/ 4 oz caster sugar
2 eggs
100 g/ 4 oz self-raising flour
25 g/ 1 oz cocoa powder
1 tablespoon instant coffee
   dissolved in 1 tablespoon
   boiling water
2 tablespoons brandy

For the glacé icing
175 g/ 6 oz icing sugar, sifted
25 g/ 1 oz cocoa powder
1 tablespoon instant coffee
   dissolved in 1 tablespoon
   boiling water
1 tablespoon brandy

Grease a 23-cm/9-in ring tin. Cream together the butter or margarine and sugar until light and fluffy. Gradually beat in the eggs, then carefully fold in the flour, cocoa powder and coffee mixture. Spoon the mixture into the prepared tin and bake in a moderate oven for 40–50 minutes or until a metal skewer inserted into the cake comes out clean.

While the cake is still hot, pour 2 tablespoons brandy evenly over it. Leave for 5 minutes, then turn out and cool on a wire rack. For the icing, beat all the ingredients together and drizzle over the top of the cake.

300 | Chocolate Cups

Preparation time
25 minutes

Cooking time
5 minutes

Makes 8

Calories
505 per cake

You will need
225 g/ 8 oz plain chocolate
225 g/ 8 oz chocolate or coffee
   cake, crumbled
1 tablespoon cocoa powder
2 tablespoons rum or sherry
50 g/ 2 oz chopped mixed nuts
1 tablespoon chocolate spread
300 ml/½ pint double or whipping
   cream
chopped nuts to decorate

Place eight double thickness paper cases (one case inside another) on a wire rack. Heat the chocolate in a basin over a saucepan of hot, not boiling, water until melted. Brush the chocolate fairly thickly around the inside of the cases, then leave to cool and set.

Meanwhile, mix together the cake crumbs, cocoa powder, rum or sherry and nuts.

When the chocolate has set, carefully peel off the paper cases, and fill the chocolate cups with the mixture. Mix the chocolate spread with 2 tablespoons of the cream. Whip the remaining cream until thick, then fold in the chocolate mixture.

Spoon into a piping bag fitted with a star nozzle and pipe swirls of chocolate cream on the top of the cake mixture and decorate with chopped nuts. Chill before serving.

Microwave Tip

To soften refrigerator-hard fat for creaming for cakes or for spreading, heat in microwave for 1–2 minutes.

Cook's Tip

When melting chocolate be careful not to over-heat it or it will go grainy. Also take care not to get any drops of water in the chocolate, always dry bottom of bowl.

301 | Iced Fancies

Preparation time
25 minutes

Cooking time
7–10 minutes

Oven temperature
220C, 425F, gas 7

Makes 16

Calories
210 per cake

You will need
3 eggs
75 g/3 oz caster sugar
75 g/3 oz plain flour

For the glacé icing
225 g/8 oz icing sugar, sifted
2 tablespoons warm water
a few drops of food colouring

For the buttercream
100 g/4 oz butter
225 g/8 oz icing sugar
1–2 tablespoons milk
1 drop vanilla essence
a few drops of food colouring

Decoration
silver balls, crystallised fruit,
grated chocolate or nuts

Line and grease a 30 × 18 × 3-cm/12 × 7 × 1¼-in tin. Whisk the eggs and sugar until pale and very thick. Carefully fold in the flour, using a metal spoon. Pour the mixture into the tin and bake in a hot oven for 7–10 minutes. Turn out on a sheet of greaseproof paper on a wire rack to cool.

Use a variety of cutters to cut out shapes from the sponge. For the glacé icing, beat all the ingredients thoroughly. The icing can be coloured if liked. Ice the cakes.

Beat the butter, sugar, milk and vanilla together until smooth. Colour, if liked, and pipe on the cakes. Decorate as shown.

302 | Meringue Snowmen

Preparation time
30 minutes

Cooking time
2 hours

Oven temperature
110C, 225F, gas ¼

Makes 20

Calories
90 per snowman

You will need
4 egg whites
225 g/8 oz caster sugar

For the filling
150 ml/¼ pint double or whipping
   cream

Decoration
chocolate drops
red bootlace liquorice
sticks of liquorice
1 packet liquorice allsorts
rice paper
a few drops of food colouring

Grease three baking trays. Whisk the egg whites until stiff but not dry, then gradually whisk in the sugar to make a stiff glossy mixture. Using two wet spoons, put spoonsful of the mixture on the trays. Using wet teaspoons put the same number of spoonsful of the mixture on the trays. Bake in a very cool oven for 2 hours, until dry. Cool on a wire rack.

Whip the cream until thick. Sandwich the large shapes together with cream to make the bodies and the small shapes to make the heads. Use cream to stick the snowmen together. Using a piping bag and a star nozzle, pipe on the features. Decorate as shown. Make hats from circles of rice paper. Cut a hole in the centre and place a liquorice allsort in the middle.

Freezer Tip

Place cut-out shapes on a wire rack and freeze, to prevent cakes crumbling when glacé icing is spooned over.

Freezer Tip

Egg yolks freeze well. Beat with either a pinch of salt or ½ teaspoon sugar and store in small pots. Mark on pots how many yolks and whether sweet or savoury.

303 | Raspberry Cream Squares

Preparation time
25 minutes

Cooking time
10–12 minutes

Oven temperature
220C, 425F, gas 7

Calories
675 per square

You will need
1 (368-g/13-oz) packet puff pastry
2 tablespoons raspberry jam, sieved
300 ml/½ pint double or whipping cream
50 g/2 oz raspberries
100 g/4 oz icing sugar
1 tablespoon water

Grease two baking trays. Roll out the pastry thinly and cut into two 7.5 × 30-cm/3 × 12-in strips. Place on the prepared baking trays and bake in a hot oven for 10–12 minutes or until well risen and golden. Leave to cool on a wire rack. Heat the jam until runny and brush on to one strip of pastry. Whip the cream until thick, then fold in the raspberries. Spread the cream filling over the pastry slice without the jam. Top with the jam-coated pastry slice, jam side up. Carefully cut into four. Beat the icing sugar and water until smooth and pour over the jam.

304 | Ginger Snaps

Preparation time
25 minutes

Cooking time
8–10 minutes

Oven temperature
190C, 375F, gas 5

Makes 12

Calories
130 per ginger snap

You will need
50 g/2 oz butter or margarine
2 tablespoons syrup
50 g/2 oz soft brown sugar
50 g/2 oz plain flour
1 teaspoon ground ginger

For the filling
150 ml/¼ pint double or whipping cream
chopped stem ginger and angelica to decorate

Grease as many wooden spoon handles as possible. Thoroughly grease two baking trays. Melt the butter or margarine, syrup and sugar over a low heat, then stir in the flour and ginger. Drop teaspoonsful of the mixture well apart on a baking tray to allow room for spreading.

Cook in a moderately hot oven for 8–10 minutes, then leave the biscuits to cool for a few seconds. Use a palette knife to lift them off very carefully, then roll around the wooden spoon handles with the top of the biscuit on the outside. Hold in position for a few minutes until set. Slip the biscuits from the handles and place on a wire rack to cool. Bake the biscuits in batches. If they set too quickly return them to the oven to melt for a few seconds.

Whip the cream until thick and use to fill the ginger snaps. Decorate with stem ginger and angelica.

Cook's Tip

To make custard slices: cook pastry as above. Spread both slices with jam and thick custard with whipped cream folded in, then sandwich together, jam sides in. Cut into 5-cm/2-in slices.

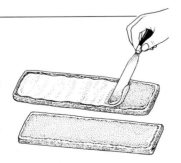

Cook's Tip

To make cups to hold ice cream or sorbet, mould hot biscuits over oiled oranges and leave to cool.

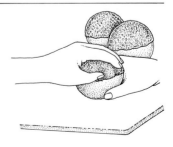

Index

Alaska, baked, 225
Almond and coffee cake, 266
  paste, 287
Apple
  and apricot charlotte, 201
  and blackberry pie, 206
  and cashew soup, quick, 12
  round, wholemeal, 260
  strudel, 209
  stuffed baked, 210
Apricot and apple charlotte, 201
  and pineapple fritters, 212
  and prune pudding, 200
  and walnut sauce, 97
  chicken pilaff with, 155
Aubergine and tomato bake, 132
Avocado dip, 34
  soup, hot, 5

Bacon and split pea soup, 22
Bakewell tarts, 274
Banana and walnut cake, 268
Battenburg cake, 293
Beans: cassoulet, 67
  curry, mixed, 143
Beef bourguignonne, 62
  cobbler, 63
  Cornish pasties, 172
  Hungarian goulash, 66
  in beer, 61
  roast, 88
  soup with dumplings, 21
  steak and kidney pudding, 170
  see also Minced beef
Beetroot soup, 9
Birthday cake, 292
Black cherry clafouti, 214
Black forest gâteau, 236
Blackberry and apple pie, 206
Boeuf bourguignonne, 62
Borscht, 9
Bourbons, 280
Bread and butter pudding, spiced, 197
  see also recipes 241–6
Broccoli quiche 185
Brussels sprouts with chestnuts, 113
Burgers, spicy, 103
  vegetarian, 136
Buttercream, 265, 301

Cabbage leaves, stuffed, 139
  peanut coleslaw, 124
Cannelloni, stuffed, 159
Carrots, buttered, 109
  cake, 261
  soup, 6
Cashew and apple soup, quick, 12
Cassoulet, 67
Cauliflower cheese, 110
Celery and stilton soup, 14
  with walnuts, 112
Cheese and chicken puffs, 189
  and fruit salad, 121
  and onion soup, 15
  and salami salad, 120
  sauce, 111
  blue, 164
  scones, 258
  Welsh rarebit, 39
Cheesecake, chocolate mint, 229
Chelsea buns, 251
Chestnuts, Brussels sprouts with, 113
Chick peas: hummus, 141
Chicken and cheese puffs, 189
  and leek soup, 18
  and lemon casserole, 79
  and rice salad, 119
  coq au vin, 70
  curry, 73
  fricassée, 72
  gougère, 192
  Kiev, easy, 83
  liver pâté, 29
  liver risotto, 145

pie, 174
  pilaff with apricots, 155
  roast, 81
  soup, cream of, 19
  tandoori, 84
  with honey, 82
Chilli con carne, 77
  stuffed peppers, 116
Chocolate cake, 265
  refrigerator, 298
  sachertorte, 296
  castles, 281
  cups, 300
  fondue with fresh fruit, 213
  log, 288
  mint cheesecake, 229
  nut crispies, 283
  orange soufflé, 224
  pots au chocolat, 218
  pudding, 195
  sauce, 232
Choux pastry, 192, 230
Chow mein, pork, 166
Christmas cake, 286
  pudding, 194
Cock-a-leekie soup, 18
Cod au gratin, 43
  steaks, grilled, with parsley butter, 42
Coffee and almond cake, 266
  and hazelnut gâteau, 285
  gâteau, 291
  ice cream, creamy, 240
Coleslaw, peanut, 124
Coq au vin, 70
Cornish pasties, 172
Courgettes, baked stuffed, 138
  fritters, 114
  quiche, 186
Crème caramel, 233
Croissants, 248
Crumble topping, 202
Cucumber soup, iced, 1
Curried parsnip soup, 11
Curry, chicken, 73
  mixed bean, 143
  seafood, 58
  vegetable, 144
Custard jam tart, 208

Date and walnut loaf, 270
Devil's food cake, 294
Doughnuts, 252
Drop scones, 259
Duck, roast, 86, 87
Dumplings, 21, 69
Dundee cake, 263

Easter cake, 290
Egg and smoked mackerel salad, 122
  mayonnaise, 31

Fish au gratin, 43
  balls, 57
  cakes, 54
  chowder, white, 24
  envelopes, 178
  kebabs, 41
  ragoût, 53
  pie, crunchy, 177
  sticks, crispy, 56
  see also Seafood and under specific fish
Fisherman's pie, 55
Flapjacks, sesame, 282
French onion soup, 16
Frosting, 294
Fruit and cheese salad, 121
  and vegetable kebabs, 142
  buns, 273
  cake, quick, 264
  salad, fresh, 237
  salad, hot, 216
  pavlova, fresh, 231
  see also specific fruits

Gammon steak with apricot and walnut sauce, 97
Ginger pudding, baked, 196
  snaps, 304
Gingerbread, 255
  men, 279
Glacé icing, 261, 265, 267, 285, 299, 301
Gougère, 192
Goulash, Hungarian, 66
Grainy bread, 243
Grape and melon cocktail, 36
Grapefruit, grilled, 35
Green salad, 125

Haddock crumble, 45
  fish envelopes, 178
  in cider, 44
  pâté, smoked, 26
Ham, spiced glazed, 96
Hazelnut and coffee gâteau, 285
Herrings with soured cream sauce, 51
Hot cross buns, 250
Hummus, 141

Ice cream, creamy coffee, 240
  nutty brown bread, 238
  pineapple, 239
Iced fancies, 301
Icing, glacé, 261, 265, 267, 285, 299, 301
  royal, 287
Irish stew, 65

Jam doughnuts, 252
  tarts, 275
  custard, 208

Kebabs, 104
  cocktail, 40
  fish, 41
  mixed, 101
  vegetable and fruit, 142
Kedgeree, 154
Kidney and sausage casserole, 75
  and steak pudding, 170
Kipper flan, 179
  with lemon butter, 59

Lamb chops, honey-glazed, 100
  Irish stew, 65
  kebabs, 104
  Lancashire hot pot, 64
  noisettes with savoury butter, 92
  roast, 89
  stuffed breast of, 91
  stuffed shoulder of, 90
Lamingtons, 276
Lancashire hot pot, 64
Lasagne, vegetable, 130
  verdi, 158
Leek and chicken soup, 18
  and potato soup, chilled, 3
  in sauce, 111
Lemon and chicken casserole, 79
  meringue pie, 226
  mousse, quick, 219
  sauce, 196
  soup, chilled, 4
Lentil loaf, 135
Liver with watercress, 76
  see also under Chicken

Macaroni cheese, 157
Mackerel, piquant, 50
  smoked, and egg salad, 122
Madeira cake, 269
Malt bread, 253
Mandarin tartlets, 227
Marbled cake, 295
Marmalade cake, nutty, 267
  sponge pudding, 198
Marrow rings, stuffed, 117
Meat and vegetable soup, 20
  loaf, 98
  pies, spicy, 171
  see also specific meats
Meatballs and peanut sauce, 102
Melon and black grape cocktail, 36
Meringue snowmen, 302
  with chocolate sauce, 232
Minced beef: chilli con carne, 77
  meatballs and peanut sauce, 102
  moussaka, 78
  samosas, 187
  shepherd's pie, 80
  spaghetti bolognese, 160
  spicy burgers, 103
  meat pies, 171
Mince pies, 205
Minestrone, 10
Mocha gâteau, 291
Moussaka, 78
Muffins, 247
Mulligatawny soup, 13
Mushroom and sherry soup, 17
  stuffed, 32
  salad, 126

Naan bread, 246
Niçoise salad, 30

Onion and cheese soup, 15
  and tomato salad, 127
  flan, 181
  quiches, individual, 33
  soup, French, 16
Orange and tomato soup, 7
  sauce, 87

Paella, 146
Pancakes, tropical, 211
Parkin, 256
Parsnip soup, curried, 11
Pasta salad, 168
  shells, stuffed, 167
Pavlova, fresh fruit, 231
Peaches, turkey with, 71
Peanut coleslaw, 124
  cookies, 284
  sauce, 102
Pears in ginger wine, 215
Peppers, chilli-stuffed, 116
Pilau rice, 148
Pineapple and apricot fritters, 212
  ice cream, 239
  upside-down pudding, 199
Pitta bread, 245
Pizza, 173
  speedy, 38
Plaice rolls, stuffed 47
  veronique, 46
Pork and dumplings, 69
  casserole, sweet 'n' sour, 68
  chops with orange and cashew nut stuffing, 95
  chow mein, 166
  parcels, 176
  roast, 93
  roll, stuffed, 94
Potatoes, baked, 105
  cakes, 137
  duchesse, 106
  fantail, 107
  Lyonnaise, 108
  salad, 128
Prawns, potted, 27
Profiteroles, 230
Prune and apricot pudding, 200

Queen of puddings, citrus, 193
Quiche, broccoli, 185
  courgette, 186
  lorraine, 182
  ratatouille, 184

Rabbit casserole, 74
Raspberry cream squares, 303
  delight, frozen, 223
Ratatouille, 115
  quiche, 184
Ravioli supper, quick, 165
Rhubarb crumble, 202
  fool, 221
Rice and chicken salad, 119
  bake, 156
  basic, 147
  cakes, 153
  pudding, 203
  see also recipes 145–56
Rock cakes, 272

Sachertorte, 296
Saffron rice, 149
Salad, pasta, 168
  see also recipes 118–28
Salami and cheese salad, 120
  flan, rich, 180
Salmon mousse, 52
Samosas, 187
Sandwiches, toasted, 37
Sauce, apricot and walnut, 97
  cheese, 111
  blue, 164
  chocolate, 232
  lemon, 196
  orange, 87
  peanut, 102
  tomato, 98, 161
  watercress and walnut, 162
Sausage and kidney casserole, 75
  layer pie, 169
  plait, 188
Savoury puff(s), 133, 191
  rice, 150
Scones, cheese, 258
  drop, 259
  plain, 257

Scotch broth, 20
Seafood curry, 58
  soup, 23
Semolina swirl pudding, 204
Sesame flapjacks, 282
Shepherd's pie, 80
Sherry and mushroom soup, 17
Shortbread, 278
  strawberry creams, 228
Shortcrust pastry, 176
Soda bread, 244
Spaghetti bolognese, 160
  with tomato sauce, 161
  with watercress and walnut sauce, 162
Spanish soup, 2
Split pea and bacon soup, 22
Sponge cake, 262
Spring rolls, 134
  salad, hot, 118
Steak and kidney pudding, 170
  grilled, 99
Stilton and celery soup, 14
Strawberry creams, chilled, 217
  shortbread creams, 228
Stuffing, apple, 94
  apricot and peanut, 90
  chestnut, 85
  orange and cashew nut, 95
  pear and lemon, 86
  prune and almond, 91
  tarragon and lemon, 81
Summer pudding, 235
Sunflower seed and vegetable bake, 131
Sweetcorn flan, 183
Swiss roll, 271
Syllabub, citrus, 220

Tagliatelli alla carbonara, 163
  with blue cheese sauce, 164
Tandoori chicken, 84
Taramasalata, quick, 28
Tea cakes, 249
Teabread, traditional, 254
Tipsy ring, 299
Toasted sandwiches, 37
Tomato and aubergine bake, 132
  and onion salad, 127
  and orange soup, 7
  rice mould, 152
  sauce, 98, 161
Treacle cake, 297
  tart, 207
Trifle, traditional, 234
Tropical pancakes, 211
Trout, baked stuffed, 48
  with almonds, 49
Tuna bake, quick, 60
  fish pie, crunchy, 177
  mousse, rich, 25
Turkey, roast, 85
  with peaches, 71

Valentine cake, 289
Vegetable and fruit kebabs, 142
  and meat soup, 20
  bake, sunflower seed and, 131
  curry, 144
  lasagne, 130
  pancakes, 129
  pie, 175
  savoury puff, 133
  soup, chilled, 2
  minestrone, 10
  spring rolls, 134
  terrine, 140
  see also main vegetables
Vegetarian burgers, 136
Veronique, plaice, 46
Vichysoisse, 3
Victoria sandwich cake, 262
Viennese whirls, 277
Vols-au-vent, 190

Waldorf salad, 123
Walnut and banana cake, 268
  and date loaf, 270
  and watercress sauce, 162
  celery with, 112
Watercress and walnut sauce, 162
  liver with, 76
  soup, cream of, 8
Welsh rarebit, 39
Wholemeal apple round, 260
  bread, 241
  pastry, 185

Yogurt fool, 222